NATIONAL DEFENSE RESEARCH INSTITUTE

ENLARGING NATO

The Russia Factor

Richard L. Ku | D1205826
with
Marianna V. Kozintseva

PREPARED FOR THE OFFICE OF THE SECRETARY OF DEFENSE

RAND

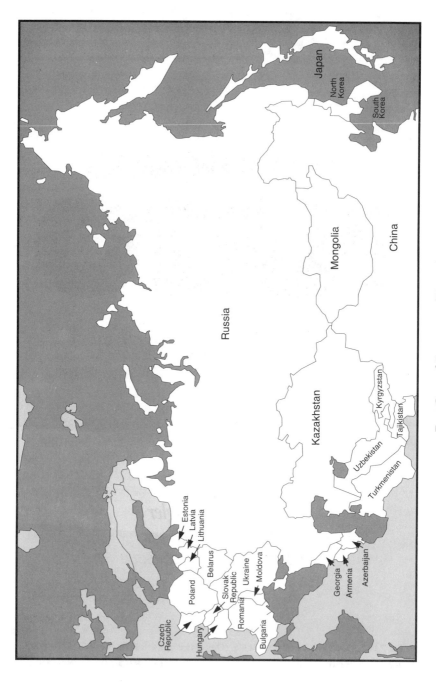

East Central Europe and Eurasia

The end of the Cold War left East Central Europe as a large neutral zone between the Western community and Russia. To promote stability and democracy there, NATO and the European Union (EU) currently are shaping plans to begin enlarging into this region by admitting new members. They already are encountering a Russia that is intent on putting its imprint on the region and therefore is opposed to major aspects of Western enlargement. As the future unfolds, the interaction between the West and Russia promises to be a defining one for East Central Europe's emerging geopolitics, and it will affect the stability of Europe as a whole. Focused on the big strategic picture, this study presents a political-military analysis of the dynamics likely to unfold and of the actions the United States can take to shape a positive outcome. It begins with a theoretical framework and an in-depth assessment of Russia's new statist foreign policy and defense strategy, including actions in Eurasia. It then examines East Central Europe's current and future geopolitics. It concludes with an analysis of alternative strategic and military "end games"—destinations coupled with plans for getting to them—that the United States and its allies can pursue for achieving their goals of admitting new members while encouraging overall regional stability, including stable relations with Russia.

This study is intended to contribute to U.S. and Western strategic, defense, and arms-control planning for NATO enlargement, an issue of growing importance. It does not advocate any single policy or plan. It will be of interest to government officials who deal with this issue and to others concerned about new-era security and defense affairs in Europe. It was prepared as part of a research project for the

Office of the Secretary of Defense aimed at developing new strategic planning concepts for Europe and Eurasia. It was conducted within the International Security and Defense Policy Center of RAND's National Defense Research Institute, a federally funded research and development center sponsored by the Office of the Secretary of Defense, the Joint Staff, and the defense agencies. This study is current as of late 1995.

CONTENTS

TABLES

One of the most momentous developments taking place in Europe is preparations by "the West"—the transatlantic community bonding the United States and its European allies—to go east. The West intends to take this step by enlarging both NATO and the European Union (EU) into East Central Europe—the zone separating Germany and Russia—in the coming years. Decisions have not yet been made, but, most probably, these bodies will begin admitting some or all of the "Visegrad Four" (the states of Poland, the Czech Republic, Hungary, and Slovakia) around the turn of the century, after which other countries might be admitted. This enlargement can help temper East Central Europe's dangerous new-era geopolitics (*geopolitics* being the process by which nations interact as they try to attain their strategic objectives). It also offers an historic opportunity to bring new European democracies into the Western family of nations. Yet it will draw the West into a region of chronic turmoil. It also will set into motion an interaction with Russia, whose foreign policy is acquiring a reawakened sense of state interests. As matters now stand, Russia is determined to put its own imprint on the region, and it is avowedly hostile to NATO enlargement there. As a result, a portentous strategic drama is beginning to take shape in East Central Europe, and the outcome will have a major effect on the future of Europe as a whole.

The alliance's *Study on NATO Enlargement* (Brussels, Belgium: NATO Headquarters, September 1995) establishes the goal of enlarging while also creating a stable European security architecture and building cooperative relations with Russia. Yet, many worried observers are raising critical questions about the entire enterprise:

lent setting seek to ensure their physical security, to dominate their immediate neighbors, and to exert influence farther out in order to keep potential rivals at bay. Statism is consistent with Russia's history before communism, reflects the presidential-style government that is taking shape (a democracy with strong central leadership deemed necessary to advance Russia's causes while offsetting pressures for restored dictatorship), and responds to Russia's long-term strategic requirements as seen by contemporary Russians. Plausibly, Russia could again embrace Atlanticism if the future yields liberal democracy at home and a tranquil environment abroad. Alternatively, Russia could revert to imperialism if the far right wins the domestic struggle and is willing to subordinate domestic economic reform to external adventures. If Russia weakens internally so that it can no longer function as a cohesive nation-state, it might have no foreign policy worthy of the name. Barring these developments, statism seems likely to be the model for the future. But exactly how it will be defined remains to be seen, because the national interest and statism can be interpreted in a variety of ways.

Russia's definition of *statism* will be affected by the resources available for national security enterprises. If Russia's government and society settle down, the development of statism might permit strategic rejuvenation and a more assertive foreign policy. Economic recovery could contribute in the same ways. Yet Russia will be struggling for the coming decade and beyond to absorb capitalism, recover lost wealth, and build a modern economy. Moreover, Russia will lack the military strength of the Soviet Union by a factor of 4 or more. Today, its defense posture has been weakened by downsizing and a major loss of readiness. Russia is embarking upon an effort to build a new military strategy and a smaller but potent force posture capable of peacetime missions, crisis interventions, and limited regional wars outside its borders. It may succeed within a decade. Even so, it will face imposing strategic requirements across its vast landmass, and it will need to refrain from developing rivalries with powerful countries and alliances. These economic and military constraints may not prevent Russia from contemplating an ambitious foreign agenda if the opportunity presents itself, but they will inhibit sweeping ventures that could incur high costs and dangers.

The likely prospect thus is that Russia will pursue statism in more-assertive, yet calculated, ways. Reintegration of Eurasia will remain

Russia's top priority; however, reintegration can occur in hierarchical or democratic ways. To the extent Russia comes to dominate the CIS, it may be better able to seek influence in East Central Europe, where it will encounter an enlarging West. A key issue will be whether Russia adjusts to enlargement by seeking normal relations with the West (accommodating itself to the situation and seeking concessions in return) or, instead, chooses to pursue a Cold Peace (standoffish relations) or a new Cold War (a Russian military threat to the West). If Russia is left profoundly dissatisfied by the outcome, it might view Cold Peace as a viable choice even if Cold War is deemed unthinkable. President Boris Yeltsin and other Russian officials already have warned of a Cold Peace, and they may have more than rhetoric in mind. Yet, Russia will have ample incentives to seek normal relations if satisfactory policies can be arranged, given that Cold Peace could cut Russia off from the world economy and lead to a bleak economic future. Such incentives can open the door to Russian strategic collaboration with the West, but only if a descent into animosity and rivalry can be avoided.

MANAGING EAST CENTRAL EUROPE'S GEOPOLITICS

Russia's statist policy heightens the need for wise planning as the West enlarges. If the West's sole goal is to mollify Russia, it likely would not enlarge into East Central Europe at all. But the West is being influenced by other objectives, which include preventing this region from sliding into a geopolitical instability that could endanger all of Europe. Today, this region is making progress in escaping from its Cold War past. A tranquil future is possible if it becomes democratic, builds prosperous economies, settles lingering ethnic frictions, and harmonizes the quadrangular relationship among Germany, Russia, Poland, and Ukraine. The entire region is threatened by deep troubles, however: Its security system is anarchical, owing to the lack of collective-defense assurances; its members are wary of Russia and each other; and it is afflicted with widespread imbalances of military power. The current situation is far from static, because great changes are possible. In the absence of Western enlargement, such changes might not be for the good.

A distant fear is that a resurgent Russia might regain control of the region, snuff out democracy, and turn the region against the West. A

Partnership for Peace (PFP), and an upgraded OSCE to promote an intensified security dialogue with them. Its goal would be to use this "web" to sufficiently support Russia, Ukraine, and other countries to ensure that the region outside the enlarged West is neither unstable nor threatening. This end game has the virtues of being feasible, affordable, and able to exert positive influence. Its drawback is that it fails to address the geopolitical basics: It says little about how security affairs and economic relationships in Eurasia are to be organized or how Russia and an enlarged West are to relate to each other in strategic terms. As a result, it runs the risk of having only a marginal influence when the basics are at stake. This end game must be part of any coherent strategic end game, because it identifies important instruments for constructive activity; however, devoid of an underlying theory, its ability to serve as a stand-alone end game is another matter.

This lack of a core theory requires that one of the two final end games supplement the institutional web: "open-door enlargement" or the "two-community solution." Open-door enlargement calls on the West to enlarge beyond the Visegrad Four, admitting Ukraine and the Baltic states, in particular, into the EU and NATO in the foreseeable future. At some later date, it might admit Russia and other CIS countries, too. An ever-enlarging West thus would become the vehicle for building a stable regional system. But the West would advance into Eurasia in slow steps, the region would remain pluralist (i.e., composed of many independent actors) in the interim, and an increasingly isolated Russia would stand near the end of the queue.

The two-community solution embraces opposite premises. It assumes that the West will not enlarge far beyond the Visegrad Four, that Europe and Eurasia will be two separate strategic clusters, and that some form of Russia-led reintegration of the CIS is inevitable. This end game grants Russia a leadership role in Eurasia if Moscow behaves responsibly. It endeavors not to block CIS reintegration but to guide it toward the democratic values and gradualism followed by the EU, and, above all, it seeks to avoid hierarchical domination of the CIS by Russia and any military bloc that might threaten the West. Its goal is to create a democratic CIS community in Eurasia that has normal, neighborly relations with the West. It postulates that Poland and Ukraine will enjoy close ties with both communities, thus blurring the separation between them. Its theory of regional stability is that of two different but cooperative and interdependent communities living side by side, peacefully.

Both of these two very different strategic end games offer plausible theories if these theories can be executed as planned. Yet the assumptions of both merit careful scrutiny. The attractions and drawbacks they offer are the reverse of each other. Open-door enlargement is attractive because it views enlargement in encompassing terms. However, to assume that the West will enlarge beyond the Visegrad Four, and that the act of moving selectively into Eurasia can be a basis for stable relations with Russia, is dubious. The two-community solution is more realistic about the West's intentions and the dynamics of dealing with Russia, but it runs the risk of presiding over the wrong kind of reintegration on CIS soil.

The choice between these two final end games resides in an assessment of their trade-offs: Is the West willing to continue enlarging after the Visegrad Four are admitted? In particular, is it willing to admit Ukraine well before Russia is considered? Will this phased enlargement yield regional stability or the opposite? Conversely, is the two-community solution too hopeful that CIS reintegration can be steered in healthy directions and that neighborly relations between two quite different clusters will be possible? If neither end game seems attractive, can some other solution be found?

Perhaps the future must become better-defined before a choice among these and other options can be made. But before many years have passed, a choice must be made. Either enlargement will continue or it will stop, giving rise to the need for some other theory for organizing Eurasia and managing security affairs between an enlarged West and a statist Russia. If the West decides that it is unwilling to enlarge beyond the Visegrad Four and that the institutional web is not strong enough, the two-community solution may offer a plausible fallback position for dealing with Russia and Eurasia. Although the two-community solution requires skillful implementation, pursuing it seems better than either accepting that Eurasia remains in interstate anarchy or acquiescing to Russia's going after the kind of reintegration that might endanger both Eurasia and Europe.

Regardless of the strategic end game chosen, the West faces the practical task of acting to ensure Ukraine's survival. Even if Ukraine does not join the West, its independence is vital to creating a stable regional security system. If Ukraine—currently a neutral state—falls under Russia's control, this status cannot endure: A critical buffer separating Eastern Europe and Russia will be lost, and the likelihood of a new bipolar confrontation between Russia and the West will grow. An independent Ukraine that serves as a bridge between Europe and Eurasia is a viable concept. But to bring it about, strong Western economic assistance to Ukraine will be needed, and a closer security relationship may be required as well. An invigorated PFP provides a vehicle for developing stronger military ties to Ukraine while not threatening Russia. Associate membership in the EU can have the same effect in the economic arena.

The bottom line is that a sensible strategic end game will require some combination of the institutional web, further enlargement, and the two-community solution. Fashioning this combination and carrying it out will require making tough choices and putting in hard strategic labor. Yet the promise is that, if these steps are taken, the West can enlarge with hope that a positive outcome—a stable overall region—can be attained.

MILITARY END GAMES

Assuming that the Visegrad Four are admitted to NATO in the next five years, the military dynamics ahead must be carefully managed in ways that help promote the West's objectives. If these dynamics acquire a life of their own and evolve in negative directions, they could inflict damage on the political climate, intensifying the incentives for bipolar rivalry and other forms of military instability. A military end game, therefore, must be planned for three arenas: NATO's defense preparations, weapon sales and modernization in East Central Europe, and conventional-arms control. The ultimate goals are clear: an enlarged West that can defend itself, a stable security relationship with Russia and the CIS, and a regional balance that minimizes the incentives to provocative conduct by any country. The challenge will be to handle the manifold military details so that these goals can be brought to life.

Pursuit of a military end game begins with the crafting of appropriate defense relationships between NATO and its new members. That NATO can be enlarged with no military appendage may be proposed, but the need to avoid a militarily hollow enlargement will argue otherwise. NATO's commitment to collective defense will require that the forces of old and new members become able to work together to carry out military missions in East Central Europe and elsewhere. The need to avoid sending provocative signals to Russia will mandate that preparations for such missions be restrained and reflect purely defensive intent. NATO will be faced with the task of balancing these goals.

Three military strategies are available to NATO for achieving a proper balance: new-member self-defense, power projection, and forward presence. The first strategy calls for new members to defend themselves with only NATO command, control, communications, and intelligence (C3I) and logistics support. The second strategy provides for NATO combat reinforcements in a crisis, but stations these forces primarily in Western Europe in peacetime. The third strategy stations large NATO forces on the soil of new members in peacetime.

New-member self-defense has the drawback of providing inadequate security guarantees, because the forces of the Visegrad Four lack sufficient strength to handle demanding contingencies. Forward presence likely will be seen as unnecessary in the absence of a major threat, too costly, and provocative. Power projection can meet NATO's security needs at affordable cost while signaling defensive intent. Yet it will require a serious, 10-year defense program aimed at upgrading new-member forces, developing a better military infrastructure in Eastern Europe, and preparing NATO's forces to project eastward in a crisis. If this strategy is pursued, an era of moderate but steady-paced military activity lies ahead as new members join NATO. The outcome can be an enlarged NATO capable of defending itself with conventional forces, thus obviating any need for undue reliance on nuclear weapons.

A sensible military end game also will require steps to exert political control over modernization of weapons and their sale in East Central Europe. In the coming years, a sizable defense market likely will emerge, owing to the need of several countries to replace obsolescent weapons with new models. The outcome of market mechanisms left unchecked might prove unhealthy: For example, some countries might acquire offensive capabilities. Effective political control requires that the sales process not damage NATO's internal cohesion or produce anger by Russia that it has been unfairly excluded from this market. The sales process must avert a polarized outcome in which some nations buy from the West and others buy from Russia, and countries must not be permitted to acquire inordinate numbers of high-technology, offensive weapons, thereby increasing already-existing military imbalances. By relying on affordable, lower-technology systems designed for defensive operations, the modern-ization process can be managed effectively, producing a region of countries capable of protecting themselves while not posing enhanced military threats to each other.

Finally, a sensible military end game argues for innovative ap-proaches to conventional-arms control, so that the Conventional Forces in Europe (CFE) Treaty framework can be more relevant to the new era. The existing framework was designed to handle the old, bipolar Cold War. Although it brought about major reductions in Warsaw Pact forces, it left a still-well-armed East Central Europe, and it does not address the problems posed by the new era. The CFE Treaty will probably have to be amended so that specific provisions that inhibit countries from meeting their legitimate defense needs are softened. The argument may be advanced that new arms-control policies should aim at more deeply cutting the inventories of all states—a proposal that is likely to encounter political resistance and that may not be a reliable path to military stability if major steps are not taken toward full disarmament. A more effective approach would try to buffer any tendency toward a competitive action-reac-tion cycle between NATO and Russia, and to control readiness and modernization across the region so that additional imbalances do not emerge. Such an arms-control agenda would be very different from that pursued by CFE negotiations when the Cold War ended, but it has the attraction of being aligned with the challenges ahead.

CONCLUSIONS

The West considers enlargement to be necessary and desirable, and properly so. Owing to the turbulent setting in East Central Europe and opposition posed by Russia, however, enlargement is not destined to unfold effectively unless the process is managed with coherent policies and viable destinations in mind. The strategic and military end games identified here are intended to help clarify the alternatives available to the West and their consequences. None of the alternatives offers certainty that, as the West enlarges, a stable regional security system will take shape around it. Yet the best of them may be able to tip the scales in this direction. Regardless of how the alternatives are appraised, the larger point is that the West will need to be astute and act wisely in dealing with the political and military challenges that it faces. To neglect this task is to ensure that trouble lies ahead.

ABM Treaty	Anti-Ballistic Missile Treaty
AD-70	Alliance Defense for the 1970s
AFCENT	Allied Forces, Central (Europe)
AFEAST	Allied Forces, East (Europe; hypothetical)
AFSOUTH	Allied Forces, South (Europe)
ALCM	Air-launched cruise missile
APC	Armored personnel carrier
ATACMS	Army Tactical Missile System
AWACS	Advanced Warning and Control System
C3I	Command, control, communications, and intelligence
CDI	Conventional Defense Initiative
Center Regions	Zone covering Germany, France, and Low Countries
CFE Treaty	Conventional Forces in Europe Treaty
CFSP	Common Foreign and Security Policy (of the European Union)
CIS	Commonwealth of Independent States (former Soviet Union; Russia is a part of the CIS)
CJTF	Combined Joint Task Forces (between NATO and WEU)
Comecon	Economic arm of the Warsaw Pact
CSCE	Conference on Security and Cooperation in Europe
Duma	Russia's parliament
EC	European Community
ECE	East Central Europe
EDI	European Defense Identity (of the European Union)

EEC	European Economic Community
EFTA	European Free Trade Association (Austria, Finland, Sweden)
ERM	Exchange Rate Mechanism (of the European Union)
EU	European Union
Eurocorps	The potential military arm of the WEU; it was the Franco-German brigade
FBIS	Foreign Broadcast Information Service
G-7	Group of Seven; major industrial powers that meet regularly to coordinate international economic policy
GDP	Gross domestic product
GNP	Gross national product
ICBM	Intercontinental ballistic missile
IFV	Infantry fighting vehicle
IISS	International Institute for Strategic Studies
IMF	International Monetary Fund
INF Treaty	Intermediate-Range Nuclear Forces Treaty
IRBM	Intermediate-range ballistic missile
IRF	Immediate Reaction Forces
KGB	Komitet Gosudarstvennoi Bezopasnosti (Soviet Secret Police)
LRC	Limited regional contingency
LTDP	Long-Term Defense Plan
MIRV	Multiple independently retargeted vehicle
MLRS	Multiple-Launch Rocket System
MOD	Ministry of Defense
MRBM	Medium-range ballistic missile
MRC	Major regional contingency
MRL	Multiple rocket launcher
NACC	North Atlantic Cooperation Council
NATO	North Atlantic Treaty Organization
NCO	Noncommissioned officer
OECD	Organization for Economic Cooperation and Development (U.N.)
OSCE	Organization for Security and Cooperation in Europe
PCI	Per capita income

PFP	Partnership for Peace
POL	Petroleum, oil, and lubricants
R&D	Research and development
RDF	Rapid Deployment Forces
RFE	Radio Free Europe
RRF	Rapid Reaction Force (NATO)
SAM	Surface-to-air missile
SLBM	Sea-launched ballistic missile
Spetznaz	Special forces (Soviet Union)
SSBN	Missile-launching nuclear submarine
START I and II	Strategic Arms Reduction Treaty I and II
TLE	Treaty-limited entitlement
U.N.	United Nations
USAF	United States Air Force
USSR	Union of Soviet Socialist Republics
Visegrad Four	The states of Poland, the Czech Republic, Hungary, and Slovakia
WEU	Western European Union (associated with the EU)
WTO	World Trade Organization

Chapter One

INTRODUCTION

As recently as 1994, common opinion held that because Russia and Europe seemed headed toward a bright future, the United States could turn its attention to other, more-dangerous parts of the world. Newer, unsettling trends, however, are calling this judgment into question, and Europe may again become a focal point of U.S. strategic policy—especially if, as seems probable, the West's[1] two key institutions, the European Union (EU) and NATO, begin enlarging into East Central Europe in the next few years.

EU ENLARGEMENT

EU enlargement is itself a momentous strategic step that will alter the geopolitical terrain of East Central Europe. At the moment, the EU's enlargement plans are unclear, and they will not be given more definitive detail until after the Inter-Governmental Conference of 1996, which will establish next-steps for carrying out the Maastricht Treaty. What can be said now is that the process of enlargement already has begun with admission of the three European Free Trade Association (EFTA) states: Austria, Finland, and Sweden. The "Europe Agreements" signed in 1993 point toward eventual admission of the Visegrad Four and, potentially, Romania and Bulgaria if these states can meet the EU's stiff criteria for membership. The three Baltic states (Estonia, Latvia, and Lithuania) also have been identified as potential admittees, as have Cyprus and Malta. This

---

[1] By "the West," we mean the transatlantic community bonding the United States and its European allies.

enlargement may take years to accomplish and may not come to full fruition. But if it does occur, it could result in the admission of eleven additional countries by the end of the next decade: five or more from the heartland of East Central Europe.

Moreover, the EU is becoming a more cohesive institution, owing to its emphasis on internal deepening (i.e., adding to the internal strength of existing institutions with current members), and such deepening will enhance the strategic significance of its entrance into East Central Europe. At its inception, the old European Economic Community (EEC) was little more than a union to regulate customs duties. But its growth into the European Community (EC) and the subsequent signing of the Maastricht Treaty have created a European Union with greatly expanded aspirations: for common monetary, economic, and trade policies, as well as a common currency; for co-operation and coordination in justice and home affairs; for a Common Foreign and Security Policy (CFSP); and for development of a "European Defense Identity" (EDI), a step that contemplates co-ordination and even integration of national defense policies. Associated with the EU is the West European Union (WEU), a collec-tive-defense alliance that involves most of the EU's members and whose treaty commitments are stronger even than those of NATO. Throughout the Cold War, the WEU existed in a limbo created by NATO's dominant role. But in recent years it has been slowly coming to life. It is now headquartered in Brussels and has a small military-planning cell that could grow. In addition, the Eurocorps has been created out of the old Franco-German brigade, and it is slowly gain-ing operational status as a potential military arm of the WEU.

Events of 1992–1993 dealt setbacks to the idea that the Maastricht Treaty would produce a unified Europe anytime soon. Reacting to discontent expressed in many countries, the EU established the principle of "subsidiarity," which dictated that the internal affairs of each country would be interfered with as little as possible. Recession across Europe slowed governmental cooperation in economic and monetary affairs. The collapse of the Exchange Rate Mechanism (ERM) in 1992 damaged early prospects for creation of a common currency. Germany, France, and other countries quarreled over the fundamentals: Whether the EU was to become a strong federation with legislative powers or a looser bloc in which member nations would retain substantial sovereignty and act mostly through executive organs. Yet 1994 and 1995 seemingly have witnessed the EU re-covering from its post-Maastricht slowdown and again moving to-ward integration. The history of the past four decades shows that the cause of European unity moves slowly, but relentlessly and with great power. As the EU enters East Central Europe, it will not only enlarge but will also deepen, magnifying its impact on the region's geopolitics because it will tend to enhance the separation between EU members and those standing outside.

One idea has been advanced that the strategic goals of enlargement can be achieved by having the EU expand without NATO also ex-panding. However, this idea apparently has been rejected, partly to avoid the problem of interlocking treaties and backdoor commit-ments by NATO. Membership in the EU will normally bring mem-bership in the WEU and, therefore, treaty commitments from coun-tries that also belong to NATO. In theory, the WEU could become involved in a crisis, which would drag NATO into the crisis, perhaps too late for NATO to control events. Especially for the United States, the need to avoid backdoor commitments argues for the EU and NATO to enlarge in tandem—a judgment now shared by many European countries that regard U.S. guarantees as critical to their own security. Equally important, the EU is still a mostly economic organization, and the WEU is a lightly equipped alliance that will remain dependent upon NATO for many of its security functions. By consensus, WEU members plan to use this body only for security missions that NATO is not prepared to undertake. Even for such missions, the WEU plans to borrow NATO military assets through use of NATO-created Combined Joint Task Forces (CJTFs).[2]

Owing to the judgment that the EU and WEU cannot perform the critical task of laying an adequate security foundation, NATO en-largement is now being viewed as a logical accompaniment to EU expansion. The converse is also true. In the final analysis, EU en-largement is a half-measure because it offers economic prosperity without security, and NATO enlargement is the same in reverse, be-cause it offers security without economic prosperity. Because pros-perity and security cannot flourish without each other, the situation

---

[2]Rick Atkinson and John Pomfret, "East Looks to NATO to Forge Links to West," *Washington Post*, July 7, 1995.

requires that the EU and NATO enlarge together, not on widely separate tracks or as substitutes for each other. This does not imply a need for identical paths in every detail of timing and new members. But it does mean basic strategic complementarity on enlargement issues that go to the heart of shaping the new strategic and economic order in East Central Europe.

NATO ENLARGEMENT

The prospect of NATO enlargement complicates matters, because NATO is a powerful collective-defense alliance whose actions can greatly affect the regional security affairs of East Central Europe. Above all, NATO is an alliance with strong internal bonds. NATO enlargement involves issuing binding treaty commitments to new members, commitments dictating that the entire alliance will come to their defense if they are attacked. Consequently, enlargement likely will involve the developing of ever-closer military relationships between NATO and its new members. Present indications are that at least Poland and the Czech Republic may gain entrance to NATO within five years or so. Hungary and Slovakia may gain entrance as well. After that, nobody knows. For the most part, those that gain access to NATO will be those that join the EU. Those left outside NATO will be those that are also left outside the EU.

A REGIONAL SECURITY SYSTEM

Enlargement can help temper dangerous new-era geopolitics in East Central Europe, and it offers a historic opportunity to bring new European democracies into the Western family of nations. But it also carries risks and challenges, because it will draw the West into a region of chronic turmoil and closer to Russia's borders. Moreover, this step is likely to set into motion complex dynamics of its own, some of them laden with the potential for trouble.[3]

---

[3]For an early optimistic appraisal of prospects for building a stable Europe in the post–Cold War world, see Richard H. Ullman, *Securing Europe*, Princeton, N.J.: Princeton University Press, 1991. For advocacy of strong U.S. efforts to aid the Russian transition to democracy, see Graham Allison and Robert Blackwill, "The Grand Bargain: The West and the Future of the Soviet Union," in Graham Allison and Gregory F. Treverton, eds., *Rethinking America's Security: Beyond Cold War to New World Order*,

East Central Europe presents a difficult challenge, because it is marked by numerous unsettled countries and geopolitical anarchy from a lack of security guarantees. As the West enters this region, it should view enlargement and relations with Russia as interrelated parts of a larger, common enterprise—designing a stable regional security system, an arrangement to promote democracy and community-building—in East Central Europe and beyond.

This book puts forth three main ideas. The first is that, owing to Russia's pursuit of a "statist" foreign policy, a policy aimed at putting its own imprint not only on Eurasia but on East Central Europe as well, the act of shaping a stable regional system will be far from easy. Its regional design will likely differ from that sought by the West. The interaction between an enlarging West and a statist Russia in fluid East Central Europe will largely influence whether a stable outcome is achieved. A danger is that if this interaction is mishandled, it could descend into confrontational relations with Russia or some other form of turbulence. This danger by no means implies that a dark future is inevitable or even likely. Rather, it means that if a bright future is to come, it will have to be achieved by intelligent statecraft.

The second idea is that in order to achieve a favorable outcome, the West will need to develop a clear "strategic end game"—a destination based on a feasible and desirable vision for attaining orderly progress not only for nations joining the West but also for the countries remaining outside—and a plan for bringing it about. As the West moves eastward—not to contain Russia but to promote stability, democracy, and community-building—it will need this strategic end game to help guide its manifold actions and goals over many years. An important component will need to be a stable relationship with Russia. Although difficulties may lie ahead because Russia opposes enlargement, Europe will be safe only if agreement is reached with

---

New York: W. W. Norton and Company, 1992. For an optimistic appraisal of developments in Russia and the U.S.–Russian partnership, see Stephen Sestanovich, "Russia Turns the Corner," *Foreign Affairs*, January/February 1994. For critiques of Clinton Administration foreign policy through early 1994, see Paul D. Wolfowitz, "Clinton's First Year" and Philip Zelikow, "Beyond Boris Yeltsin," *Foreign Affairs*, January/February 1994. For an official Russian perspective for a U.S.–Russian partnership, but with a Russia that asserts its interests, see Andrei Kozyrev, "The Lagging Partnership," *Foreign Affairs*, May/June 1994. Also see Andrei Kozyrev, "Partnership or Cold Peace?" *Foreign Policy*, Summer 1995; Zbigniew Brzezinski, "A Plan for Europe," *Foreign Affairs*, Vol. 74, No. 2, January/February 1995.

Russia on the basics—security affairs and economic relationships. Yet Russia is not the only country in the calculus; others—Ukraine among them—will need to be made secure as well. The challenge lies in fashioning a strategic end game that has a positive, regionwide effect, thereby ensuring that an enlarged West is not left with a dangerous frontier on its new borders. The West's strategic end game needs to be thought about carefully, because a variety of alternatives are available that have very different implications for how the West should behave, and the choice among them is not obvious.

The third idea is that, regardless of the strategic end game chosen, the West will need to devote attention to emerging military affairs as it enlarges into East Central Europe. If it can foster a stable military situation, the chances for a favorable political outcome will be enhanced. The West will need to cooperate with many nations, including Russia. In essence, it will need to develop a military end game, one that goes along with its strategic end game.

APPROACH AND ORGANIZATION

This book is about the strategic and military fundamentals of European security east of NATO's current borders. It deals with the long term: the next one or two decades. It is not written for Russia specialists, and it does not place that country under a microscope, as would a traditional area study. Written for those engaged in the task of forging long-range U.S. policy toward Russia and Europe, it performs the estimation and planning functions for the regional security system as a whole. Accordingly, its approach is macroscopic, deriving from the academic discipline of foreign policy and international relations theory, and employing a geopolitical framework. That is, this study views Russia as one actor in a larger European security system of many nations interacting in a structural setting that influences the conduct of each country. It postulates how and why Russia's strategic policy might unfold and how the overall security system might be affected. Using this estimate, it offers strategic-planning insights into how the United States can carry out enlargement, deal with Russia, and help shape unfolding events by steering them in favorable directions.

This volume combines theory, inference, facts, forecasting, and policy evaluation. It draws on the existing literature, history, primary sources, and many discussions with senior government officials and outside experts who deal with these matters. It offers judgments, but its purpose is to illuminate and inform, not advocate. Its central thesis is that keen strategic thinking and wise planning will be needed in order to bring about a successful conclusion. The West needs to think in comprehensive terms focused on the long term, because it has multiple objectives and interests at stake, and multiple requirements to harmonize.

Chapter Two provides a theoretical framework for the strategic thinking about Europe's new geopolitics and insights into how that strategic thinking can be accomplished. Because a firm understanding of Russia's new foreign policy in Europe and Eurasia is needed before we can assess the options facing Western enlargement policy, the next three chapters cover this subject in considerable depth. Chapter Three examines the essence of Russia's new statist foreign policy. Chapter Four assesses that policy's determinants and long-range staying power. Chapter Five appraises Russia's resources, including its emerging military strategy and force posture. Chapter Six analyzes the new geopolitics of East Central Europe, including the quadrangular relationship among Germany, Poland, Ukraine, and Russia. Chapter Seven deals with Western policy toward Russia and Europe, including alternative strategic end games. Chapter Eight focuses on military affairs in the new geopolitics and describes three possible military end games. Chapter Nine provides conclusions and recommendations.

Chapter Two

A THEORETICAL FRAMEWORK

The issue addressed by this book—NATO's interaction with Russia as the alliance enlarges eastward—is not only controversial but also complex. Although the public debate over NATO enlargement is becoming passionate, it is often too simplistic. A deeper and more comprehensive understanding is needed to grasp the fundamentals. Accordingly, in this chapter, we develop a theoretical framework for gauging the issue—a framework that not only synthesizes many subordinate topics but also probes beneath appearances to examine underlying trends and first principles. Within this framework, we can view the dynamics now emerging in East Central Europe, including the NATO-Russian interaction over enlargement, as an exercise in modern-era geopolitics: the search for a stable security order by many participants with differing agendas. Precisely because a new type of geopolitics is at work, the United States and its allies need to think in truly strategic terms. That is, they need to embed NATO enlargement in a larger policy aimed at managing the region, and Russia, as a whole. The following pages develop this theoretical framework as it applies to the enlargement debate. They provide an organizing context for the following chapters, which examine the subordinate issues.

THE ESSENCE OF GEOPOLITICS

Precisely because it sounds forbidding and because it is used in a specific way here, the term *geopolitics* requires definition. Some decades ago, *geopolitics* was regarded as the narrow study of how geography affects foreign policy and military strategy. Alternatively,

strategic stage in a particular way. But it does not determine the play that will unfold, and many different scripts are possible, with radically dissimilar plots and climaxes. For good or ill, geopolitics is what its participants make of it.

EUROPE'S NEW GEOPOLITICS

The United States has a compelling strategic interest in achieving a stable and peaceful Europe, but is Europe's new geopolitics headed toward stability or instability? The Balkans disaster is a grim reminder of the historical forces that can be brought back to life if not kept under control.[5] Europe's troubles, moreover, are not limited to the Balkans. Potential trouble is brewing in North Central Europe, and that trouble will be neither localized nor the province of minor powers. Today, Europe is best seen as standing at a crossroads: capable of moving toward either peaceful stability or chronic turmoil. Much will depend on how the United States and its Western allies act, because they will have the capacity to affect the outcome. But before they can act wisely, they will need to think and plan for the long term, the next one or two decades.[6]

The assertion that difficulties could lie ahead with Russia will come as no surprise to anybody aware of recent events.[7] Evidence of a more assertive Russian diplomacy is obvious, as the daily news demonstrates. Russia itself could be a partial cause of an unwelcome future; however, the central problem is not solely Russia, but that the currently anarchical security system in East Central Europe—the troubled zone between Russia and Germany—appears unsound at its very foundations because it safeguards the vital interests of almost

---

[5]See Robert D. Kaplan, *Balkan Ghosts: A Journey Through History*, New York: Vintage, 1993; Warren Zimmermann, "Origins of Catastrophe," *Foreign Affairs*, March/April 1995; David Gompert, "How to Defeat Serbia," *Foreign Affairs*, July/August 1994.

[6]For an analysis of the debate between international optimism and pessimism, see Richard L. Kugler, *Toward a Dangerous World: U.S. National Security Strategy for the Coming Turbulence*, Santa Monica, Calif.: RAND, MR-485-JS, 1995.

[7]See Zbigniew Brzezinski, "The Premature Partnership," *Foreign Affairs*, March/April 1994; Paul Wolfowitz, "Clinton's First Year," Philip Zelikow, "Beyond Boris Yeltsin," and Dmitri Simes, "The Return of Russian History," *Foreign Affairs*, January/February 1994; and Andrei Kozyrev, "The Lagging Partnership," *Foreign Affairs*, May/June 1994.

nobody, including Germany.[8] Poland and Ukraine, to name only two countries, are using diplomacy to search for better security arrangements. Meanwhile, Germany's influence is spreading eastward even as Russia prepares to reassert its interests westward, portending more changes in how all countries are likely to see things. Some observers began pointing to this systemic problem two years ago, but their warnings were mostly abstract and speculative. Only as the meaning of events since then has become clear have their warnings gained currency.

East Central Europe has a dubious historical legacy. Its land has been the battleground for many conflicts, it was the catalyst of two world wars, and it was subjugated to communism throughout the Cold War. Today, its residents are trying to escape this history by making the conversion to market democracy and by establishing a peaceful region for themselves. Although, in many ways, their progress is encouraging, market democracy is taking hold only gradually, it is hard to implant in an atmosphere of insecurity, and it alone will not yield regional stability. Moreover, negative trends are at work not only within several countries but also in the overall security system. Few of the countries feel safe, and signs of renewed rivalry among the major powers (United States, Russia, Germany, Ukraine) for influence in this region are beginning to appear. Heady optimism is fading, and real concern is mounting in many quarters. The key question is: What lies ahead?

As of 1993, Europe was divided into three separate parts that were not interacting a great deal: an inward-looking Western community, a neutral East Central Europe, and an internally consumed Russia. An interaction is now starting, and it seems destined to intensify in the coming years: The West is preparing to enlarge by expanding NATO and the EU to encompass at least parts of East Central Europe. This prospect is welcomed by impatient East Europeans, who are becoming restive about their anarchical situation and may be prone to taking steps independently to gain security if membership in Western institutions is not offered. Originally, Russia did not seem likely to object, but it is now becoming a complicating factor in the

---

[8]As defined here, *East Central Europe* includes Belarus and Ukraine. *Eurasia* is defined as including the entire Commonwealth of Independent States (CIS). Hence, Belarus and Ukraine straddle both regions and are a part of each.

enlargement equation. It is coming out of its diplomatic slumber to pursue a new statist foreign policy, a policy aimed at preventing Western enlargement. The impending interaction among these three actors—an enlarging West, an East Central Europe mostly eager to join, and an opposing Russia—promises to be a defining feature of Europe's new geopolitics over the coming decade or two.

NATO'S STANCE TOWARD ENLARGEMENT

NATO enlargement can be seen as one part of the West's effort to manage Europe's new geopolitics. The alliance's *Study on NATO Enlargement* (Brussels, Belgium: NATO Headquarters, September 1995) lays down key postulates to govern the process. It refrains from saying who will be admitted and when. Indeed, it spells out no specific criteria for admission to NATO. But it does make clear general principles. The broad goal is to enlarge in ways that strengthen the alliance, promote democracy, and contribute to a stable Europe. As a result, the study proclaims, NATO will consider countries that can contribute to these objectives while also carrying out the duties and obligations that come with membership. The practical effect is to underscore the status of Poland and the Czech Republic as initial invitees, and to suggest that Hungary and Slovakia might also be invited if their evolution meets NATO's standards. As for other countries, whether the door to NATO is left open will depend on events over the coming years. NATO's standards for enlargement thus are being established. Less clear is how the study's accompanying goals—building a stable European security structure and cooperative relations with Russia—will be accomplished.

The idea of enlarging NATO and the EU eastward remains controversial to some, but it seems destined to occur. *Enlargement* reflects the premise that Western Europe and Eastern Europe are no longer separable, and that if the former is to be stable, the latter must be stable, too. Enlargement already has gained widespread official endorsement and has contributed to expectations that Western institutions will remain relevant to Europe's new problems and opportunities. It reflects many strong and irreversible forces at work in Europe today and tomorrow. It offers to make the West's eastern flank more secure while protecting its growing interests to the east and fostering greater stability there. It also offers the prospect of an enormously positive change for the better: that of bringing new but endangered democracies into the Western family of nations, where they will be able to nurture common values. Enlargement thus seems necessary because it is required by the precarious situation in East Central Europe; it seems desirable because it is the proper vehicle for capitalizing on the opportunity to spread democratic values. For both reasons, it is likely to be a central feature of the West's strategy for dealing with Europe's new security affairs.

While enlarging into East Central Europe may be part of the solution, it is not the whole solution. The benefits of enlargement could be diluted if the by-product is a polarized relationship with Russia and/or if the CIS remains in chronic turmoil. The West will then have brought democratic stability to Eastern Europe, but it will also be threatened with a dangerous frontier on its new eastern border. Even as it carries out enlargement, the West will need to work with Russia to avoid a new bipolar confrontation and a chaotic CIS. Yet it may also have to guard against Russia's pursuing its interests with disregard for its neighbors. Thus, the task of enlarging while dealing with a statist Russia in the new geopolitics will be far from easy, because Russia may be both part of the problem and part of the solution.[9]

RUSSIA'S ROLE IN THE NEW GEOPOLITICS

Russia will likely derive its stance toward NATO enlargement from its own role in Europe's new geopolitics. Notwithstanding its many problems, Russia will remain Europe's largest country—and one of the most influential. The Russian nation is being reborn with a statist foreign policy—as a "normal political actor" (i.e., state-centered and geopolitical) on the Eurasian and European scene, a common player from the eighteenth century until 1917.[10]

---

[9]For an appraisal of Western policy toward Russia, see Rodric Braithwaite, Robert D. Blackwill, and Akihiko Tanaka, *Engaging Russia: A Report to the Trilateral Commission*, New York: Trilateral Commission, June 1995.

[10]For a discussion of the role of interests in foreign policymaking, see Arnold Wolfers, "The Pole of Power and the Pole of Indifference" and Thomas W. Robinson, "National Interests" in James N. Rosenau, ed., *International Politics and Foreign Policy: A Reader in Research and Theory*, New York: Free Press, 1969, pp. 173–190. For a similar discussion of Russian interests from a Russian perspective, see Mahmut Gareyev, "Russia's Priority Interests," *International Affairs* (Moscow), June 1993. For a Western

To be sure, this is not the only way that Russia and its foreign policy could turn out. For example, Russia might succumb to its internal troubles and collapse from within, becoming no longer a country or a state. Alternatively, it might emerge with a new xenophobic ideology, perhaps a modern fascism under a new authoritarian government. Or, if Europe itself makes great strides toward building a unified community from the Atlantic to the Urals, Russia might become a truly democratic country committed to the ideals of integration and not deeply preoccupied with its own interests.

All of these outcomes are plausible. Yet all seem less probable than the statist model. Without implying that the issue should be foreclosed, this study therefore focuses on the characteristics of this model and the implications it poses for European strategic affairs. The issue is not whether Russian foreign policy has changed recently but whether this change is *enduring.* As we argue in Chapter Four, there are reasons for judging that statism may be on the scene for a long time. For the foreseeable future, Russia will be striving to reintegrate the CIS and to keep East Central Europe as a neutral zone into which the West does not enlarge.

The impact of Russia on Europe will depend on the health of Europe itself. A healthy Europe can absorb and channel a Russia in pursuit of its own interests, but an unhealthy Europe may be another matter. What then is the strategic character of Europe, not only today but some years from now? The idea that Europe may be vulnerable to sliding into another era of fragile geopolitics will be dismissed by optimists who judge that the current era has made history anachronistic. They argue that the combination of democracy, market economics, communications, technology, multilateral institutions, learned lessons, new attitudes, and other developments may be transforming international politics for the good. Yet, ethnic hatred and romantic nationalism have produced rampant slaughter in the Balkans, suggesting that even if history is not springing back to life, it is definitely not yet dead.

---

appraisal of recent trends in Russian foreign policy, see Leon Aron and Kenneth M. Jensen, *The Emergence of Russian Foreign Policy,* Washington, D.C.: U.S. Institute of Peace, 1994. For analysis of the early debate over Russia's interests, see Suzanne Crow, "Russia Debates Its National Interests," *RFE/RL Research Report,* July 10, 1992; Jeff Checkely, "Russian Foreign Policy: Back to the Future," *RFE/RL Research Report,* October 16, 1992.

The underlying structure of the European security system will have an important bearing on how the new geopolitics takes shape. Despite friction over Bosnian policy and many internal matters, Western Europe and the transatlantic community today remain united and secure, owing to NATO and the EU. But the situation in East Central Europe looks precarious: Although the countries there are moving toward market democracy and want to join the West, the security system is structurally unstable owing to the lack of security assurances. The countries there are vulnerable and lack collective-defense guarantees, so all suffer from chronic insecurity today, and their problems will grow worse if tomorrow's geopolitics sour. Vulnerability of this sort can unhinge democracy and damage community-building impulses.

It also can lead desperate countries to act controversially in anticipation of a sour future. An immediate worry is that a variant of the Balkans ethnic politics may spread northward and thereby consume the region in anti-democratic nationalism and reborn local rivalries.[11] A more distant fear is that a rejuvenated Russia may rebuild an imperial empire within the CIS and then restore control over Eastern Europe in the manner of Catherine the Great and her czarist successors. But before this restoration could come to pass, steps likely would be taken to head it off, and these steps might themselves have disastrous consequences: remilitarization, new alliances, or Germany's resuming its old role as an independent actor in Central Europe and falling into conflict with Russia.

The existing East Central European security system is neither stable nor static. The taking-hold of democracy and market prosperity will have a calming effect, as will growing economic ties with the West. Yet this transformation will take years, and even then may still not provide security. Moreover, this transformation itself remains fragile, depending on strategic stability for its own success. If the existing security system is subjected to too much stress, it may mutate, and the outcome might be worse than what exists today, going far beyond the strategic realm. A wholesale change could not occur overnight; changes might take place over a period of years, perhaps in silent and cumulative ways that could escape notice in the early

---

[11]See Daniel Patrick Moynihan, *Pandaemonium: Ethnicity in International Politics,* New York: Oxford University Press, 1993.

stages. The issue is not whether something should be done to head off a dangerous future—Western policy already accepts this premise. The real issue is: How can NATO enlargement take place so that it does not produce a new bipolar rivalry with Russia or chronic turmoil throughout the region?

STRATEGIC END GAMES AND MILITARY END GAMES

This question confronts the United States with profound strategic dilemmas. The task of handling an emerging geopolitics requires the blending of power and restraint, the balancing of contending forces, and the negotiating of complex arrangements. Yet the very idea of geopolitical management is somewhat alien to the U.S. foreign-policy style, which was mostly one of implementation, not strategic design. Moreover, the United States sat on the sidelines in the years before World Wars I and II. As a result, it has little experience in grappling with the peacetime problems of bringing geopolitical order to East Central Europe, a region that formerly was assessed as lying outside the strategic perimeter of U.S. vital interests. The United States thus needs to think deeply before it acts.

At the moment, the public debate in the United States seems to miss the point. It is mostly posed in terms of modalities, instruments, and tactics: Should enlargement be carried out by NATO, or the EU, or both? Who should be admitted first and when? What side deals should be made with Russia, and what consolation should be given to those not included in enlargement? These questions are important, but the still-unresolved issues confronting the West are not procedural—they are truly strategic: What is the overall concept for a regional security order? What are the objectives to be served? What is to be accomplished? Above all, what strategic end game is being sought? How is the new security system to appear in its entirety once the process of change has unfolded? How is it to operate so that it produces a satisfactory outcome?

At its core, the long-term strategic task facing the West involves pursuing multiple objectives. If the only goal were to maintain tranquil relations with Russia, the choice would be easy. Indeed, enlargement probably would not be pursued at all, out of concern that the effort would anger Russia. If the goal is to achieve enlargement irrespective of the larger consequences, the effort would become the

West's sole concern and Russia's reaction could be discounted. If the goal is to achieve Russia's acquiescence to enlargement, then Russia could be offered a cynical deal: In exchange for the West absorbing Eastern Europe, Russia would be allowed to rebuild an empire on CIS soil if its power proves adequate to the task.

None of these approaches will work, because each ignores a critical objective in what seems likely to be the West's calculus: the task of designing an appropriate strategic end game. That task is to shape a balanced policy so that, when events *have* run their course, all of the West's multiple objectives are attained satisfactorily.

Dealing with Russia's objections to enlargement will be an important part of fashioning a strategic end game. Notwithstanding the potential difficulties ahead, Russia's current opposition does not ensure a calamity—if enlargement is carried out responsibly. The assertion that democracy in Russia may collapse if the West moves east seems overblown. Russia's form of government will be determined by domestic factors. The more-valid worry is that Russia's foreign policy may tilt in an unwelcome direction. Yet Russia today ostensibly has its new strategic bearings straight. It is acting as a geopolitical power with purposeful intent and is animated by self-interest. The task of dealing with Russia, therefore, is one of managing an already-existing geopolitics with Moscow, not preventing geopolitics from emerging.

How Russia Views Enlargement

Russia seems far more apprehensive about NATO enlarging than about the EU enlarging—a relativity that may stem partly from the realization that any eastward EU growth is years off and, when it does occur, will pose no military threat to Russia. Yet over the long term, an EU presence in East Central Europe could pose an economic threat if it denies Russia access to profitable trade, commerce, and financial relationships with that region. Much will depend on Russia's economic recovery. As for NATO, Russia still seems to regard it as an alien Cold War institution, not an organic part of the Western community with whom Russia professes a desire for intimate ties. This negative stance doubtless reflects geopolitical imperatives rather than a serious belief that NATO is contemplating military aggression against Russia.

The exact nature of these imperatives is unclear. The signals now coming from Moscow suggest that the Russian government may be forging a systematic strategy for contesting NATO enlargement by either blocking it entirely, by diluting it, or by channeling it in acceptable directions. Russia likely will continue warning of dire consequences if enlargement occurs, demanding a special relationship with NATO if it does take place. It may warn of the collapse of arms-control agreements, the formation of a CIS military bloc led by Russia, and other provocative steps. It can be expected to argue in favor of NATO becoming a loose pan-European structure if it enlarges, and to promote the Partnership for Peace (PFP), the WEU, and the Organization for Security and Cooperation in Europe (OSCE) as alternatives. And it probably will play upon the sympathies of NATO's own doubting Thomases, especially southern-region members who see no personal benefit in their alliance going east.

Anti-NATO Stance: Russia's Double Zone of Security

Underlying these stratagems, however, is an unbalanced geopolitical position that likely will weaken Russia's anti-NATO stance in the eyes of others. Russia has a legitimate right to oppose any steps by NATO that might pose a direct military threat to its borders. But it is asking for a good deal more. It is insisting upon what amounts to a double zone of security between it and NATO. The inner layer is to be provided by Belarus and Ukraine—CIS members that will have close ties to Russia and, if anything, are vulnerable to being controlled by Moscow. The outer layer is to be provided by a neutral zone of medium-sized East European states that are to be left potentially vulnerable—not only to Russian military power but also to their own anarchical neighborhood. Russia's opposition to these countries joining NATO implies that these countries have no legitimate right to improve their precarious situation through the collective-defense guarantees that NATO could provide. Russia thus is seeking absolute security for itself, but at the cost of absolute insecurity for others.

Russia's claim to legitimacy implicitly rests on the proposition that the 2+4 Agreement of 1990 provided an enduring basis for organizing the future security order in East Central Europe. The main purpose of that agreement was limited: to unify Germany and withdraw Soviet forces from Eastern Europe in a setting of stability and reassurance—not to freeze the resulting geopolitical terrain in perpetuity, especially if great additional changes occurred and subsequent problems were encountered. Today, the East European states seeking entrance into NATO have a well-based legal and geopolitical right to a more secure existence. Russia's demand for an accepting interpretation of its interests is eroded because East European entrance into NATO can be designed in ways that pose no plausible military threat to Russia—a huge, nuclear-powered nation with an amply demonstrated capacity to defend its own borders. Russia's hostility to NATO enlargement appears to stem in part from lingering animosity from the Cold War, not from a well-grounded strategic theory for organizing security in the new era.

Perhaps these considerations will have no affect on Moscow's calculus, but they likely will influence Russia's ability to assemble sympathetic allies on its behalf.

The Limits of Enlargement

Some indicators suggest that Russia is grudgingly coming to accept that some of Eastern Europe will be joining the West and that, provided Russia is neither threatened by NATO nor excluded from Europe, it can live with the outcome. Russia's deeper worry may be: What comes next? Who else will be joining NATO, the EU, and the Western community? Where does the enlargement process end? How will Russia and the CIS region fare in the aftermath?

Russia's true reaction will not be known until NATO begins announcing concrete decisions on the scope and timing of enlargement in 1996–1997. Perhaps Russia may choose to dig in its heels ever deeper as the moment for admitting new members draws near. Yet it would be bucking a powerful tide and provoking a crisis that could be self-defeating. An equal likelihood is that Russia will use diplomacy to make the best of the situation by seeking reassurances that its other interests will be respected. If so, a fruitful dialogue about the security and economic arrangements to accompany enlargement may be possible.

Before a far-reaching dialogue can get under way, the West will need to fashion a strategic concept for the overall region that advances its own goals but also shows respect for Russia's legitimate interests, has a regionwide focus, and sets forth a positive vision for the future. As history shows, geopolitical solutions are hard to forge if their focus is narrow. When enduring solutions were forged, the reason normally was that larger issues were addressed and a comprehensive vision was established. The dialogue over Western enlargement will need to reflect these lessons.

Effective Western Planning Is Needed

Effective Western strategic planning is needed, therefore. *Effective planning* begins with clear objectives. The West is likely to have three primary objectives: to maintain the cohesion of the transatlantic alliance and community; to promote stability, market democracy, and pro-Western ties in East Central Europe; and to preserve constructive relations with Russia while seeking a stable CIS that respects the independence of states on Russia's periphery.

The current public debate over how to achieve these objectives centers on whether to rely on enlargement of the EU, of NATO, or of both. One argument favors the EU because economics is deemed more important than security and because NATO enlargement is opposed by Russia. Another argument favors NATO because security is deemed more important than economics and because EU enlargement could be vastly more expensive than relying on NATO. Both arguments miss the critical point: The two institutions work together and perform complementary functions, and neither can operate effectively in the absence of the other. East European economic ties to the West will be ineffective in the absence of greater security. Conversely, security will have a far less stabilizing effect in the absence of the economic renewal that EU membership can bring. As a result, the logical conclusion is that both institutions should move eastward in tandem. Both, moreover, should begin moving within the next few years to avoid a paralyzing delay.

Western policy reflects awareness that NATO and the EU must enlarge together, not apart. It also has a coherent stance toward timing: that enlargement should move fast enough so that new members are not left wondering, but slow enough so that Russia does not get unduly alarmed. It also seems to be moving toward a decision on who should join first: some or all of the Visegrad Four—Poland, the Czech Republic, Hungary, and Slovakia.

The real debate, therefore, is not over these issues but over strategic end games—and it has not yet really begun. The West cannot afford to muddle eastward without a sense of destination and an overall theory of stability. To have neither could court geopolitical trouble with Russia and a still-fragile security structure. The West might wind up worse off than before by acquiring entangling commitments in a region still prone to fragility from lingering problems left unresolved and new troubles generated. Accordingly, what is the destination for enlargement and the theory of stability behind it? A variety of alternative strategic end games can be imagined, and they need to be scrutinized carefully: The choice is not obvious.

A military end game may be as important as a strategic end game. As history shows, geopolitics and defense planning are intertwined. If not kept aligned, they can infect each other with instability. Despite the common perception that the Conventional Forces in Europe (CFE) Treaty has fashioned enduring military stability, East Central Europe remains an armed camp. Of the many countries, the forces of nearly all are out of balance with their immediate neighbors. To the east is Russia, which is far stronger than any single country or plausible coalition of them. NATO expansion is intended to bring orderly stability to this chaos by reassuring new members and PFP participants of their security, but the associated military issues must be handled effectively.

SUMMARY

The task of enlarging NATO while dealing with Russia thus should be seen within a geopolitical framework. With this framework in mind, we now focus our analysis intently on Russia and its emerging foreign policy.

Chapter Three

RUSSIA'S NEW FOREIGN POLICY OF STATISM

Russia is adopting a new foreign policy of "statism," a key change taking place in Europe that promises to affect events in East Central Europe and poses challenges to Western enlargement. In basic ways, Russia's strategic affairs promise to be similar to those of the old Russian state in the centuries before communism took over. That is, they will be driven by pragmatic interests as defined by Russians themselves rather than by a transcendent ideology.

STATISM DEFINED

A statist foreign policy draws its inspiration from the often-competitive strategic requirements of the parent country and views cooperation as conditional. Its stance toward community-building is the same: It rejects neither cooperation nor community-building in principle, but it judges these ventures by whether they benefit the nation. Statism typically begins with an intense focus on the internal integrity of the state. Looking outward, it seeks a secure environment that will allow the state to live safely and prosper. Accordingly, it often aspires to dominate the areas near its borders and to exert influence farther out. Statism can be imperial, but need not be so. Its outward strategic thrust has geopolitical aims, especially that of great powers worrying about their external setting and having the resources to contemplate trying to control it.

Statism often is equated with nationalism, but the two are not synonymous. *Nationalism* is an ideology that attaches extra-high value to the moral worth and communal bonds of a people. It can produce a statist foreign policy. But it can also produce quite different policies, both less assertive and more assertive. Countries not possessed by nationalism can pursue a statist foreign policy and can muster the willpower to carry it out. Statism requires domestic support, but on behalf of strategic priorities rather than lofty visions or values. *Statism* thus is Palmerstonian: It sees a world not of permanent friends or permanent enemies, but of permanent interests—a world in which consensus is preferred, but conflict is sometimes the case.

The means of statist statecraft tend to be utilitarian: seeking to persuade others, to negotiate, and to take steps that benefit other countries if there is reciprocity. Statism often recognizes the need for restraint. It values stability, provided its interests are protected, and it is aware that order will be achieved only when the legitimate interests of several states are safeguarded. Yet it does not embrace stability as an end in itself, and it is willing to seek change when change is needed to secure high-priority state interests. In the quest for change, it sometimes is prepared to resort to coercion when necessary. When push comes to shove, it is keenly aware of power relationships. It is not necessarily militaristic, but it can regard war as an acceptable instrument of statecraft.

In this chapter, we analyze how Russia currently is defining *statism* for itself. We first appraise the strategic debate in favor of a shift to statism in Russia since 1993, and the Russian government's reaction to this debate by embracing statism's tenets. We then assess how Russia has begun to carry out its new policy in Eurasia and Europe: the two regions of principal concern here.[1]

THE STRATEGIC DEBATE IN RUSSIA

Russia today is preoccupied with its domestic economics and politics, but its government recognizes that a coherent foreign policy is needed. It is confronting weighty questions: What is Russia's proper role in the world? What are the main purposes to be served and what resources should be applied? What goals are to be pursued, priorities

---

[1]Good chronologies of Russia's developments in domestic politics and foreign policy are provided in the annual reviews conducted by the International Institute for Strategic Studies (IISS), *Strategic Survey, 1992–1994*, London: Brassey's Inc. The material presented here draws on these reviews, Western press accounts, Russian press accounts, and discussions with Russian government officials and security experts.

set, and means employed? Russia is not alone in facing these questions. Indeed, the need to craft a new foreign policy for the post–Cold War era has bedeviled countries around the world. Many have encountered trouble figuring out how to react now that bipolarity and ideological confrontation have gone. As Zbigniew Brzezinski and others have written, the dominating feature of the new era is chaos and potential turbulence. Great uncertainty about where international politics is headed creates powerful incentives for many countries to fall back on national interests as a determinant of foreign policy. This trend is already noticeable even within the Western community. Elsewhere, the incentives for statism are stronger. The national interest provides a criterion for shaping diplomacy toward many age-old strategic dilemmas that are resurfacing. Nowhere are the incentives to statism more powerful than on the Eurasian landmass, which is experiencing nearly all of the drawbacks of the new era and few of its benefits.

Until the Soviet Union's last days, President Mikhail Gorbachev hoped that the Soviet Union would remain both a strategic power and communist, but he urged collaboration with the West. He seemed to sense a distant clash pitting European civilization against a China-led Asia and an Islamic fundamentalist world. In his view, a close strategic relationship that joined the Soviet Union to the United States and Western Europe offered a vehicle to contain this menace and produce an enduring era of peace in which the Soviet Union would gradually become more pluralist and prosperous.

Gorbachev's vision was based on the premise that communism would remain viable and that the Soviet Union would continue to exist. Both premises collapsed in late 1991. Communist rule disappeared overnight, and the Soviet Union was disbanded. In its stead came a reborn Russia and a newly created Eurasian structure called the Commonwealth of Independent States (CIS). The new Russia was to be a democratic country with a market economy. But it was beset with huge uncertainties about how to overcome its authoritarian past.

The CIS was envisioned as a body of democratic states enjoying close ties—but it was nothing more than a cloudy vision. The reality is that the CIS had no political shape. The entire region surrounding Russia was now an anarchical mass, with most countries spinning away from organized relationships with Russia. This profound transformation greatly altered the strategic calculus of the new Russian government led by Boris Yeltsin. Owing to its own reform policies, Russia found itself in the middle of an explosive struggle over how market democracy was to be built at home. The effect was to magnify the strategic dilemmas facing Russia. Although initial labors were focused on the domestic scene, Yeltsin's government also tried to grapple with foreign policy amid the turmoil. It did so from a position of weakness, for the once-mighty Soviet empire was now gone. Indeed, Russia itself had as yet no firm identity. Nor did an obvious foreign policy beckon as a way for Russia to deal with the new environment surrounding it.[2]

Atlanticism

In the months after Russia emerged, Foreign Minister Andrei Kozyrev began sketching a foreign policy. In his public statements, Kozyrev seemed preoccupied with creating the international conditions that would allow Russia's internal drama to yield a happy ending. While not oblivious to Russia's interests, he soft-pedaled any hint of statism in favor of cooperation. He stressed two priorities. The first was Russia's need to develop close relations with the United States and Western Europe. The second priority was to establish good relations with the newly independent CIS. Kozyrev stressed that the West should help Russia become a democratic country and a responsible actor on the world scene. This transformation, he said, could aid Russia in overcoming the imperial legacy of the czars and the Soviet Union, thereby contributing to a stable global climate in which Russia could achieve economic reform and respect as a new member of the Western community. Kozyrev's stance came to be called "Atlanticism."[3]

---

[2]For a Russian appraisal, see Alexei Arbatov, "An Empire or a Great Power?" *Novoye Vremya*, December 1992. See also Sergei Karaganov, "After the USSR: Search for a Strategy," *Krasnaya Zvezda*, February 1993.

[3]See Andrei Kozyrev, "A New Russian Foreign Policy for a New Era," Russian Federation Permanent Mission to the United Nations, Press Release No. 41, September 24, 1992; Andrei Kozyrev, "Russia: A Chance for Survival," *Foreign Affairs*, Spring 1992.

In mid-1992, Kozyrev launched an internal study aimed at writing a definitive statement of Russian foreign-policy interests and priorities for the coming era. The document was issued in January 1993, under the title "Concept of Foreign Policy for the Russian Federation." A shorter version offering key tenets was approved by President Yeltsin in April. Inward-looking, it rejected both isolationism and any new ideological dogma. Of the nine tenets laid down, most focused on creating a viable state and achieving economic reform. One tenet, however, addressed security policy. It called on Russia to maintain a reliable defense capable of protecting national borders and to promote a stable system of international relations. Although cast in less forthcoming and supplicant terms to the West than Kozyrev's earlier statements, the document carried forth his Atlanticist theme.[4]

Although Kozyrev's stance reflected a general consensus, its priorities were not fully shared even in 1992. Some Russian analysts were beginning to think in more-calculating terms. For example, Vladimir Lukin, then ambassador to the United States, published an article in the U.S. journal *Foreign Policy* that came across as more guarded. Lukin called for market democracy in Russia not only to make life better but also to help protect Russia from its imperial past. Yet he also expressed doubt that the conversion would come quickly. He endorsed a foreign policy of partnership with the United States, but his reasons were grounded less in idealism than in realism. He said that Russia should become a great power again, not only to promote its interests but also to play a stabilizing global role. Surveying the globe, Lukin found many trends to worry about, including the European transition to a new security architecture and a more powerful role for Germany, a tenuous balance-of-power situation in Asia, an unstable Middle East, and an unsettled CIS, where many new states allegedly were failing to grasp the need for friendly relations with Russia.[5]

Lukin called for the United States and Russia to work together to contain these dangers. He said that Russia was to play the role of a geopolitical stabilizer on the Eurasian landmass and a counterweight

---

[4]Leon Aron and Kenneth M. Jensen, *The Emergence of Russian Foreign Policy*, Washington, D.C.: U.S. Institute of Peace, 1994, pp. 17–34.

[5]Vladimir Lukin, "Our Security Predicament," *Foreign Policy*, Fall 1992.

to menacing countries in surrounding regions. The U.S.–Russian relationship was to be a partnership of equals, and Lukin's tone suggested something more pragmatic than Kozyrev's vision. Lukin pointed to the emergence of three foreign-policy schools in Russia: ideologized democratic internationalism, traditional Russian chauvinism, and enlightened self-interest. The third, he judged, should be the basis for Russia's foreign policy.

Similar sentiments were expressed by Sergei Stankevitch, a close Yeltsin adviser. Rejecting ultranationalism and imperialism, Stankevitch identified two schools worth considering: Atlanticism and Eurasianism. The former, he said, pulls Russia west, and the latter, east and south. He rejected the extremes of both. Atlanticism would not suffice, because Russia was now too far separated from Europe and behind the West in economics. Conversely, Russia could not afford to become a solely Eurasian and Asian power. The task, he said, is for Russia to react to its geographical position by striking a proper balance on an east-west axis and a north-south axis. The overall goal, he said, is to bring security to Russia and stability to neighboring regions.[6]

Growing scrutiny of the Atlanticist model was manifested in a lengthy report issued in early 1993 by the Foreign and Defense Policy Council, an advisory group composed of 37 experts. Orchestrated by Sergei Karaganov, the document was candid about Russia's situation. It asserted that Russia needed to recapture its strategic bearings before it could begin a long effort to shape the surrounding regional environment to suit its interests. It began with the admission that "in the foreseeable future Russia will be a moderately authoritarian state with a mixed state-capitalist type of economy" beset by serious problems. It perceived no threat from the United States and Europe, but worried that the Western alliance was turning so inward that it would not support Russia's reform efforts. In Asia, it expressed concern about Russia's relations with Japan and China. In Central Asia and the Caucasus, it forecasted local instability and the rise of Islamic fundamentalism. Overall, it judged that Russia faces the

---

[6]"State Counsellor Views Foreign Policy Goals," *Nezavisimaya Gazeta*, March 28, 1992.

danger of being written off as a serious power because of its weaknesses and problems.[7]

The report rejected isolationism and imperialism in favor of pragmatic engagement with the outside world. Within the CIS, it endorsed a "post-imperial reintegrationist course" aimed at establishing normal relations with the new states. Noting the pro-Western stances of East European states, it declared that Russia was not interested in seeing them join any security system of which Russia was not a member. It urged a policy of close relations with the West and a constructive dialogue with Asia, South Asia, and the Middle East. It allowed that a semi-authoritarian Russia might experience "recurrences of authoritarianism and harsh acts of force against neighbors or even temporary splashes of imperial ambitions." It concluded that emerging prospects "do not allow us to hope for cloudless relations with the West even despite the hopefully predominant partnership elements in such relations." Its bottom line was that "Russia will be forced to rely on its own possibilities and will go through several stages of improved or worsened relations with the outside world."

Different Schools

Because this influential report was an attack on Atlanticism, it helped set the stage for the full-blown debate over foreign policy that took place in the following months. By mid-1993, three major schools of thought had emerged. The Atlanticist school remained one of them. The second, the "Eurasianist" school, urged Russia to develop a separate strategic identity focused on its internal needs and security management of its immediate region. It rejected a restored empire within the CIS but called for partial reintegration. In Europe and Asia, it called for active participation, with Russia's interests to be the beacon. The third school, which can be called the "Extreme Nationalist" or "Neo-Imperial" school, rejected internal totalitarianism, but its external policies were outright nationalistic. It called for

---

[7]See "Document Presents Theses of Council," *Nezavisimaya Gazeta*, August 19, 1992.

reabsorption of the CIS and a rearmed Russian empire that would act as a global power, in opposition to the West, if necessary.[8]

By early 1994, a further differentiation seemingly had emerged. Writing in *Foreign Policy*, Alexei Pushkin proclaimed four schools. The first school, he said, was the "radical democrats," led by Kozyrev, Yegor Gaidar, and Gennaday Burbulis and still clinging to Atlanticism. The second school in Pushkin's scheme was the "moderate or statist democrats," led by Vladimir Lukin, Sergei Stankevitch, Yevgeny Ambartsumov, and Vladimir Volkov and advocating a strong state, partnership with the West only if Russia was treated as a co-equal, and pursuit of Russia's core interests in Eurasia. The third school, the "statist bureaucrats," was composed of officials from the military-industrial complex, the Army, and the power ministries (defense, intelligence, and internal security). Pushkin said that its stance was similar to that of the second school but was dominated more by vested institutional interests than by strategic theory. The fourth school, he alleged, was composed of the communists and ultranationalists, whose stance was imperial and anti-United States.

Pushkin's spectrum was not the only one to emerge in this period. Alexei Arbatov, for example, saw four schools of his own: a "pro-Western group," a "moderate-liberal group," a "centrist and moderate conservative group," and a "neo-communist and nationalist" group. What stands out is the similarity in how both Pushkin and Arbatov saw the consensus shifting away from Atlanticism. Both asserted that the extremists—the communists and nationalists—were a minority on the periphery. But they also observed that the Atlanticists, once the majority, were rapidly losing strength. They asserted that the statist center was becoming a majority. Indeed, the statist center includes, said Pushkin, "almost all of Russia's leading foreign affairs experts as well as important political figures."[9]

---

[8]For further analysis, see Alexander Rahr, "Atlanticists vs. Eurasianists in Russian Foreign Policy," *RFE/RL Research Report*, Vol. 1, No. 22, May 29, 1992; Suzanne Crow, "Russia Plans to Take a Hard Line on Near Abroad," *RFE/RL Research Report*, Vol. 1, No. 32, August 14, 1992.

[9]See Alexei Pushkov, "Russia and America: The Honeymoon's Over," *Foreign Policy*, Winter 1993/94; Alexei Arbatov, "Russia's Foreign Policy Alternatives," *International Security*, Vol. 18, No. 2, pp. 5–44.

The importance of this shift in elite opinion was magnified by the role it played in the domestic political drama unfolding in Russia. Throughout 1993, Yeltsin had fought an increasingly bitter battle with the hard-line parliament inherited from the Soviet Union.[10] Led by Ruslan Khasbulatov and Alexander Rutskoi, Yeltsin's political opponents called for a slowing of economic reform and diminished presidential latitude in domestic policy, but they also badgered Yeltsin because of his allegedly Atlanticist foreign policy. The crisis came to a head in September, when Yeltsin dissolved parliament, took emergency powers, and called for December elections. The parliament retaliated by impeaching Yeltsin and anointing Alexander Rutskoi president. In early October, violence erupted and Yeltsin turned army tanks against his opponents holing up in the parliamentary White House.

Yeltsin won that bloody encounter, and it freed him to call for a new constitution and election of a new parliament. Yeltsin succeeded in writing a constitution to his liking, calling for substantial presidential authority. But the elections backfired. Whereas reformist parties were left in minority status, parties cautious about reform acquired a plurality, and Vladimir Zhirinovsky and his nationalist supporters showed surprising strength. The effect was to shift Russian politics to the center and right, thereby influencing Yeltsin not only to slow domestic reforms but also to alter his foreign policy.

Signs of a shift in official doctrine had begun to emerge some months before. On September 28, 1993, Kozyrev addressed the United Nations General Assembly. His address came on the heels of speeches by President Bill Clinton, National Security Council Advisor Tony Lake, Secretary of State Warren Christopher, and U.N. Ambassador Madeleine Albright—all of which endorsed close relations with Yeltsin and Russia. Kozyrev heralded partnership with the United States, but he asserted special Russian prerogatives in Eurasia and the CIS. His speech included a plea for U.N. financial support

---

[10]See Margaret Shapiro, "Yeltsin Appeals for Truce on Powers," *Washington Post*, February 13, 1993, and "Russia Congress Moves to Reduce Yeltsin's Power," *Washington Post*, March 11, 1993; Fred Hiatt and Margaret Shapiro, "Yeltsin Assumes Special Rule Over Russia," *Washington Post*, March 21, 1993; Michael Dobbs, "Yeltsin Survives Impeachment Vote," *Washington Post*, March 29, 1993; Margaret Shapiro, "Yeltsin Vows to Protect Reforms," *Washington Post*, May 6, 1993, and "Yeltsin Sets Constitutional Talks in June," *Washington Post*, May 12, 1993.

for Russian peacekeeping operations in the CIS. When U.S. officials later asserted that multinational U.N. forces should perform this mission, the Russian government rejected the idea in favor of its own troops.

On October 12, eight days after the Moscow shoot-out, a revealing article by Kozyrev appeared in the *Washington Post*. Entitled "And Now: Partnership with Russia's Democrats," it claimed that Yeltsin's victory had opened the way to enduring Western partnership with a democratic Russia. But he also added a new twist on how Russia would define this partnership:[11]

> We do have and shall continue to have our special interests, differ-
> ent from Western interests and at times even competing. We intend
> to advance them not through confrontation but through partner-
> ship as other states are doing.

Kozyrev thus stated that partnership with the West would be a two-way street, not only serving Russian interests but becoming the way for *advancing* those interests. The implication was that if adjustments are to be made, the Western states will have to do their fair share of the adjusting. Kozyrev again denied any neo-imperial ambitions or nationalism. But he pointed out that Russia would remain a nuclear superpower and should not be treated like a backward, Third World country. His article closed by asserting Russia's special responsibility for Eurasia, which he defined as a single geopolitical space, not a zone of separate states. He asserted that, in this space, Russia has the right to protect Russian-speaking minorities, to engage in peacemaking, and to pursue economic reintegration.

In the following weeks, the Russian Army unveiled a new military doctrine that had been in the making for eighteen months. The timing suggested the extent to which Yeltsin was now beholden to Army support. The new doctrine underscored the professional military's intent to rebuild a strong force posture that could defend the homeland and support Russia's national security strategy, and laid claim to the necessary funds. In an expression of gratitude for the Army's support in the October showdown, Yeltsin conducted a series

---

[11]See Andrei Kozyrev, "And Now: Partnership with Russia's Democrats," *Washington Post*, October 13, 1993.

of high-profile visits to military bases and announced that salaries would increase and conversion of the defense industry to civilian use would slow. In the aftermath, Marshal Pavel Grachev, Russia's military chief, announced that troop levels might be higher than the 1.5 million originally scheduled by the year 2000.

The Move to Statism

In mid-January, President Clinton journeyed to Moscow after first stopping in Brussels to preside over a NATO summit that adopted the Partnership for Peace initiative.[12]   Clinton also signed (with Yeltsin) a trilateral agreement with Ukraine in which that country would yield nuclear weapons on its soil in exchange for border guarantees and financial support ($350 million from the United States, later upgraded to $700 million). Yeltsin expressed support for PFP over NATO expansion, but he left unclear Russia's willingness to join. In early February, Kozyrev proclaimed that Russian foreign policy would maintain its current course, but he was now portraying himself as a pragmatic statist. The clamor coming from the Duma was decidedly statist. Vladimir Lukin, now chairman of the Foreign Affairs Committee, said that Russian reform would never reflect the U.S. ideal. He denounced PFP as a "rape of Russia" and accused the United States of trying to push Russia out of the Caucasus and Central Asia. Lukin was a centrist on the Russian spectrum. His views were more strident than those of the outnumbered liberals, but they were more mellow than those of many conservatives and rightists. Indeed, Zhirinovsky was calling for a foreign policy of outright nationalism, irredentism, and imperialism.[13]

---

[12]See Ann Devroy, "President to Urge Yeltsin to Press Reform Agenda," *Washington Post*, January 6, 1994; Fred Hiatt, "Yeltsin Promises to Hold Course Despite Election," *Washington Post*, December 22, 1993; Lee Hockstader, "Will Yeltsin Try to Save Russia or Himself?" *Washington Post*, January 3, 1994; Ann Devroy and Margaret Shapiro, "Yeltsin Says Reforms to Continue," *Washington Post*, January 11, 1994; and Fred Hiatt, "Yeltsin Names Cabinet of Reformers," *Washington Post*, January 16, 1994.

[13]Daniel Williams and Lee Hockstader, "NATO Seeks to Reassure East as Russia Warns Against Expansion," *Washington Post*, January 6, 1994. Vladimir Lukin, "No More Delusions: Reform in Russia Will Never Fit American Ideals," *Washington Post*, August 1, 1994.

In late February, Yeltsin gave his State of the Union speech to a combined session of the Duma and Federation Council. Speaking in a stern tone, he proclaimed that Russian foreign policy would be based on protection of the national interest. He warned Eastern Europe not to join NATO unless Russia also joined. He said that cooperation with the West would continue, but that "Russia has the right to act firmly and toughly to defend the national interest." His earlier language of Atlanticism and dependence on Western economic help was toned down. In its place was firm statism, implying that there would be Russian solutions to Russia's problems in domestic policy and an unapologizing assertion of vital interests in diplomacy. The following months saw a steady stream of similar doctrinal statements by senior Russian officials. Kozyrev continued to strive for a balance between Atlanticism and statism. Yeltsin aside, his was the official voice. But most Russian security experts were talking as though statism was without serious rivalry from Atlanticism, and the only real competition was from the political right.[14]

In September, Clinton and Yeltsin met in Washington. With both sides now backing away from the idea that a U.S.–Russian partnership already existed, Yeltsin supported the idea of an "emerging partnership."[15] But he also acknowledged that both countries could make difficult partners. Speaking to the U.N. two days earlier, Yeltsin asserted that Russia's foreign policy would be based on its own interests. He proclaimed that its ties with the CIS are more than a traditional neighborhood relationship—they are a "blood relationship." His remark suggested how Yeltsin viewed claims by the CIS to full independence from Russia. As an East Central European diplomat quipped, "Where and when do blood relationships end?"[16]

Within two months, official rhetoric on both sides was beginning to reflect the mounting strains in U.S.-Russian relations. On December 5, a Conference on Security and Cooperation in Europe (CSCE) summit meeting was held in Budapest. Denouncing NATO expan-

---

[14]Fred Hiatt, "Yeltsin Promises Assertive Russia," *Washington Post,* February 24, 1994.

[15]Hiatt, "Yeltsin Promises Assertive Russia," 1994.

[16]John Goshko, "Yeltsin Claims Russian Sphere of Influence," *Washington Post,* September 26, 1994.

sion, Yeltsin warned of a "Cold Peace" if Russian interests were trampled by the West. Afterwards, Clinton and Vice President Albert Gore pronounced U.S.–Russian relations as being still on track.[17] But a few weeks later, Russian troops poured into Chechnya. Washington at first granted Yeltsin's right to preserve the integrity of the state, but as the violence mounted, it protested with growing vigor.[18] The United States was not alone, but none of the West's complaints seemed to have much effect on the Russian government's determination to quash Chechen separatism.[19] Both governments resolved not to let Chechnya destroy the ties that still bound.

The Chechen crisis did, however, produce soul-searching about Clinton's plans to travel to Moscow in May for a celebration of the fiftieth anniversary of World War II's end. Clinton went, but the tone of the meeting was businesslike, not euphoric like those in the past. The meeting focused mostly on tough security issues (e.g., NATO expansion and Russian sales to Iran), not economics. Some specific deals were signed, but a sense of trouble was also in the air. Afterwards, Clinton praised Russia's domestic reforms and called for continued U.S.–Russian cooperation. Yet he added that "we will have differences," but we are "managing matters which can be managed in a relationship that is quite good for the world and that has made us all safer." Yeltsin's comment was cooler: "Even after the summit, differences on a number of issues have not disappeared.

---

[17]See Daniel Williams, "Russia Minister Balks at NATO's Expansion Plans," *Washington Post*, December 1, 1994, and "Yeltsin, Clinton Clash Over NATO's Role," *Washington Post*, December 5, 1994; Charles Krauthammer, "The Romance with Russia Is Over," *Washington Post*, December 16, 1994.

[18]See Lee Hockstader, "Russia Pours Troops into Breakaway Region," *Washington Post*, December 11, 1994; Fred Hiatt and Margaret Shapiro, "Move on Chechnya Shifts Political Alignments in Moscow," *Washington Post*, December 15, 1994.

[19]For a Russian analysis of how collapse threatens Russia in the aftermath of the Chechnya crisis, see Andranik Migranyan, "Chechnya as Turning Point for Russian State," *Nezavisimaya Gazeta*, January 17, 1995. The author blames the allegedly antistatist policies of the radical democrats (e.g., Gaidar and Kozyrev) and recommends the assertion of presidential power and authority to prevent both collapse and a possible takeover by the communists and ultranationalists.

The important thing is that we seek to address these problems while maintaining a balance of interests."[20]

Writing in *Foreign Policy*, Kozyrev summed up Russia's new strategic doctrine as of mid-1995. The title of his article, "Partnership or Cold Peace?" suggested his tone.[21] Launching his article with a call for continued democratization of his country, he then asserted that democracy cannot flourish without internal order. While acknowledging the legitimacy of dissent, he cited Moscow's treatment of Chechnya as an example of the lawful pursuit of order. The challenge for reformers, he said, is to carry out the task in a civilized manner, or "others will do it for them with a firm hand." Turning to foreign policy, he said that "people in Russia want their country to be a self-confident power capable of championing the interests of their society in the international arena." The challenge facing Russian democracy, he reasoned, is to accomplish this championing task so that a return to authoritarianism does not become tempting.

A democracy, he said, has a legitimate right to pursue its interests. Brushing aside "lofty declarations of partnership," he called for a diplomacy focused on promoting Russia's concrete interests in security, trade, and protection of citizens abroad. He said that today's partnership with the United States resembles a marriage after the honeymoon, when life's day-to-day problems emerge. The solution, he said, is to get down to practical business.

What is to be the practical business? Kozyrev proclaimed that NATO should abandon enlargement unless it becomes a "pan-European organization." He said that Cold Peace can be avoided, but only if the United States and Russia avoid the twin dangers of living an illusion or falling back into ideology. He called for a "partnership that really works." His final sentence proclaimed such a partnership a feasible goal, but only if partnership is based "on equality and a balance of interests." His sober article revealed a great deal about how far Russian strategic thinking had come in only three years.

---

[20]Ann Devroy and Fred Hiatt, "U.S., Russia Cite Discord at Summit," *Washington Post*, May 10, 1995.

[21]Kozyrev, "Partnership or Cold Peace?" *Washington Post*, May 10, 1995.

DEALING WITH EURASIA AND THE CIS

Just as Russia's statist doctrine did not arrive in a single "big bang"—evolving, rather, in stages and still developing—its diplomacy shows a similar pattern. Change started in late 1992, picked up pace in 1993, and intensified in 1994 through 1995. The cumulative effect suggests that although statism has not yet grown into a mature policy, it is showing up in several arenas. In Asia and the Middle East, Russia is starting to carry out policies that reflect statist thinking. The trend is more noticeable in Eurasia and Europe, regions in which Russia has been more active and in which its policies will interact with Western enlargement.

Throughout most of 1992 and 1993, domestic politics pushed foreign policy to the backburner. Yeltsin's government was desperate for Western financial help, however, and thus was quite active in foreign economic policy. In 1992, President George Bush promised Russia $1.5 billion in credits and an additional $1.5 billion in various types of direct aid. In 1993, Clinton upped U.S. aid by $300 million and urged the G-7 to act likewise. Clinton and Yeltsin met in Vancouver, where they laid plans for a U.S.–Russian partnership.

The subsequent G-7 meeting in Tokyo, held at mid-year 1993, was also a success for Russia. The year before, the G-7 had promised $24 billion in aid to Russia. By April 1993, only one-half of that aid had been delivered. The principal shortfall came from aid to be given by the International Monetary Fund (IMF) and the World Bank, aid that was denied because Russia's economic reforms had been judged sluggish. At their 1993 Tokyo summit, the G-7 members increased the total to $28.4 billion and promised faster delivery if Russia acted to put its economic house in order. Of this total, $4 billion was to be made available by the IMF and World Bank under more-relaxed rules, $10 billion was to be long-term loans, and $14 billion was to be used for structural reforms (e.g., to oil-drilling and heavy equipment). In addition, $4 billion was promised as bilateral aid from the United States, Japan, and Britain. Also, $15 billion of Russian debts were to be rescheduled. Critics from Russia and the West grumbled that this increased aid was still far short of being adequate, and that all of it was unlikely to be delivered. But such aid offered the prospect of helping Yeltsin's government stem Russia's downward economic spiral and stabilize the situation.[22]

The following year, 1994, saw a similar pattern, again influenced by Clinton's support. Russia was granted technical rights to information and consultation by the U.N.'s Organization for Economic Cooperation and Development (OECD). Yeltsin attended the G-7 summit meeting as an observer and was given assurances of continued financial support. As a reward for its successful efforts to reduce inflation, Russia was granted greater aid from the IMF. Perhaps most important for the long term, Russia signed an agreement with the EU calling for economic trade, partnership, and cooperation.[23] EU Commission Chairman Jacques Delors proclaimed the deal as historic. The immediate benefits to Russia were unclear because the EU countries have been slow to expand economic ties to that country, but the deal opened the door to improvements in the future.

Russia's international economic position still suffered from major liabilities—among them, an unstable currency and economy, a lack of exportable products aside from natural resources and weapons, and few foreign investments pouring into Russia. But at least Russia was moving toward becoming a member of the world economy. The effects of Western aid are hard to measure, but, at a minimum, it has played a role, along with Russia's own market reforms, in helping bring about the improved economic picture that seemed to be emerging by mid-1995.

The CIS

During the years in which this economic drama has unfolded, Russia began an effort to define its goals and policies within the CIS. The Soviet Union's collapse represented not only the end of communist rule but also the unraveling of a Russian empire built long before the Bolsheviks took power in 1917. Czarist Russia had absorbed Belarus and Ukraine during the seventeenth and eighteenth centuries, and

---

[22]See Dan Oberdorfer and Ann Devroy, "Clinton Said to Have Ordered Bolder Ideas on Russian Aid," *Washington Post*, April 2, 1993.

[23]William Drozdiak, "Russia, European Union Sign Historic Pact," *Washington Post*, June 25, 1994.

Central Asia and the Caucasus in the eighteenth and nineteenth centuries. The dismantling of the Soviet Union resulted in both the tearing down of a centuries-old political structure and rejection of any legitimate right by the new Russia to establish a similar system of authority in the coming era.

The act was done by the newly independent states, all of whom took advantage of the situation to assert their independence from Moscow's control. Preoccupied by its domestic dilemmas, the Yeltsin government acquiesced in this abrupt departure, having little leverage to prevent it. Yet the outcome dealt a blow to Russia, because it yielded a huge loss of territory and status. It also gave rise to troubling questions about the future. Left unclear was how far the disintegration process would go, whether the new states could establish effective governments, and whether Eurasia would be stable. The events of the past three years suggest that Russia is recovering from the shock of lost empire to conclude that it still has bedrock interests in most parts of the CIS, and that an activist approach is needed to protect those interests.

Judging from the debate in Moscow and the Yeltsin government's actions, Russia's basic aim has been to reconstitute strategic order in a huge region that became anarchical when the Soviet Union collapsed. Russia seemingly has minimalist and maximalist objectives. Its minimalist objectives have been to prevent a wave of chaos and violence from sweeping over the region and to prevent the newly independent states from aligning with Russia's adversaries. Its maximalist objectives are less clear but fall under the general rubric of reintegrating the region: drawing the states into closer bilateral and multilateral relations with Russia. Although Russia's weakened condition left it without political and military resources to apply to its causes, its behavior suggests a capacity to use the instruments at its disposal with some skill.

Overall, Russia's strategic position vis-à-vis its minimalist objectives either improved during 1993–1995 or at least did not deteriorate further. Local violence erupted in the Caucasus and parts of Central Asia, but the region has not been swept by widespread conflict, toppling governments, and fracturing states. Belarus remains a loyal buffer, and Ukraine remains a neutral state between Russia and Europe. The Caucasian states have not aligned with Turkey or Iran.

Nor have the Central Asian states aligned with Iran or China, or shown any capacity to join with each other against Russia. Most of the CIS countries recognize that they will remain in Russia's security orbit, or at least that they are located in a bordering zone of great strategic importance to Moscow. Russia's worst strategic nightmares about Eurasia thus have not come to pass.

Russia thus far has been less successful at advancing its maximalist objectives of reintegration, especially for multilateralism: Although the CIS has acquired an institutional facade, it has remained a largely hollow shell. This situation partly reflects skepticism among the CIS powers, but it also reflects Russia's own uncertainty about what the CIS should become. Yeltsin and Kozyrev have spoken of following the path by which the European Community was built. Whether this vision is more than rhetoric is unclear.

Unresolved questions have characterized the public debate among Moscow's foreign-policy experts. Exactly how are Russia's interests served by reintegration? How important is the enterprise, given Russia's other priorities? Who is to be reintegrated: only Belarus and Ukraine, also parts of the Caucasus and Central Asia, or all of both regions? Is reintegration to be political, military, or economic, or a combination of all? How is the relationship to work after reintegration? Is Russia to be the director of a hierarchy, or is a relationship of equals to evolve? Until these questions are answered and adequate resources are applied, Russia's pursuit of CIS integrationist goals likely will be opportunistic, not systematic. Its success will be constrained not only by Russia's lack of power but also by its lack of a clear strategic concept.

The original idea behind the CIS was to create a framework for the new countries to coordinate policies in a variety of areas. Apart from the Baltic states and Georgia, all ten countries agreed to join with Russia. Throughout 1992, heavy blows were dealt to the idea that the CIS would quickly become a vehicle for building close ties between Russia and its new neighbors. Indeed, the term "Commonwealth" was a misnomer, for the CIS fell short of being even a loose confederation. A variety of enacting agreements were signed at the Tashkent summit, including a nebulous five-year collective-security pact. But enthusiasm to bring the CIS to robust life was lacking. Indeed, Russia itself seemed ambivalent, because some of the new states on CIS soil came closer to being economic albatrosses than strategic assets.

The CIS today has several high-level bodies that meet regularly: a Heads of State Council, a Heads of Governments Council, Ministerial Councils, and an Interparliamentary Assembly. What it lacks is a bureaucracy: ministries and agencies similar to those of the EU. The effect is to make the CIS a forum for debate but to deny it the capacity to develop and carry out policy on its own. Its charter document calls for cooperation in many fields: foreign policy; economics, markets, and customs; transportation and communication; environment and ecology; migration; and crime control. Its high-level councils are directed to shape common policy in these areas, but decisions are made by consensus of co-equal members, and implementation authority lies in the hands of the countries. The CIS thus is intended to be only what its members want to make of it, and most members have not sought much.

From the outset, defense policy has been an area where Russia sought cooperation. Russia proclaimed the CIS a common strategic space, but this concept received a mixed reaction from its partners. During the CIS's early days, control of the Soviet Union's nuclear weapons was the highest priority. Agreement was reached that Russia would have operational control over those weapons, but that it would be required to seek CIS-wide approval to use them. By mid-1992, tactical nuclear weapons were being shipped back to Russia. The intercontinental ballistic missiles (ICBMs) and bombers based in Ukraine, Kazakhstan, and Belarus became a more serious sticking point. But by early 1994, agreements had been reached that these countries would all be non–nuclear powers.

Russia's efforts to promote other forms of CIS defense cooperation have encountered tough sledding. Initially a CIS joint military command was established, but it was abolished in June 1993. In its place came a Defense Council and a "provisional joint staff" for coordinating national policies. Ukraine has distanced itself from cooperation, but the smaller countries thus far have been drawn into multilateral and bilateral ties with the CIS and Russia. In 1994, most CIS members endorsed an agreement envisioning Russian bases in several countries, joint training, a CIS air defense system, and combined peacekeeping troops. For the most part, progress in these areas has been slow. A number of states in straitened circumstances have wanted financial support that Russia has been unenthusiastic about giving. Russia, on the other hand, has wanted control over a wide range of their military activities. Except for limited forms of cooperation, however, these countries have mostly insisted on maintaining national defense forces. The CIS thus is far short of a military alliance similar to NATO or the Warsaw Pact.

In the economic arena, the CIS has met with somewhat greater success. Initially, the CIS countries drifted apart. National currencies were established; tariffs and other barriers to commerce were created. Russia, Belarus, and Ukraine proclaimed their zone a single economic space. Kazakhstan, Uzbekistan, and Kyrgyzstan launched an economic federation as an alternative to the CIS. By 1993, interest in CIS-wide cooperation was starting to appear. Summit meetings endorsed proposals for an interstate bank, a CIS radio and television network, and a court to arbitrate interstate disputes. In September 1993, agreement was reached on a "ruble zone" for seven countries, with the Russian Central Bank to be the sole issuing authority. Widespread agreement also was reached on a framework for a CIS-wide economic union, including the gradual removal of tariffs. The concept laid down was to move from monetary union, to a free-trade zone, and eventually to a Common Market. In late 1994, a CIS Interstate Economic Committee was created as the CIS's first supranational executive body and was given the charter of presiding over future CIS policies.

By mid-1995, nonetheless, the CIS remained a zone of countries with separate economies only loosely tied together through multilateral arrangements. A CIS summit meeting in May produced three agreements, but each was signed by only a subset of the entire body. Seven countries signed an agreement on joint monetary policies; six endorsed a human-rights charter; seven agreed to Russian-led military patrols of the CIS's outer borders. This outcome reflected a pattern prevalent in the CIS from the outset: accords signed by subgroups but not by the entire body. Before the summit, Yeltsin had sketched a picture whereby the CIS would become something like the EU, "where countries have full independence, but put all their problems in one bag." Afterwards, he voiced his disappointment with the summit, saying that if integration is to be achieved, agreement on a full monetary alliance cannot be postponed indefinitely. His vision of an EU-like community seemed a long way off.[24]

Eurasia—Belarus

Because the CIS thus far has not come to robust life, Russia's efforts to pursue its interests in Eurasia have been carried out mostly through its bilateral dealings with the individual countries. In this area, Russia's record has been mixed but, on the whole, fairly successful. One reason is Russia's skillful ability to pull the diplomatic, military, and economic levers at its disposal. Another reason is the CIS countries themselves. All want national independence, but many have come to accept that close ties with Russia are unavoidable and, in varying ways, desirable.

Only Belarus appears to value an enduring bond with Russia, and this stance seems to have deepened over the past three years. A national referendum in early 1995 overwhelmingly endorsed not only close political and economic ties with Russia but actual reunification. The principal barrier is Russia, which has displayed ambivalence about whether it wants Belarus back anytime soon.[25]

Eurasia—Ukraine

By contrast, huge Ukraine, with 54 million people and deep cultural ties with Russia, was intent on establishing independent sovereignty from the outset. Of all the defections, Ukraine's seemingly dealt Russia the worst psychological blow. The Caucasus and Central Asia always had seemed distant parts of the Russian and Soviet empires: of strategic and economic importance, but not part of Russia's cultural heritage. Ukraine was different, because its history and population caused it to be viewed as part of Russia, not an extension of empire.[26] Accordingly, Ukraine's defection was greeted with in-

---

[24]"Russia, Belarus Scrap Border Checkpoints; Ex-Soviet States Reach Partial Accords on Rights, Debt," *Los Angeles Times,* May 27, 1995.

[25]Margaret Shapiro, "Belarus Voters Support Renewed Ties to Russia," *Washington Post,* May 15, 1995.

[26]"Narodnoe Khoziaistvo SSSR za 70 let: Yubileiny statistichesky yezhegodnik," *Finansy I Statistika,* Moscow, 1987, pp. 219–263. *Ukraine and Ukrainians: A Reference*

credulity in Russia, and with outright dismissal of the idea that Ukraine could be a separate state. That Ukraine saw matters differently set the stage for tension between the two countries and for issues that remain unresolved today.[27]

Although Ukraine has joined the CIS's ruble zone and free-trade zone, and has endorsed economic union, its stance toward security relationships with Russia and the CIS has been for national independence. Ukraine pointedly stood outside the 1992 Tashkent Summit's collective-security pact, and has demanded reassurances from Russia about its security. In 1992, Kiev and Moscow disputed the disposition of former-Soviet military hardware left on Ukraine's soil. ICBMs attracted the greatest public attention, but bitter wrangling also took place over the Black Sea Fleet, as well as the large ground and air forces in Ukraine.[28]   Whereas Russia wanted much of the equipment returned to it, Ukraine wanted to keep a large amount for its own defense posture. The nuclear and Black Sea Fleet negotiations bogged down as 1993 unfolded, but Ukraine managed to keep enough ground and air equipment to build a large defense posture—one transparently aimed at signaling Ukraine's new status as a sovereign country able to defend itself. The nuclear issue was settled by the 1994 trilateral deal among Russia, the United States, and Ukraine, in which Ukraine agreed to cede the ICBMs and bombers on its soil in exchange for security assurances and economic aid. The Black Sea Fleet issue remained a thorny one, but, as 1994 unfolded, it

---

Outline, Ukrainian National Association, February 1993, p. 5. "The Economy of Ukraine in January Through September 1994," *Uryadovyy Kuryer*, Kiev, October 27, 1994. Orest Subtelny, *Ukraine: A History*, Toronto: University of Toronto Press, 1988, p. 44. Michael Hrushevsky, *A History of Ukraine*, Kiev: Ukrainian National Association/Archon Books, 1970, p. 43. Michael Hrushevsky, *A History of Ukraine*, 1970, p. xi. David Saunders, *The Ukrainian Impact on Russian Culture 1750–1850*, Edmonton: Canadian Institute of Ukrainian Studies, University of Alberta, 1985, p. 2. Stephen Velychenko, *Shaping Identity in Eastern Europe and Russia: Soviet-Russian and Polish Accounts of Ukrainian History, 1914–1991*, New York: St. Martin's Press, 1993, p. 14. Helen d'Encausse, *The End of The Soviet Empire*, New York: BasicBooks, 1993, p. 127.

[27]For analysis, see Charles F. Furtado, "Nationalism and Foreign Policy in Ukraine," *Political Science Quarterly*, Spring 1994; Adrian Karatnycky, "The Ukrainian Factor," *Foreign Affairs*, Vol. 71, No. 3, Summer 1992; I. S. Koropeckyj, *The Ukrainian Economy: Achievements, Problems, and Challenges*, Cambridge, Mass.: Harvard University Press, 1992; Eugene Rumer, "Will Ukraine Return to Russia?" *Foreign Policy*, Fall 1994.

[28]See "The Black Sea Fleet: Documents and Comments," *UCIPR Survey*, Kiev, Ukraine, June 1995.

was secondary to the larger political, economic, and strategic issues affecting the Ukraine-Russian relationship.[29]

Spring 1994 saw Russian pressure being applied to Ukraine, enough to lead Ukrainian President Leonid Kravchuk to complain to President Clinton that Russia was a strategic threat to it. Russia denied this accusation. But in March 1994, it announced a major cutback of fuel supplies—gas and nuclear rods—to Ukraine. Russia's rationale was $1 billion of unpaid bills, but the effect was to throw the Ukrainian economy into further turmoil. Critics charged that Russia was playing internal politics in Ukraine by trying to split Crimea off and to orchestrate the election of pro-Russians to the presidency and parliament. In April, a military face-off occurred in which a Russian hydrographic ship was harassed by Ukrainian airplanes and naval vessels as it tried to travel from Odessa to Sevastopol. Russian warships came to the rescue, and the incident ended without violence. Two weeks later, the two nations signed a deal whereby Ukraine would get 15–20 percent of the Black Sea Fleet's 300 vessels, and Russia would make a large cash payment to Ukraine for keeping more than 50 percent. This was the third deal signed to dispose of the fleet; the first two deals collapsed. The fleet issue since then has been relegated to quiet negotiations over money, port facilities, and basing rights.

The great strategic issue in Ukrainian-Russian relations continued to be whether Ukraine will survive as an independent nation or, instead, collapse internally and be reabsorbed by Russia. Ukraine had come to life in 1991 amid an outburst of national zeal: After three centuries of almost-continuous subjugation to Russian rule, it finally had recaptured the independence it had held for several centuries before Russia came into existence. It had the advantage of being large, well-populated with an educated workforce, and endowed with rich natural resources. Yet its government chose to avoid serious political reform and economic shock therapy. The result was a political standoff between the presidency and a fragmented parliament largely opposed to reform, and a serious downward economic spiral as 1993 ended and 1994 began. Indeed, Ukraine's economic

---

29 For analysis of nuclear issues, see John J. Mearsheimer, "The Case for a Ukrainian Nuclear Deterrent," and Steven E. Miller, "The Case Against a Ukrainian Nuclear Deterrent," in *Foreign Affairs*, Vol. 72, No. 3, September 1993.

plight soon became worse than Russia's, and some observers worried that it was headed toward collapse. The economic downslide, in turn, magnified Ukraine's internal cleavages. Heavily affected were industrial workers living in Ukraine's eastern districts, many of whom are ethnic Russians. The consequence was growing talk that the Donets region, as well as Crimea, might secede and join Russia.

The July 1994 election of Leonid Kuchma to replace Kravchuk as president seems to have led to a turnabout in Ukraine's plummeting fortunes. Kuchma embarked on accelerated market reforms and budget stringency.[30] By early 1995, Ukraine's economic situation was starting to stabilize. Kuchma slammed the door on Crimean separatism when he dissolved its constitution and presidency, thereby overthrowing a 1993 resolution proclaiming Crimea as Russian territory.[31] Kuchma also took steps to draw closer to the United States by speeding up the removal of nuclear weapons on Ukraine's soil and signing the Non-Proliferation Treaty. The result was an upsurge of Western economic aid to Ukraine. Kuchma visited the United States in fall 1994, afterward announcing a policy of drawing closer to the West in economic and political terms.[32] In May 1995, Clinton reciprocated by visiting Kiev. The atmosphere was noticeably warmer than Clinton's Moscow summit with Yeltsin the day before.[33]

Ukraine's relations with Russia are unclear. Kuchma entered office proclaiming a desire to draw closer to Russia. Ukraine remains dependent upon Russia for many resources, and Russia is a natural market for Ukrainian goods. Also, Ukraine's neutral status is a source of great concern that leads Ukrainians to contemplate closer relations with Russia if deeper ties to the West are not forthcoming. Yet overall political relations between the two countries seem to have

---

[30]James Rupert, "Ukraine Votes Austerity Spending Bill," *Washington Post*, April 6, 1995.

[31]James Rupert, "Between Russia and Ukraine's Key Region in Crimea Is Focus of Diplomacy," *Washington Post*, March 30, 1995. James Rupert, "Striking at Separatists, Ukraine Abolishes Crimea's Charter, Presidency," *Washington Post*, March 18, 1995.

[32]For analysis of Ukrainian affairs through late 1994, see IISS, "Ukraine: Rising from the Ashes," *Strategic Survey*, 1994–1995.

[33]For analysis, see Anders Aslund, "Eurasia Letter: Ukraine's Turnabout," *Foreign Policy*, Fall 1995.

deteriorated during Kuchma's first year. Ukraine remained standoff-ish toward the CIS. Although Russia was responsive in rescheduling Ukraine's debt, it was unresponsive to Ukraine's requests for border assurances in drafting a bilateral friendship and cooperation treaty between them. Yeltsin's protest of Kuchma's handling of Crimea was damaging, because it suggested a Russian willingness to meddle in Ukraine's internal affairs.[34] Russia may try to influence Ukraine's domestic politics. But the idea that Ukraine will implode, and therefore allow Russia to pick up the pieces, is fading.

Eurasia—Central Asia and the Caucasus

Russia's relations with the Central Asian and Caucasian states have been marked by these states' politics of disintegration and reintegration. Nearly all these states took advantage of the Soviet Union's collapse to distance themselves from Moscow. Some (e.g., Kazakhstan) were more irreversibly dependent upon Russia than others or more welcoming of the stabilizing assistance that Russia could provide. Nonetheless, virtually all treated the CIS as an à la carte menu for preserving a limited set of economic and security relationships. Sensing that many of its own interests would be endangered if the region became a permanent anarchy, the Russian government was left frustrated. Russian analysts pointed to the millions of Russian citizens still living in these states, Russia's many economic interests and entanglements, the violence on Tajikistan's border, and the threat of spreading ethnic warfare in the Caucasus. They also spoke of the threat to Russia's southern flank if the two regions descended into local violence or fell under the sway of Islamic fundamentalism. The troubled situation created incentives for the Russian government to forge a better policy employing the limited assets at its disposal and aimed at dealing with the separate countries on a bilateral basis.[35]

As 1993 unfolded, some Russian security experts began describing the CIS region as Russia's "Near Abroad," contending that Russia

---

[34]James Rupert, "Yeltsin Criticizes Ukraine's Crimea Policy," *Washington Post*, April 15, 1995.

[35]For more analysis, see Sherman Garnett, "Russian Power in the New Eurasia," *Carnegie Endowment for International Peace*, Washington, D.C., Fall 1994.

should apply a "Monrovsky Doctrine" to it, the equivalent of the U.S. Monroe Doctrine for Latin America. This stance seemed to give Russia special geopolitical privileges in the region—not only the right to keep out unwelcome foreign intruders but, perhaps also, the right to orchestrate the domestic arrangements of its countries. Russian spokesmen denied the latter interpretation; yet Russia was undeniably involved in the region's affairs.

Whereas its large population and other resources enabled Ukraine to deal with Russia from a position of strength, a different situation prevailed in the Caucasus and Central Asia, with these far-weaker countries finding themselves more vulnerable. Russia's involvement with them was carried out primarily with economic and political means. Yet Russia also retained a measure of military strength that could be used selectively as a diplomatic tool. Russian troops remained in Central Asia, and another 15,000 troops were based in the Caucasus: enough to give Moscow some influence in the countries hosting this presence. With both regions showing signs of instability, it became evident that Russian involvements were aimed at promoting not only general stability but also Russia's interests and favorite sons.[36]

For example, Russia prevented Moldova from leaving the CIS by threatening punitive economic sanctions and by using the 14th Army based there to fashion an internal settlement favorable to Moscow's interests. Moldova threatened to withdraw because it was angry over Russian support for separatist activity in Transdneister. It backed away from the idea when it realized that withdrawal would provoke further trouble from its Russian neighbor. As the situation in Moldova stabilized, Russia signed an agreement in August 1994 to withdraw the 14th Army on a three-year timetable.[37]

In the Caucasus, Russia became entangled in efforts to calm both strife between Armenia and Azerbaijan over Nagorno-Karabakh and unrest in Georgia.[38] Its efforts were advertised as peacekeeping, but

---

[36]For analysis of emerging Russian policy in CIS conflicts, see Suzanne Crow, "Russia Seeks Leadership in Regional Peacekeeping," *RFE/RL Research Report*, April 9, 1993.

[37]For an analysis, see Charles King, "Moldova with a Russian Face," *Foreign Policy*, No. 97, Winter 1994–95. See "Great Russia Revives," *The Economist*, September 18–24, 1993.

[38]See IISS, "Transcaucasus: Hell Is Other People," *Strategic Survey*, 1993–1994.

critics complained that Moscow was taking advantage of the situation to pull all three countries closer to Russia and the CIS, and to ensure that all three countries were led by people friendly to Russia.

Of the three countries, Armenia has attained the greatest success at establishing an independent and democratic government. Its vulnerable location—next to Azerbaijan, Georgia, Turkey, and Iran—gives it an incentive to rely on Russia for support, however.

Russia's involvement in Azerbaijan has been marked by its handling of the Armenia-Azerbaijan dispute over Nagorno-Karabakh. Armenians living in Karabakh began fighting for independence from Azerbaijan in 1988. By 1993, their military operations had become successful enough to spill over into Azerbaijan, causing massive migration of refugees and an embarrassing defeat for the Azerbaijan military. In June, a military uprising led to the overthrow of Azerbaijan's first democratically elected president, Abulfaz Elchibey. His replacement, Geidar Aliyev, is a former local KGB chief and Communist Party leader. Aliyev immediately reversed an earlier parliament vote against ratification of the CIS pact in 1992. In exchange for Azerbaijani sympathy toward Russia's interests, Moscow said it was ready to send peacekeepers to monitor a cease-fire in Nagorno-Karabakh. By mid-1994, Moscow had brokered a cease-fire, but the underlying political problem of Nagorno-Karabakh has not gone away, and Azerbaijan was left more dependent upon Russia than even Aliyev wanted.

A similar situation prevailed in Georgia, a multiethnic state racked by civil war. Fighting erupted shortly after Georgia's first democratically elected president, Zviad Gamsakhurdia, came to power. South Ossetia quickly broke free, and Russian peacekeepers were sent to the region to keep order. In 1992, Gamsakhurdia was forcibly deposed and was replaced by Eduard Shevardnadze, formerly Gorbachev's foreign minister. Gamsakhurdia's supporters retreated to western Georgia, where they waged civil war against Shevardnadze's government. The northwest province of Abkhazia then started fighting for its independence. Owing to its weak military forces, the Shevarnadze government suffered one reversal after another. In late September, Abkhazian rebels, allegedly supported by Russian volunteers, had overrun the town of Sukhumi on Georgia's eastern coast. Shevardnadze dispatched forces to contain the uprising, but they were quickly defeated. With the rebels advancing, by mid-October an alarmed Shevardnadze had retreated to Tbilisi, the capital, where he asked Russian forces based nearby for help. Some 1,000 Russian soldiers were sent to protect the railroad to Tbilisi, thus keeping supply lines open and stemming the rebel tide. Shortly thereafter, a subdued Shevardnadze cast aside his former opposition to the CIS and, bowing to Russian pressures, agreed to join, and also to provide Russia with military bases and port facilities on Georgian soil.[39]

The following February, Marshal Grachev unveiled a plan for five Russian military bases in the Caucasus. When Russia and Georgia signed a treaty of friendship and cooperation, the deal evidently included three bases in Georgia. Russian troops were slated to patrol the border with Turkey and to help train a national Georgian army. Fighting between Georgia and Abkhazia dragged on, but in April 1994, Georgia and Abkhazia signed a cease-fire accord. In June, Russia agreed to send peacekeepers to Abkhazia. Although that step helped stabilize the situation, Shevardnadze was left weak and dependent upon Russian help to keep his country together. Through 1994 and early 1995, tensions remained high in the Caucasus, and the Chechen crisis further intensified the atmosphere. Azerbaijan experienced a coup attempt and seemed on the brink of civil war. Relations between Azerbaijan and Armenia remained volatile. Russia, however, enjoyed a position of influence across the region.

In Central Asia, violence continued along Tajikistan's border: By early 1995, 25,000 Russian troops were deployed there. The remainder of Central Asia was in a state of precarious, yet peaceful, equilibrium. Russia's efforts were focused on propping up preferred regimes, encouraging more-favorable candidates and policies, and shaping better economic relationships. All five countries were more active in the CIS than Ukraine. The two countries most important to Russia, Kazakhstan and Uzbekistan, continued to be led by entrenched governments that, while wanting independence, viewed Russia as a guarantor of stability in the region. Facing Islamic threats from the south, Turkmenistan and Tajikistan embraced a similar cal-

---

[39]See Lee Hockstader, "Rebels Overrun Georgia City," *Washington Post*, September 26, 1993; "Russia Troops to Guard Georgia Rail Line," *Washington Post*, October 21, 1993; "Moscow Ties Return to Mount Georgia," *Washington Post*, October 24, 1993.

culus. Stable Kyrgyzstan remained of indeterminant importance to Russia, and no threat. For the moment, the strategic equation in Central Asia seemed fixed. Although it did not please Russia in its entirety, it did not pose any near-term menace to Russia's vital interests.

Immediate focus shifted from border disputes to disputes over construction of an oil pipeline from the Caspian Sea, so that the region's rich oil reserves could be exploited. Azerbaijan found itself with lucrative offers from Iran and Turkey—a Turkey backed by a consortium of wealthy Western businesses—to build the pipeline westward through their countries. But Russia applied pressure to build the new pipeline northward, across its territory, that would be linked to its existing network between Kazakhstan and the Black Sea. Along with enriching Russia, this outcome promised to leave Azerbaijan, Kazakhstan, and Turkmenistan permanently dependent upon Russia and, thereby, less able to build strong ties to Turkey or Iran.

The effectiveness of Moscow's pressure on Azerbaijan was enhanced because Russia was backing Armenia in its struggle with Azerbaijan over Nagorno-Karabakh. In addition, because it relies on the existing Russian pipeline to export all its current oil, Kazakhstan could scarcely afford to alienate Russia. As of mid-1995, Russia seemed poised to coerce Kazakhstan and Azerbaijan to honor its wishes for an emerging deal calling for two pipelines: one through Russia and one through Turkey. The international consortium was forging a deal that would allocate a sizable share of new oil fields to Russia, muscling out Iran.[40]

A New Great Game?

A Russian spokesman characterized the complex mixture of oil, money, and politics as classical geopolitics: a revival of the great game in the nineteenth century that marked Central Asia and the Caucasus. The old "great game" was focused on the dynamics of Russia absorbing the Caucasus and Central Asia as parts of its expanding empire. If a new great game is emerging, its immediate

---

[40]David Southerland, "Azerbaijan Picks Exxon over Iran for Oil Deal," *Washington Post*, April 11, 1995.

focus appears to be on practical matters, not on a restored Russian empire. Across the entire CIS, countries that earlier could be dismissed as short-lived and destined for prompt reabsorption by Russia are still holding their own. In East Central Europe, Belarus wants to return to Russia, but Ukraine's prospects for enduring independence are brightening. In the Caucasus, Georgia, Armenia, and Azerbaijan all face troubled futures but are determined to preserve their sovereignty. In Central Asia, early hopes for a flowering of democracy are fading, because most countries are drifting toward strong presidential rule and even renewed authoritarianism. Their economic prospects are mixed, their governments face internal opposition, their societies are racked by ethnic tensions, and some of the states have troubled relations with each other. Many continue to depend on Russia for economic help and even security. But none faces imminent collapse or widespread turmoil of the sort that could invite or necessitate a Russian takeover.

A reversal could still occur, because all CIS countries remain vulnerable to internal troubles and, in the long run, to a Russia that might regather enough strength to overpower them. Yet, for as long as the current situation prevails, it alters the strategic calculus facing Russia within the CIS, closing the door on hopes of Russia's nationalists for any early restoration of empire. Consequently, Russia's strategic thinking is being compelled to focus on reintegration of surviving states, not on picking up the pieces of failed efforts at independence.[41]

DEALING WITH EUROPE AND WESTERN ENLARGEMENT

Evidence of growing statism also has come from Russia's diplomatic activities with the "outside world" from 1993 through 1995. Russia's actions point to a country coming out of its diplomatic shell but still uncertain of itself. Bilateral U.S.–Russian relations from late 1994 onward manifest continuing cooperation in controlling nuclear weapons on Russian territory and in the United States purchasing

---

[41]Ann Devroy, "U.S., Russia Sign Variety of Pacts," *Washington Post,* September 28, 1994.

Russian nuclear materials.[42]   The Clinton-Yeltsin meeting in September 1994 produced several agreements in the security arena: mutual inspection of plutonium-storage facilities, accelerated nuclear-arms drawdowns, nuclear retargeting away from each other, shutdown of Russian nuclear reactors, and U.S. financial help for defense conversion. In addition, Clinton and Yeltsin signed an accord to help speed U.S. private-business investments in Russia. Their subsequent meeting in May 1995 produced fewer concrete accords but did help promote a better dialogue on contentious security issues.

In exchange for Clinton's assurances that the door would remain open for Russia to someday join NATO, Yeltsin voiced expectation that Russia would soon join PFP. Although Yeltsin expressed his intent to sell nuclear reactors to Iran pending further review, he agreed not to sell a gas centrifuge, which the United States feared would be used to make nuclear weapons. The two sides also discussed Russia's complaints about CFE limits on its force deployments in the Caucasus, and Clinton expressed willingness to take up the issue at the upcoming CFE review conference. Another subject was the Anti–Ballistic Missile (ABM) Treaty. Without agreeing on the specifics, the two sides concluded that the treaty could be interpreted to provide room for theater defenses—a U.S. request. Clinton and Yeltsin also agreed to press their respective legislatures to ratify the Strategic Arms Reduction Treaty (START) II.[43]

Arms-Control Slowdown

Despite this apparent meeting of minds, momentum seemed to be slowing in the bilateral arena that thus far had been key to U.S.–Russian cooperation: arms-control negotiations. Many specific issues were involved in the numerous negotiating forums, but an underlying reason for the slowdown was political. To U.S. observers, Russia seemed to be losing interest in the entire venture. Since Gorbachev's days, the Soviet Union and Russia had been forthcom-

---

[42]For analysis, see IISS, "Fissile-Material Protection: A New Challenge," *Strategic Survey*, 1989–1990.

[43]Michael Dobbs, "Summit Negotiators Agree on Security Issues, but Hill GOP Opposes Deal," *Washington Post*, May 4, 1995.

ing on arms control, agreeing to a set of historic treaties—e.g., Intermediate Range Nuclear Forces (INF), START I, and CFE—that had dramatically stabilized the old Cold War military balance. But those had been special times, and Russia's stance had reflected the high priority attached to reaching political accords to end the Cold War and stabilize the new era. Also important, Russia was agreeing to disarm excess nuclear and conventional forces and was willing to retire them for budgetary reasons.

The times seemingly are changing. Russia appears less attracted to the political glow of further arms-control progress, and it is in the throes of trying to define defense requirements for the uncertain future. Also, Yeltsin has been under pressure from conservatives to toughen his stance: anti–arms-control Duma protagonists, for example, have been calling for START II to be shelved. All three factors probably have played a role in Russia's less-eager approach. Russian observers have countered that the U.S. side is responsible for any loss of momentum in arms-control negotiations. They have blamed congressional pressure and U.S. efforts to foist disadvantageous deals on their country. The larger truth may be that existing negotiating forums are carryovers from the Cold War and several may not adequately address the emerging security issues of the coming era.

By contrast, control of proliferation is a relevant issue and has not suffered a comparable slowdown. Virtually all of today's other issues are highly technical, not arenas for strategic decisions that will shape world events. In an atmosphere of unengaged top-level political interest, such issues can be intractable or slow-moving under the best of circumstances.

Russia's slowdown may reflect trends that are more basic than a shift in its arms-control strategy. Russia today is trying to dispel the impression that it is in permanent strategic retreat, and being less eager for and less compliant with arms control may be part of this effort. Conceivably, Russia is also reaching the conclusion that its bilateral relations with the United States are becoming less important and that regional affairs, involving interactions with many countries, will mark the new era. If so, prospects for U.S.–Russian cooperation will be determined by how regional affairs play out and by how Moscow's interests and policies square with those of Washington. In any event,

Russia is becoming more active in regional politics, even if its emphasis on the United States may be changing. Its principal focus has been on Europe.

Russia and the Retreat from Europe

When Russia was reborn, it inherited the policies of a Soviet Union in strategic retreat from Europe. The Soviet military withdrawal and the accompanying dismantling of the Warsaw Pact and East European communism amount to the biggest and fastest retreat of any nation in modern peacetime history. The resulting upheaval not only destroyed the Cold War bipolar order but also called into question the peace structure in Eastern Europe, which was fashioned at Versailles, after World War I. With the new order still amorphous and no immediate menaces to Moscow's interests, Russia went into a temporary hibernation from Europe. Yet Russia has a long-standing involvement in Europe's security affairs, going back to the days of Czar Peter the Great, in the early 1700s. It was inevitable that, sooner or later, Russia would begin reasserting itself on behalf of its traditional geopolitical interests.

The first signs of such reassertion came with Russian diplomacy to end the war in the Balkans, where Russia has a lengthy history of entanglement and a long-standing friendship with Serbia. As Yugoslavia unraveled, Croatia and Bosnia emerged as two new countries with intermingled ethnic populations. When heavy ethnic fighting broke out in 1992, the West was slow to intervene. But with violence mounting and Bosnian Serb forces pursuing ethnic-cleansing, the U.N. mounted a diplomatic campaign aimed at a political settlement, imposed an arms and economic blockade, and dispatched peacekeepers to help protect civilians and abate the fighting. The U.N. intervention was officially neutral, but, by early 1993, most Western governments were branding the Serbs as aggressors. In late February 1993, Kozyrev offered to send Russian soldiers to help support the U.N. peacekeeping mission. Along with this gesture came concerns by Kozyrev that U.N. policy should not take sides against the Serbs.[44] Russian diplomacy in the Balkans became

---

[44]See Daniel Williams, "Russia Vows Bosnia Peace Role, Sidesteps U.S. Military Force Proposal," *Washington Post,* May 6, 1993.

more active as time passed, and, by mid-year, Russia had established itself as an influential shaper of U.N. policy. It portrayed itself as one of the few countries able to work with the Serbs, calm them down, and persuade them to accept a reasonable diplomatic settlement that would leave Bosnia at least partly intact. It worked toward this end, but to some observers, its efforts seemed skewed toward a settlement more favorable to the Serbs than envisioned in many Western capitals.[45]

Russia's intervention led to creation of a body for coordinating Bosnian diplomacy, the "Contact Group," made up of the most-influential outside participants: the United States, France, Britain, Germany, and Russia. In a larger sense, the Contact Group became an encouraging departure in new-era geopolitical cooperation. It helped buffer against disruptive steps taken by individual major powers. But it also retarded the ability of any single country to take decisive action without the consensus of the others. Russia backed the goal of containing the fighting, and it supported a U.N.–sponsored negotiation aimed at reaching a political settlement. But the negotiations failed to reach a deal, and the fighting dragged on throughout 1994. Russia sided with Britain and France in opposing the growing U.S. interest in lifting the arms embargo and using NATO air power to help the outgunned Bosnian Muslims, who were steadily losing ground. U.N. policy moved toward securing enclaves for the beleaguered Muslims while continuing negotiations. NATO patrolled the seas and skies, and offered to respond when the U.N. called—but no calls for decisive military intervention came. The large U.N. peacekeeping effort did help deliver humanitarian aid and dampen fighting. Yet, with no major NATO military interventions under way, the Serbs steadily consolidated their hold on Bosnian territory and the Muslim position weakened. As of mid-1995, the Bosnian situation had continued to deteriorate. The Croats and Muslims were showing greater military power, and fighting intensified. Concern was mounting that a disastrous outcome lay ahead, and that a wider conflict might erupt across the Balkans.

---

[45]See Daniel Williams, "Bosnia: Europe's Lesson or Problem?" *Washington Post,* December 7, 1994, and Ruth Marcus and John F. Harris, "Behind U.S. Policy Shift on Bosnia: Strains in NATO," *Washington Post,* December 5, 1994.

The role played by Russia and other major powers is a matter of debate. The larger point is that the Bosnian war has marked the new Russia's rite of passage as a strategic player in Balkan affairs and as a country willing to engage in multilateral crisis management, but with its own interests and agenda to serve. It also has marked Russia's re-entrance into European security affairs in general, because at the height of the Balkans conflict, another drama with far-reaching strategic implications had been building to the north, in East Central Europe.[46]

From Neutral Zone to Western Zone?

At the time the 2+4 Accord was signed in 1990, Moscow apparently assumed, or at least hoped, that Eastern Europe would remain a strategic neutral zone after its military withdrawal was completed. The collapse of the Soviet Union one year later greatly reduced the ability of the new Russia to prevent the East Europeans from going their own way, but in the West's rush to help Russian democracy in 1992, few noticed that the opportunity was being taken seriously. By mid-1993, East European drumbeating to join the West was growing louder, and the West was starting to take notice. The idea of retaining a neutral zone made geopolitical sense to the West as long as Soviet military power still cast a dark shadow westward. But with Soviet power gone, a key gain of Cold War victory could be realized: the liberation of Eastern Europe. And with Russia being viewed then as a democratizing country with a still-Atlanticist foreign policy, and hence unlikely to pose big objections if the step was portrayed as an extension of Western community-building, the step toward the West could not be viewed as a strategic threat to Russia.

NATO enlargement was later to attract great controversy. But in mid-1993, the EU was the first institution to begin considering enlargement to the east. The process began at the time the Cold War was ending in the late 1980s, with initial writing of the Maastricht Treaty, which pointed the EU to both deepening (i.e., adding to the internal strength of existing institutions with current members) and broadening (i.e., adding new members). The concept of deepening

---

[46]For a sympathetic account of Russia's role in the Balkans, see Charles G. Boyd, "Making Peace with the Guilty," *Foreign Affairs*, September/October 1995.

soon encountered trouble when several nations began worrying about losing too much sovereignty to a "power-hungry Brussels bureaucracy" and to collectivist policies that were insensitive to differing national requirements.

As momentum for deepening slowed, interest in broadening grew. The first candidates were the already-rich countries of Sweden, Finland, and Austria, all of which were slated for entry within two years. Next in the queue were tiny Cyprus and Malta, followed by ten East European countries, including the Baltic states. By 1994, the EU had signed trade, cooperation, and technical-assistance agreements with all of them. It also had awarded Associate Membership status to the Visegrad Four and to Bulgaria and Romania, called for free trade with them in ten years, and labeled all as potential EU members. The Baltic states were scheduled for similar status in 1995. Because all the countries need to upgrade their economies and pass through a lengthy qualifying process, their entrance may be delayed a decade or more. Yet Germany's growing position in the EU means that the East Europeans have a powerful backer, and West European businesses already are beginning to make investments in the Visegrad Four. An era of flourishing trade and mutual profitmaking appears to be ahead, and will be enhanced as the EU enters Eastern Europe. The EU may be moving in slow motion, but the wheels of its enlargement *have* been set into motion.

NATO initially was slower to respond. Its new strategic concept, signed at the Rome Summit in late 1991, had called for NATO to become a more political alliance, with broader security missions than defense of old Cold War borders. But this concept was primarily viewed as guidance to prepare NATO's forces for involvements in outlying areas: e.g., the Balkans, North Africa, and the Persian Gulf. Military operations in Eastern Europe were seen as one possible contingency; throughout 1992, however, making collective-defense guarantees was not on the agenda. NATO's principal outreach program to the east was the North Atlantic Cooperation Council (NACC), which held regular political consultations for all eastern nations but did not envision membership for any.

The lobbying of the East Europeans played a big role in changing this position by putting expansion on the agenda in 1993. Poland's Lech Walesa and the Czech Republic's Vaclav Havel were especially forceful in arguing for enlargement and warning that failure to bring Eastern Europe into the NATO fold would amount to a sinister new Yalta agreement. NATO's nations began listening to these pleas. Although their reactions varied, a number found reasons of their own for warming to the idea. Even so, NATO enlargement promised to be a serious step involving the extension of collective-defense guarantees into not just a new region, but a historically unstable one.

The enlargement idea was not uniformly shared, but, during 1993, it gained important backing in the United States and Germany, the alliance's two most influential members. For many reasons, the obvious first target was East Central Europe, including Poland and the other three Visegrad states. Unlike the EU, NATO has no associate membership status: Admission is an all-or-nothing proposition. This constraint influenced the alliance's options as the fall 1993 summit approached. Three factors were influential in inhibiting any early endorsement of expansion:

- Lack of uniform consensus within NATO

- The inability of Eastern Europe to meet the standards for admission anytime soon

- Concern about a negative reaction from Russia.

NATO thus fastened on the Partnership for Peace as an initial step, which had the advantage of fostering better defense relationships not only with prospective members but also with many other countries. The summit communiqué announced PFP, but it also made clear that NATO expected to expand eventually and that Russia would not be given veto power over NATO's plans.[47]

PFP enabled NATO's cooperative military activities to move eastward, including Russia and the CIS countries. But it offered no collective-defense assurances, and it was focused on such operations as peacekeeping and rescue, not protection of entire nations. The initiative also got off to a slow start and did little to mollify the East Europeans, who saw it as a weak, temporizing device. A debate

---

[47]See Steve Vogel, "U.S. Proposes NATO Partnership for Former Warsaw Pact Nations," *Washington Post*, October 20, 1993; William Drozdiak, "Yeltsin Warns NATO in Expansion," *Washington Post*, December 9, 1994.

erupted in the United States, and votes in the Congress showed widespread support for expansion. The German position solidified, and support gained ground elsewhere in the alliance. By mid-1994, President Clinton was saying that NATO expansion definitely would occur in the foreseeable future. At its fall 1994 summit, NATO strengthened its commitment to eventual expansion and launched a study aimed at providing answers to the *whys* and *hows* of expansion. A study to address the related questions of who and when was set for 1996. By mid-1995, German Chancellor Helmut Kohl was promising the Poles major progress on both NATO and EU enlargement by 2000, a date commonly heard in Western circles for admitting new NATO members. The wheels of NATO enlargement thus had also been put into motion.

The Russian Response

When talk of NATO enlargement first surfaced in mid-1993, Russia seems to have been caught off guard, and its initial reaction was ambivalence. In a meeting with Walesa, Yeltsin expressed no enthusiasm for the idea but acknowledged that the East Europeans had a right to choose for themselves. His reaction implied that Russia would pose no serious barriers as long as its legitimate interests were respected. Days later, the Russian government began backing away from this forthcoming stance. But even so, it did not portray NATO enlargement as deeply inimical to an orderly future. This ambivalent reaction, however, took place before the events of Bloody October and Russia's subsequent rightward foreign-policy shift. By early winter 1994, Yeltsin's government was sternly warning against NATO expansion unless Russia also was invited to join and was otherwise compensated. Kozyrev's main argument was that enlargement would result in the creation of newly divisive geopolitical lines in Europe, isolate Russia, push it into an anti-Western foreign policy, and weaken prospects for democracy there.

In his January 1994 meeting with Clinton, Yeltsin expressed approval of PFP as an *alternative* to NATO enlargement and, immediately after, grumbled less in public than before. But Russian security experts wrote many articles debunking enlargement and arguing instead for a new, all-European collective-security pact in which NATO's importance would recede. When Clinton endorsed enlargement only six months later, the matter became more troublesome in Russia's view. Clinton's endorsement heightened the prospect that both the EU and NATO would move eastward in tandem and that, within a few years, Eastern Europe would become bonded to Western Europe, thereby eradicating the neutral zone and permanently altering Europe's geostrategic structure. As a result, the Russian government began digging in its heels deeper: Grachev threatened to tear up the CFE Treaty, and Duma pressures mounted against ratifying START II. As part of its outreach to Russia, the Clinton Administration led an effort to rechristen CSCE as OSCE (the *Organization* for Security and Cooperation in Europe), thereby raising the prospect of a stronger collective-security institution to accompany NATO enlargement. The Russian response was to accept OSCE but to complain even louder about NATO.[48]

Although PFP was attractive to many countries seeking military co-operation with NATO, it was given a lukewarm reception by Russia's military, which apparently was coming to question the value of largely symbolic military interactions with NATO. Russian diplomacy entered the picture as well, with similar questions. As 1994 unfolded, Russia latched onto PFP as a device to press its arguments against NATO enlargement. Over twenty European countries chose to join PFP during that year, and Yeltsin originally had indicated potential acceptance by his country. Russia now switched tactics by stalling on joing PFP and not participating unless NATO dampened its commitment to enlargement and, above all, slowed the process in order to give Russia more time to adjust.

Throughout 1994, Russia danced a complex minuet with PFP, alternately offering to join and then rejecting it with loud complaints about NATO. Early in the year, Russia first endorsed PFP, then backed away as part of its disagreements with Western policy in Bosnia. It then reendorsed PFP, but backed away again and postponed U.S.–Russian military exercises. By late March, it again was

---

[48]See Fred Hiatt, "Russia Speeds Plan for Link to NATO," *Washington Post*, March 17, 1994; "Russia May Now Delay Joint NATO Program," *Washington Post*, March 31, 1994. See also Lee Hockstader, "Yeltsin Vents Anger at NATO," *Washington Post*, April 12, 1994; William Drozdiak and John F. Harris, "Russia Asks Fuller Ties with NATO," *Washington Post*, May 25, 1994; Daniel Williams, "Russia Joins NATO Plan," *Washington Post*, June 22, 1994.

expressing interest in PFP, but was demanding a special relationship with NATO that would have left NATO formally consulting with Russia about its policies toward European security affairs. Grachev asserted that PFP should not focus purely on military cooperation, but on larger regional and global matters. He and other Russian spokesmen proclaimed that NATO should become subordinate to OSCE. Kozyrev later downplayed that idea, but still insisted on a special Russian status in PFP.

Russia agreed to join PFP in June 1994, but was unlear about the extent of its participation. NATO rejected a formal role for Russia in alliance decisionmaking but acknowledged Russia as a major power entitled to appropriate treatment. Negotiations proceeded throughout the summer, and Russia seemed to be actively participating in PFP in the fall. Attending a NATO foreign ministers' meeting in December, Kozyrev stunned his hosts by switching positions at the last moment. He said that, owing to NATO's growing flirtations with enlargement, Russia would not participate in PFP. He further complained that NATO had not adequately consulted with Russia in drafting a communiqué inaugurating a study on NATO enlargement. A few days later, the OSCE summit took place, and there Yeltsin thundered about the risk of a "Cold Peace" if NATO enlargement took place against Russia's wishes.

Early 1995 witnessed more Russian complaints about NATO enlargement and further-protracted negotiations over PFP.[49] The informal signals coming from Brussels suggested that NATO enlargement would come slowly, thereby reassuring Russia at least on the pace of the effort. The issues were taken up at the Clinton-Yeltsin meeting in May. Yeltsin continued to warn against NATO enlargement but did agree to participate in PFP. At the subsequent NATO foreign ministers' meeting three weeks later, Kozyrev signed two documents that brought Russia into active PFP participation. The first called for creation of an individual partnership program to cover such endeavors as joint training and maneuvers. The second document spelled out specific areas of cooperation: information exchanges on budgets, defense doctrine, and industries; cooperation

---

[49]Michael Dobbs, "Christopher Predicts Progress on NATO Expansion Issues at Russian Summit," *Washington Post*, April 27, 1995. Rick Atkinson, "Russia Warns NATO on Expansion," *Washington Post*, March 20, 1995.

on peacekeeping; and consultations on nuclear, biological, and chemical weapons. The meeting resulted in endorsement of a two-track approach whereby NATO will enlarge but also will carry out a parallel dialogue with Russia aimed at maintaining a stable relationship. A special "16+1" meeting was held in which Kozyrev met with NATO's foreign ministers to discuss the new approach. Afterwards, Kozyrev expressed satisfaction with the summit, but again voiced his opposition to NATO enlargement by asserting that it would be an anti-Russian step leading to new geopolitical divisions in Europe.[50]

By mid-year, the atmosphere seemed to have improved further. In addition to joining PFP, Russia upgraded its trade agreement with the EU and opened talks for entrance into the World Trade Organization (WTO).[51] Yet Russia's long-range stance toward Western enlargement remained a big question mark. In his *Foreign Policy* article of mid-year, Kozyrev warned against Russia being locked out of satisfying trade relations with Europe, thus signaling that EU enlargement is a worry for Moscow. But his strongest lines were reserved for NATO. Again railing against NATO expansion, he put forth an alternative approach, endorsing the idea of a "special relationship" that would be codified by a security treaty between Russia and NATO and also calling for further steps: a transitional process aimed at reaching a "qualitatively new level of relations between NATO and Russia." Only then, he said, would it be possible for Russia to withdraw its objections to East European states' joining the alliance.

This interaction with Russia, he wrote, would transform NATO into a pan-European security organization and a joint instrument for handling such common challenges as ethnic conflicts, terrorism, nuclear proliferation, and drug trafficking. He made no mention of what was to become of NATO's collective-defense obligations and practices. He outlined a two-stage process. In stage 1, PFP would be activated. In stage 2, lasting three to five years, NATO's transforma-

---

[50]Michael Dobbs, "NATO Has Initial Talks with Russia," *Washington Post*, May 31, 1995.

[51]William Drozdiak, "Russia, European Union Sign Historic Pact," *Washington Post*, June 25, 1994.

tion would occur. The "16+1" arrangement designed to grow out of NATO's existing Program for Bilateral Dialogue and Cooperation would evolve into a mechanism for regular consultation at all levels. A permanent consultative body would be created. It would aim for harmonized positions between Russia and NATO on the alliance's transformation, including political-military and military-technical concerns. He thus was saying that, to gain Russian acceptance of enlargement, NATO not only would have to agree to its transformation in principle but also would have to allow Russia to participate in shaping the details and perhaps to enjoy veto power over them.

Kozyrev expressed flexibility about how his plan would be carried out, but, even so, his long-range vision for changing NATO as a precondition for enlargement seems destined not to go down well in Western circles. Kozyrev's vision suggests that although Russia may be recognizing that it will be hard-pressed to halt expansion, it is aspiring not only to slow it down but also to shape how it is implemented. In all likelihood, Russia will aim to limit the number of new members brought in. It may also seek to prevent new members from being taken into the NATO integrated military command and to bar NATO from deploying nuclear weapons, forces, and other military assets onto East European soil. The signals coming from Moscow in mid-1995 suggest efforts to craft an organized Russian diplomatic strategy around these damage-limiting principles while holding out the option of Russian military counteractions if adequate success is not achieved. If so, the drama over enlargement has not ended. Indeed, it may only just be starting.

The final months of 1995 brought further ambiguity and controversy. For NATO, these were months of growing assertiveness in European security affairs. In September, the alliance published its long-awaited *Study on NATO Enlargement*, addressing the why and how questions. The study called for development of cooperative relations with Russia in tandem with enlargement, yet it also proclaimed NATO's intent to fashion close military ties with new members to ensure that Article 5 commitments can be carried out. At the same time, NATO intervened decisively in the Bosnian war. The summer had witnessed successful operations by Croatian and Bosnian Muslim forces aimed at taking back previously lost ground. The Serbs retaliated with brutal counterattacks against vulnerable Muslim sectors. NATO responded with heavy air strikes against Serb positions. In the aftermath came the Dayton peace accords and a treaty aimed at ending the conflict. The treaty created a multi-national Bosnian state, divided into two parts: a Muslim-Croat federation and a Serb republic. By December, NATO troops—led by 20,000 U.S. soldiers—were entering Bosnia with the mission of maintaining the peace during the period in which the new Bosnia's political institutions are created.

Russia responded by seeking a military role in the Bosnian peace-making mission. After prolonged negotiations, it agreed to send 1,500–2,000 troops who would operate with U.S. forces in Bosnia's northeast sector. This step suggested a willingness by the Yeltsin government to work with NATO in areas of common concern. Yet Yeltsin and his associates continued to complain about NATO enlargement, urging that the process unfold slowly and, preferably, not at all. By the end of the year, diplomacy was taking a backseat to the domestic drama unfolding in Russia over parliamentary elections. With Yeltsin hospitalized due to illness, the liberal reformist parties did poorly. In the elections, the Communist Party sprang back to life by winning 145 Duma seats: over 100 move than it had previously held. With other conservative parties doing well, the liberals were left in the distinct minority, holding only about one-third of the Duma's 450 seats. The outcome primarily signaled a further shift toward caution and gradualism in domestic reform, but it also implied that a foreign policy of statism is now even more prominent than before. Shortly afterward, Foreign Minister Kozyrev was replaced by Yevgeny Primakov, a man noted for more-conservative views. As a result, Russia's opposition to NATO enlargement seems likely to intensify, not diminish.

THE COMPOSITE PICTURE

The trends thus suggest that Russia likely will continue to contest NATO enlargement, including how that enlargement is carried out. It may come to resist "distasteful" forms of EU enlargement as well, because EU enlargement will also reshape the economic and strategic terrain of East Central Europe. These trends reflect a Russia that is against a Western enlargement unsuited to its tastes—a stance that stems from a new, statist foreign policy for asserting Russian interests that is being carried out in comprehensive ways, not only in

Europe but elsewhere. The effect is to firmly found Russia's emerging efforts to contest enlargement in a Russian strategic doctrine based not on ideology for its own sake but on perceptions of national interests and geopolitical dictates.

The West will need to evaluate the unfolding interaction with Russia over enlargement in the context of this bigger strategic picture. The benefits to the West of Russia's earlier Atlanticism have been lost in more than one area, and the consequences are already being felt in many ways. The current version of statism is not imperialism, however. Whether this difference is due to constraints on Russia's appetites or to its capabilities—or to a combination of the two—can be debated, but the key point is that Russia's objectives currently are limited. Its strategy within the CIS is aimed at halting disintegration while promoting reintegration, not at any early restoration of a new empire. In East Central Europe, Russian strategy is defensive, aimed at preserving the existing neutral zone, not restoring Russian control over the region. Both objectives are thorny issues for the West, but they do not yet have the deeply menacing features that might lead the United States and its European allies to conclude that Russia's new foreign policy is transforming the country into a major adversary of the West.

How successfully is the new Russian foreign policy being carried out? Because Russia today lacks sufficient resources to implement this strategy with great vigor and comprehensiveness (see Chapter Five), its performance thus far has been mixed, and doubtless frustrating to Moscow. Nonetheless, Russia has been far from impotent in achieving the concrete objectives it is seeking. While it has not been able to attain its maximalist objectives, it has enjoyed a fair measure of success at attaining its minimalist objectives. Within the CIS, for example, Russia has not been able to achieve early reintegration, but it has prevented the region from drifting into open disrespect for Russia's interests, into widespread instability, or into the camps of Russia's major adversaries. In Europe, Russia has not been able to block Western preparations to enlarge eastward, but the actual enlargement process has not yet begun. Russia has made the West aware that it has interests and stakes in the outcome. It has levers at its disposal that will permit a serious effort aimed at influencing how enlargement is carried out.

So long as this statist policy remains in place, the Russian-Western interaction over enlargement promises to be difficult, but it can be influenced by the pragmatic give-and-take of strategic dialogue. If a more relaxed foreign policy is adopted, enlargement will become easier and less contentious. If a more strident policy is adopted, enlargement will become harder and more prone to causing deep conflict with Russia. So the key question is: Is the current policy destined to be permanent, or is it likely to change in some fundamental way? The next chapter turns to finding answers to this question.

Chapter Four

THE STAYING POWER OF STATISM

Surface appearances suggest that Russia's new statist foreign policy could be a temporary departure. Statism came into existence as Russia's domestic politics were shifting to the center-right, in 1993–1994. If this internal shift is the primary cause and sustaining force of statism, then a subsequent shift away from the center-right might result in statism being rejected in favor of a policy that reflects the new domestic scene. In theory, a move to faster, democratizing reform might beget the return of Atlanticism or some variant of it. Alternatively, a lurch to the far political right—to restored authoritarianism and virulent nationalism—might bring about a quite imperial and belligerent policy.

Closer inspection reveals that although Russia's foreign policy will be affected by its domestic affairs, statism may prove to have considerable staying power. If the Yeltsin government's efforts to create a presidential-style system succeed, that system may reinforce a statist foreign policy. If it fails, internal pressures may arise to alter the policy.

The idea behind a presidential-style system is reflected in a quote from Yeltsin:

> I favor strong presidential power in Russia, not because I am the president, but because I am convinced that Russia would never survive and rise without it. The president is the only popularly elected leader and the only symbol of Russia's unity and integrity.[1]

---

[1] Fred Hiatt, "Pitch for Pragmatic Partnership," *Washington Post*, March 19, 1994.

Initial steps to lay the foundation for this system were taken from 1993 to 1995.[2] The system's essence more than its specific structure is clear. A presidential-style system is intended to be a democracy, but with the strong central leadership that is deemed necessary to advance Russia's causes. It thereby is intended to offset pressures for restored dictatorship while avoiding the twin dangers of democratic paralysis and internal chaos that allegedly could destroy Russia. It seemingly provides a safe, reassuring midpoint between Western liberal democracy and restored authoritarianism, and responds to the need for market democracy reforms while respecting Russia's unique traditions.[3]

Irrespective of how the internal political drama plays out, strategic factors will also play an important role in shaping foreign policy and security. They could argue for continuity whether the Yeltsin model is retained or altered.

Statism was adopted not only to counter transient partisan politics but also to comply with a large number of Russia's top security experts, who favored it on strategic grounds after in-depth deliberations—a factor that greatly enhances statism's staying power. Beyond this, statism seemingly rests on powerful structural foundations that give it the potential to last beyond the consensus of the moment. Russia will remain a normal state acting to protect its interests in an unsettled region, employing the means at its disposal, and dealing with many countries. A less assertive policy may fail to do justice to Russia's interests, and a more assertive policy could be unaffordable and counterproductive. As a result, statism likely will make strategic sense for a long time, regardless of who occupies the Kremlin. Especially if Eurasia and Europe remain unsettled, statism may prove robust. Indeed, the central meaning of the past two years may not be that statism has been adopted but that it is well-situated to become a lasting feature.

The prospect that statism may endure for the long term, however, does not mean that the current interpretation of it will remain static.

---

[2]For analysis of earlier events, see Islam Shafiqul, "Rough Road to Capitalism," *Foreign Affairs*, Vol. 72, No. 2, Spring 1993.

[3]For analysis of Russian internal trends, see Michael McFaul, "Why Russia's Politics Matter," *Foreign Affairs*, January/February 1995.

As a strategic doctrine, statism is flexible. It allows the ends and means chosen for any specific period to vary widely within fairly broad parameters, from cooperation to self-serving behavior. It thus adjusts to new priorities as time passes and conditions change. Because the current version embodies limited ends and constrained means, the chief worry facing the West is that future conditions might lead this policy to mutate in unwelcome directions. Conversely, the challenge facing the West is to orchestrate the future geopolitics—preferably expanding on its willingness to work constructively with Russia's neighbors in Eurasia and Europe—so that this policy does not become more threatening.

In this chapter, we examine the key factors for determining the staying power of statism. By examining insights provided from political theory and history, we establish an orienting framework but do not guess at Russia's specific conduct in the coming era. The insights illustrate the reasons statism often endures in general and that the old Russia carried out a statist policy of its own for three hundred years. We explain how this history bears on the future. We then turn to contemporary Russia, and to the internal and external structural factors that will be influencing statism's prospects in the coming years. Finally, we assess other ways in which Russia could define its interests and interpret its statist policy in the future.

INSIGHTS FROM THEORY AND HISTORY

Statism may endure because it seems to be the policy of choice for countries lacking either a transcendent ideology or satisfying membership in an all-encompassing community of nations. This, at least, is the reason suggested by textbooks on the theory of international relations, many of which are preoccupied with the fundamentals of how regional security systems operate. The very essence of the nation-state is interest-based policies, because the state is an authority structure serving its own national society, not the world at large. Moreover, the state has the capacity to mobilize national assets and thereby project power outward, preventing enemies from controlling outside zones, for its society's safety and betterment. The international arena, in turn, creates powerful incentives for statist conduct: Its structural anarchy, brought about by the lack of governing authority and common values, fashions a "self-help" situation in which all countries are on their own and must take responsibility for safeguarding their own welfare. Internal authority and power, coupled with external anarchy, thus create conditions that push countries toward statist foreign policies.

In today's world, the only region heavily exempted from this rule is the Western community, whose bonds alleviate the propensity for unilateral statism and greatly enhance the incentives for cooperative conduct by making universal gains possible. Within this community, all countries benefit by cooperating; none is left fearing risks down the line by helping neighbors grow stronger. Outside this community, however, the traditional dynamics of structural anarchy prevail—definitely the case in today's Eurasia and East Central Europe. Russia seems a likely candidate for enduring statist conduct, because it is both a major power and a country surrounded by turbulence. Minor powers normally lack the physical power to pursue statism with any ambition or assertiveness. Conversely, countries within tranquil settings face no compelling need to launch organized efforts at attaining what is given them automatically. But major powers possessing both impressive resources and chaotic, yet malleable, environments have strong incentives to act in statist ways.

Enduring statism for Russia would be consistent with the insights of the three main contemporary international relations theories: realism, idealism, and geopolitics. *Realism theory* goes beyond interests and anarchy to portray a world of perpetual uncertainty and competition in which war always threatens and a balance of power must be carefully maintained if peace is to be preserved. Realism's polar opposite is *idealism*, which argues that the dynamics favoring peace can be different, stronger, and more capable of being fostered through cooperative conduct than through rivalry. However, it does not quarrel with the proposition that when national interests are at stake and cannot be secured by anything other than an activist foreign policy, the propensity to statist conduct increases. None of idealism's three subschools, moreover, questions national interests and statist behavior as basic building blocks for international politics. *Institutional theory* holds that peace is built by creating networks of norms, practices, and organizations that temper belligerent conduct through establishing incentives for mutually beneficial cooperation. *Collective-security theory* maintains that organizations can be fashioned that seek peace through a regionwide pact aimed at deterring aggression rather than through a military balance of rival coalitions. *Critical theory* postulates that peace can be achieved by altering basic ideas about acceptable norms of national conduct. All of these subschools quest for peaceful cooperation, but all acknowledge that this quest depends critically on the ability of the major powers to safeguard their interests and harmonize them with each other.[4]

Of the three schools, *geopolitical theory*, which falls midway between the poles of realism and idealism, views differentiated patterns of national conduct and is least likely to make assumptions about how regional interactions are destined to unfold. Regardless, all three theories see statism as a normal foreign policy for a region suspended between deep competition and perpetual peace. *All three appraise statism as the special province of major powers facing trouble with their environments.* To the extent they judge matters correctly, they underscore the prospect that for today's Russia, statism or some variant may be here to stay.

Europe's and United States' History

Whether Europe's history offers an accurate way to forecast Russia's future behavior can be debated, but that history does illuminate how statism can entrench itself in the policies of many countries when a regional security system is unstable. That history also illuminates how the old Russia defined *statism* for itself.

The past 60 years have not witnessed a great deal of unilateralist statism in Europe; World War II and the Cold War were both exercises in ideology and bipolarity. In the three centuries before these conflicts, the opposite conditions prevailed, giving rise to a continued pattern of statism in all its many variants. That some of these historical conditions may be coming back to life in structural terms— in the basic building blocks of a system, albeit not necessarily in outcomes—adds force to the likelihood that statism will return to the

---

[4]For analysis, see John J. Mearsheimer, "The False Promise of International Institutions," *International Security*, Winter 1994/95. Also see the following articles in *International Security*, Summer 1995: Robert O. Keohave and Lisal Martin, "The Promise of Institutionalist Theory"; Charles A. Kupchan and Clifford A. Kupchan, "The Promise of Collective Security"; and John J. Mearsheimer, "A Realist Reply."

modern scene, and will infect many countries in different ways, including Russia.

Indeed, these centuries lend credence to an even bolder judgment about statism's staying power: Countries tend to form not only interest-based policies for a single era but also ongoing grand strategies that can last for many eras. And, once again, it is the major powers confronted with continuing external problems that are the actors most inclined to forge grand strategies, not for months and years but for decades and centuries.

Russia is one such country, but by no means the only one. That a general pattern appears to prevail enhances the likelihood that Russia will be affected irrespective of how its current internal politics play out. Authoritarian countries seemingly are good at shaping grand strategies, but as history shows, democracies can develop a taste for the art as well. What matters in shaping grand strategy is not the internal political structure of a country but its geostrategic circumstances and the enduring requirements for keeping the nation-state alive and healthy in a world whose geopolitics can change dramatically as the decades pass. This general propensity to strategic conduct can be illustrated by first discussing major powers other than Russia—Britain, France, Germany, and the United States—all of which have shown a predilection for grand strategy.

Britain, whether it was ruled by monarchy or democracy, pursued a maritime grand strategy reflecting its island status, its need to keep the Low Countries free of domination by an enemy, and its quest for global markets. France carried out a continental strategy that began with imperialism during its heyday as Europe's strongest power, then reverted to defense as Germany gained supremacy. Germany's behavior also reflected a continental strategy as a large but vulnerable country in the middle of Europe. In its own way, the United States also has carried out a grand strategy during its history, beginning as an isolationist country intent on gaining control over its own continent, then moving gradually outward to establish control over the seas and to influence the European and Asian landmasses.

This continuity in the basic grand strategies of all four countries should not be confused with policies designed to carry out the strategies. Those policies varied substantially. All four countries went through periods of oscillating activity and inactivity. All four had imperial phases, and two of them, France and Germany, briefly pursued ideological crusades. In all four countries, democracy in its infancy gave rise to breast-beating nationalism, but then matured. Democracy did not strip these countries of grand strategy; instead, it channeled their grand strategies toward defensive goals, restraint in using military power, and cooperation with each other. The great achievement of the post–World War II era is Germany's becoming a democracy and these four powers' joining together to forge a unified Western alliance. An important contributing factor is that this step both upgraded the interests of all four powers and provided a vehicle for them to continue carrying out their still-enduring grand strategies in altered form, in collaboration with each other. Indeed, Western state interests, geopolitical imperatives, and grand strategy have not gone entirely away even today. They provide a glue that continues to help hold the alliance and community together.

Russia's History

In the centuries before communism, Russia also had a long history of interests, statist policies, geopolitical conduct, and grand strategy. Russia became a nation-state about the time that European countries were doing the same, but its experience was different in two respects. First, initially separated from Europe by a long distance, it faced different geostrategic imperatives because it was confronted with an unoccupied continent rather than with many powerful nearby neighbors jostling for elbow room. Therefore it pursued a continental strategy of steady outward expansion for two centuries before it became deeply engaged in Europe in the early 1700s. Second, even with European engagement, Russia remained embedded in czarist autocracy and economic backwardness, rather than becoming democratized and modernized. These important differences aside, Russia's history is similar to that of the four Western powers in that it, too, is rich in statist lore.[5]

---

[5]A voluminous literature has been written on Russian history, including domestic politics and foreign policy. Two valuable studies are the source of the history given here: Nicholas V. Rissanovsky, *A History of Russia*, London: Oxford University Press, 1984; and Herbert J. Ellison, *History of Russia*, New York: Holt, Rinehart and Winston, New York, 1964. A classic study is Ivo J. Lederer, ed., *Russian Foreign Policy: Essays in*

A millennium ago, the Eurasian region was dominated by the Kievan Rus state, whose capital was today's Kiev. Large and quasi-democratic, Kievan Rus was animated by commercial trade and by militarism to ward off invaders and gain access to foreign markets. When it lost its political cohesion, it was overrun by the Mongols in 1240. Two centuries later, as the Mongols began retreating, Russia rose in its place.

The original Russia was a small Moscovy principality whose leader organized a group of Russian princes to defeat the Mongols in battle. After its victory, Muscovy began expanding outward, often by subjugating local warlords barring the way. By the early 1500s, the new country had a czar. He presided over a land that had been cut off from Europe's liberalizing renaissance and reformation, and that had continually to confront internal warring and foreign invasion. As a result, the czar was a reactionary dictator. Backed by an army and a police force, he ruled a weak economy and an uncohesive, ill-educated society. A small nobility was in service to the state, there was no middle class, and the large peasantry was impoverished. A pattern of autocracy that was to prevail for 400 years was set in place.

Russia displayed a propensity for statist conduct from its earliest days. Its first two centuries under the statist mantle were mostly spent building the Russian state, securing it from invasion, and enlarging its size on the Eurasian landmass. Despite continuing turmoil in Moscow over who would rule, Russia quickly grew as new lands were absorbed. As this expansion took place, autocracy, militarism, and imperialism reinforced each other. As of 1400, the Muscovy state occupied a small and fragmented parcel of land extending outward about 200 miles to the north and northeast of Moscow. By 1450, its territory had roughly doubled. By 1533 it had doubled yet again, to a size similar to the that of the Kievan Rus, but farther to the north. The next 50 years witnessed a series of military campaigns aimed at completing the expulsion of the Mongols from European Russia. By 1600, Russian territory included part of the current Baltic states, and extended eastward to the Ural Mountains

---

Historical Perspective, New Haven, Conn.: Yale University Press, 1962. See also Hugh Ragsdale, ed., *Imperial Russian Foreign Policy*, New York: Woodrow Wilson Center Press, 1993.

and southward to the Black Sea, the Caucasus Mountains, and the Caspian Sea.

The early seventeenth century witnessed sharp clashes between Russia and Poland over control of White Russia, the land separating them. Although Poland had a strong military that drove to the gates of Moscow, it failed to break the Russians, eventually retreating strategically. In 1654, Russia gained control of modern-day eastern Ukraine; by 1670, it controlled a line running from Kiev to Smolensk. While this fighting was in progress, Russia was also expanding eastward. Early in the 1600s, its border had reached 300 miles east of the Urals. What followed was a largely peaceful, but immensely strategic, colonization. This colonization was checked by Kazakh, Mongolian, and Chinese opposition to the south. But the Russians were free to march eastward, the effort led by peasants freed to seek better living conditions. By 1650, Russian settlers had reached the Pacific Ocean. By 1700, they had reached the Kamchatka Peninsula. The result was to transform Russia into a huge Eurasian country with the largest landmass in the world.

Despite this internal expansion, Russia was not yet regarded as an empire that could cast a strategic shadow outside its borders and onto Europe. It was Czar Peter the Great who won the title of empire, thus marking Russia as a state to be reckoned with. He sought to modernize the state and the economy while not democratizing or otherwise weakening autocracy. He also rebuilt the army and navy, thereby transforming Russia into a first-class military power. His foreign policy was one of war aimed at improving Russia's western flank. After a prolonged struggle, he defeated Charles XII of Sweden, then Europe's most-feared military power. The war began in 1700 when Charles XII marched into the Baltic region and defeated Peter the Great in initial encounters. But the tide turned at the Battle of Poltava in 1708. In 1714, the Russians occupied Finland and destroyed Sweden's navy. These successes brought about a diplomatic transformation as Prussia, Poland, and Denmark all joined Russia against Sweden. The war ended in 1720, when Russian forces invaded Sweden. Although similar efforts to push back Turkey in the Black Sea and Caucasus were unsuccessful, Peter the Great proclaimed himself as emperor in 1721. Only Prussia recognized his title immediately. By 1750, his title was accepted across Europe—

acknowledgment that Russia had irreversibly become a major player in Europe's power politics.

The mid-1700s saw Russia expand upon the definition of *outward-looking statism* established by Peter. Russia participated in a number of important European wars, including the War of Polish Accession, the War of Austrian Succession, and the tumultuous Seven Years' War, in which Russia, Austria, and France fought Prussia and Britain over control of Silesia. Russia made only modest territorial gains, but it succeeded in intimidating many countries and establishing itself as a bona fide player of *realpolitik.*

In a fashion reminiscent of Peter, Catherine the Great's rule in the late 1700s brought a second wave of outward-thrusting statism and great strategic gains in Europe. Prior to her rule, Turkey remained a threat to Russia's southern region. Catherine fought two wars against Turkey, both of which ended victoriously. Russia gained the Crimea and the northern shore of the Black Sea. Equally important, Catherine joined with Prussia and Austria to partition internally divided Poland three times. Before being partitioned, Poland was a large country stretching from Danzig to Smolensk. Afterward, it ceased to exist as a separate state. Prussia and Austria absorbed its western half; Russia was awarded its east. Russia's border moved 300 miles westward, thereby bringing White Russia, Lithuania, and western Ukraine into its sphere.

The eighteenth century thus was highly successful for Russia's statist policy and grand strategy. By skillfully blending military power and diplomacy to take advantage of Europe's geopolitical rivalries, Russia quashed mortal enemies Sweden and Poland, occupied the Baltic region, and took the Black Sea away from Turkey. Russia gained not only valuable new territory but also a deeper security belt on its western borders and seaports. Partitioning of Poland left Russia on good footing with Prussia and Austria, thereby consolidating a three-way axis that brought considerable security from Europe's turbulence.

Yet all was not well. Subjugation by hated neighbors left Poland's people thirsting for sovereignty and revenge. To the south, the Ottoman Empire was angry over its setbacks at Russia's hands. More important, France's Bourbon monarchy had been overthrown by a bourgeois and peasant rebellion. Out of the chaos came a republican state whose ideology posed a great threat to the reactionary autocracies of the east, including Russia. At France's head stood one of the most brilliant military leaders in Europe's history: Napoleon Bonaparte. The stage was set for an equally turbulent nineteenth century, one that would tax Russia's grand strategy and draw it ever deeper into Europe's affairs.

Russia was quick to see the danger when Napoleon emerged as France's dictator, his powerful army fired by nationalism. After defending France's borders, Napoleon used his army to embark upon a great imperial crusade across Europe. Russia's reaction was to project its military power westward in an effort to join other conservative monarchies so that the danger of Europe's being dominated not just by France, but by a revolutionary France, could be contained. By 1799, Russian troops were fighting as part of an anti-French coalition in the Low Countries, Switzerland, and Northern Italy. The conservative powers, however, proved incapable of maintaining a common front, and Napoleon kept them at bay. After a brief peace, the War of the Third Coalition broke out in 1805. Fighting his enemies one at time, Napoleon inflicted crushing defeats on Austria, Prussia, and Russia. By 1807, Napoleon was in control of Europe up to Russia's borders. The peace lasted until 1812, when Napoleon attacked Russia and seized Moscow. The harsh Russian winter drove him out, and his retreat ended in a rout. Determined to crush the French Republican menace, Russia joined with Prussia and Austria to defeat Napoleon at the Battle of Leipzig. The three allies then launched a long drive of endless battles that carried to Paris and Napoleon's exile. Napoleon briefly returned to France and regained power, but he was defeated a second time at Waterloo and was permanently removed from the scene.

Napoleon's departure opened the door to the famous Congress of Vienna, a parley of major powers that, to promote harmony and restore monarchy, redrew the map of Europe. Russia played a key role as a statist power now involved in the peacetime task of shaping Europe's security architecture to suit its own tastes and to serve a larger design. Russia, Prussia, and Austria once again divided Poland among themselves. A German confederation, formed under Austrian leadership, defended Prussia but prevented it from gaining a powerful German empire of its own. Britain was granted the neutrality of the Low Countries. Defeated France lost some territory but was treated mildly, on condition that the Bourbons be restored. In the aftermath came the Quintuple Alliance and the Concert of Europe, which fostered regular consultations among Europe's monarchs, including Russia's czar.

Because this diplomatic outcome left all the major actors satisfied, it fashioned a geopolitical equilibrium of conservative powers that was to keep Europe stable for over three decades. During that time, Russia played a role amounting to policeman of Europe, keeping not only instability at bay but democracy at bay, as well. Russia put down upheavals in Poland and Ukraine in 1830, and in Hungary, Moldavia, and Wallachia in 1848. Meanwhile, Russia improved its position in the Caucasus. After defeating Turkey twice, then Persia, Russia annexed Georgia, Azerbaijan, and Armenia. It also acquired extensive naval and commercial rights on the Caspian Sea. Mid-century thus found Russia enjoying a favorable strategic position and being recognized across Europe for its diplomatic prowess and military power.

The following fifty years were to be far less kind to Russia and its statist goals. In 1854, Britain and France acted to block Russia from dominating Turkey, whose decaying empire had become the sick man of Europe. The resulting Crimean War led to Russia's defeat and major damage to its military reputation. Russia turned away from European geopolitics as Czar Alexander II moved to address the need for political, social, and military reforms at home. Russia remained active in promoting imperial designs on its southern neighbors. It pacified the rebellious Caucasus, and its forces swept over the weak states of Central Asia, which became part of the Russian empire. Nonetheless, Russia largely stood on the sidelines as Germany unified and thereby transformed the European strategic scene.

Signs of the negative implications for Russia became apparent in 1875, when Russia came to Serbia's defense and defeated Turkey. At the resulting Congress of Berlin, Britain and Austria joined to redraw the map of the Balkans by taking away territorial gains from Russia and its friends, Serbia and Bulgaria. Owing to Germany's support, Austria was accorded an influential role in the Balkans, and Turkey was given economic and political concessions. Russia, the victor in the war, came away with few spoils—a sign of its declining prestige.

Because Otto von Bismarck had the good sense to maintain an equilibrium with Russia, his actions helped keep Europe stable for another two decades. But, gradually, the stabilizing mechanism became diplomatic intrigue rather than political accord. In 1872, the Three Emperors' League was formed, which joined Germany, Austria, and Russia in a security pact that would collapse in 1887 as Russia and Austria drifted apart, owing to conflicts in the Balkans. Bismarck found an alternative arrangement to keep the three countries at peace. He signed a treaty with Russia, plus a treaty with Austria guaranteeing its defense against attack by Russia. Meanwhile, Britain was so consumed by rivalry with France that it drew close to Germany, whose relations with France remained tense after the Franco-Prussian War of 1870. The European security structure thus became a shaky spider web, with Bismarck at the center, holding together the fabric.

When Bismarck was dismissed by the youthful and callow Kaiser Wilhelm, this diplomatic web came unstrung. As Russian-Austrian relations worsened, the Kaiser decided to side with Austria, thus choosing not to renew the treaty with Russia. Sensing Germany drifting into opposition with it, Russia entered into an alliance with France. Britain at first tried to retain its traditionally close ties with Germany. But the Kaiser's naval buildup and bullying conduct drove Britain into alliance with France. As the twentieth century dawned, Bismarck's diplomatic web had been replaced by two polarizing alliances kept in check by a military balance of power that operated in mechanical ways, unguided by diplomacy. Contemporary observers felt that the balance was stable. Although several small crises almost erupted into fighting, the observers judged that Europe's civilization had ascended to a high moral plateau that ruled out large-scale war. They were to be proven wrong in 1914, when Archduke Ferdinand's assassination, interlocking treaties, offensive military strategies, and incompetent crisis management sent Europe to catastrophe, taking Russia along with it.

At the start of the war, Russia faithfully tried to honor its pledges to France. It mobilized its large army and marched westward on Germany and Austria. Fearing invasion by the Russian "steam roller," Germany invaded France, hoping to knock France out of the war quickly so that it could meet the Russian onslaught. Germany's offensive campaign stalled north of Paris. Russia's offensive, however, met the same fate: It was halted in Poland by a small German force fighting alongside the ponderous Austrian army. The result was degeneration into a two-front stalemate, coupled with widespread war in the Balkans that had little effect on the bigger bloodbath in Europe. For four years, the war dragged on in a series of failed offensive attacks against impenetrable defensive trench lines. The casualties on the Western Front were staggering, but they were also high in the east. With no political solution in sight, war-weariness and rebellion against centuries of repressive autocracy brought down czarist government in Russia. The stage was set for communism and the transformation of Russia from a statist power into an ideological leviathan.[6]

Conclusions for Staying Power

What does this historical record suggest about the staying power of the new Russia's statist foreign policy in today's setting? Clearly, the fallacy of historical determinism (that history repeats itself to such a degree that it can be used to predict the future) should be avoided in judging whether and how the past can influence the present. Europe's past experience is not destined to be repeated, and neither is Russia's. The negative lessons to be learned from the past *have* been learned. Too many things have changed for any easy resurrection of Europe's multipolar politics or Russia's role in it. Nonetheless, three centuries of experience powerfully demonstrate that statist foreign policies and geopolitical conduct can endure when any country brings demanding interests and ambitious goals to its strategic calculus. Equally important, such policies and conduct can also be enduring consequences of an unsettled security situation laid atop a structural foundation of interstate anarchy. In essence, even countries that lack assertive ambitions can be dragged into robust statism if their external setting leaves them little recourse.

---

[6]For analysis, see Adam B. Ulam, *Expansion and Coexistence: The History of Soviet Foreign Policy, 1917–1967,* New York: Praeger, 1968; Zbigniew Brzezinski, *The Grand Failure: The Birth and Death of Communism in the Twentieth Century,* New York: Collier, 1990.

History shows that while Russia is hardly alone, it has a long and well-established record of acting in statist terms, and it is no neophyte to geopolitical conduct in either Eurasia or East Central Europe. Under the czars, Russia showed a distinct propensity for imposing control over neighboring territory, gaining valuable seaports and other vital strongpoints, pushing enemies away from its borders, and using coercive power for strategic and economic purposes. It regularly relied on military strength not only to protect itself but also to get its way in outside geopolitics. Over centuries, it invested immense strategic labor to consolidate and improve its geostrategic situation—one reason for not parting company lightly with long-prized assets and for trying to gain them back when temporarily lost. Russia also suffered greatly at the hands of Europe's geopolitics. The collapse of the nineteenth-century balance-of-power system especially dealt Russia a heavy blow, giving rise not only to World War I but also to communism, Hitler's bloody invasion of Russia, and the ultimately disastrous Cold War.

This experience gives Russia reasons to be apprehensive and defensive about how Europe's future is unfolding, because Russia has seen hopeful optimism turn to ashes many times before. Its history by no means dooms Russia to a repeat performance of old ways: European nations with similar records have shown an ability to change their behavior when they adopted new goals and their strategic conditions enabled them to act otherwise. Nonetheless, if Russia's past behavior reflects attitudes and structural conditions that endure, it also suggests that statism in a new form will not be a fresh departure for Russia. It also suggests that the potential may exist for old ways to reappear. As with other countries pursuing grand strategies animated by statist designs, Russia's conduct unfolded in a predictable sequence of events: Russia first secured its homeland, then sought to dominate the surrounding countryside, then built a security buffer separating it from outside dangers, and finally endeavored to ward off distant threats by influencing strategic relationships farther out. To the extent this calculus is brought back to life and pursued in coercive ways, it could set the stage for assertive behavior again. The key point is that while the new Russia is not controlled by history, it does have a history to overcome.

What also stands out from history is both Russia's relentless persistence and the two-edged consequences of that persistence. For three centuries, Russia regularly set ambitious strategic goals and worked hard to achieve them. It fought many wars with a staggering number of opponents. It won many, lost some, and suffered diplomatic reversals along the way. But when it lost, it usually did not give up when important interests and goals were at stake. It learned lessons from its reversals, made corrections in its approach, and performed better the next time around. This capacity for hard strategic labor and prompt rebounding probably accounts for Russia's success more than any brilliant capacity for geopolitics or war. In the end, nonetheless, Russia's persistence proved to be its Achilles' heel, because its collapse was partly owed to imperial overextension that depleted its economy and society. The Soviet Union suffered from the same fatal flaw during the Cold War. Even if the new Russia has not abandoned its old goals and fears, realization of the risk of overextension may well be the most important inhibitor of its willingness to make the same mistake a third time.

THE INTERPLAY OF INTERNAL POLITICS, EXTERNAL CHALLENGES, AND STRATEGIC REQUIREMENTS

Both theory and history suggest that statism may endure. Nonetheless, this policy's staying power will be determined primarily by the interplay of Russia's internal (domestic) politics, the external setting, and strategic requirements. Of the three, Russia's domestic politics is by far the most difficult to predict. What can be said is that if a presidential-style government is created, it will favor statism.

Presidential-Style System and Statism

The new constitution adopted in 1993 reflects the vision of a presidential-style system. Loosely patterned after the French model, it allocates more power to the president and his executive branch, as opposed to the parliament and judiciary, than do most Western democracies. It establishes the president as dominant over the prime minister, and gives him substantial authority, free from parliamentary interference. In particular, it grants the president considerable latitude over foreign policy and national security affairs. The constitution gives the parliament authority to determine the annual budget, new laws, and legislation. But although the parliament can compel the prime minister to resign through a vote of no confidence, it cannot force the president to resign or submit himself to immediate national elections. The president, however, is granted the authority to call for parliamentary elections in the event of stalemate with the Duma. These features leave the president with the upper hand in Russia's politics. His powers are greater than those of the French president, who does not control the prime minister in the same way, and greater than those of the U.S. president, who cannot dismiss Congress.

This system enjoys the support of powerful actors in Russia, including vested interests that view it as an acceptable substitute for authoritarianism's alleged virtues. As of mid-1995, however, strong forces have been at work pulling in opposite directions: toward parliamentary democracy, which would dilute presidential authority, and toward authoritarianism, which would put an end to democracy. In addition, an ongoing struggle is pitting Moscow against outlying districts and provinces over division of powers between central and local government.

As with any new political system, this system's future will be influenced by whether and how it becomes institutionalized, thereby surviving the personalities that created it. As of mid-1995, Yeltsin's approval ratings had sunk to low levels and speculation was growing that a new president might be elected in 1996, provided elections are held. What matters over the long term will be structural factors.[7]

This system is anchored in Russia's executive agencies and tradition of central authority. Democratic institutions seemingly have been implanted and are growing, but at an uncertain pace and toward an unclear destination. Much will depend on whether the Duma becomes effective and whether Russia develops a manageable number of stable political parties. Notwithstanding the complaints about political reform in Russia, little interest in restored dictatorship seems to exist outside right-wing circles. The outcome probably will be determined by whether a presidential-style system can fulfill its vision, and whether its vision captures and holds widespread sup-

---

[7]For an appraisal, see Jacob W. Kipp, "The Zhirinovsky Threat," *Foreign Affairs*, Vol. 73, No. 3, May/June 1994.

port. Its own potential staying power creates reasons for contemplating its influence on Russian foreign policy.[8]

If this system survives, the president will, in theory, have leeway to select the foreign policy of his choice, statist or otherwise. Yet the incentives for him to pursue statism will be strong. Under this system, the central mission of the president will be to rise above partisan debate by shaping policies for the good of Russia as a whole. He is to be animated by the national interest and by concern for protecting the stability of the Russian state. His job, therefore, will be to promote statism at home.

Any approach aimed at carrying out this job at home will beget a similar philosophy of promoting statism abroad. Practical political dynamics, moreover, will compel the president to seek widespread consensus, and this consensus normally will lie at the center of the political spectrum. Compared with the alternatives, statism is a centrist policy and, thus, a natural focal point for consensus politics. In addition, the president will be turning to executive agencies to develop and carry out his foreign policy. Although national security bureaucracies can develop agendas of their own, they tend to gravitate toward statism, which is a policy that serves their vested interests. Neither are they shy about promoting the national interest abroad, but their emphasis on technical professionalism typically begets an arm's-length stance toward extremist ideologies. Russia's "power ministries"—a term used by observers to denote the custodians of national security policy—have reputations for conservatism, but fall into the category of institutions that favor a professional and technical form of statism. All these factors seemingly tilt the odds in favor of enduring statism if a presidential-style system takes hold.

What will happen if a quite different style of government emerges? In theory, the polarized forces opposing statism could quash a statist

---

[8]For an academic analysis of Russian internal politics, see Richard Sakwa, *Russian Politics and Society*, London and New York: Routledge, 1993. A good theoretical analysis of the transition from communist totalitarianism to democracy is presented in Alexander J. Motyl, *Dilemmas of Independence: Ukraine After Totalitarianism*, New York: Council of Foreign Relations Press, 1993. Motyl's book deals with Ukraine, but many of his judgments apply to Russia. For an optimistic assessment, see Anders Aslund, "Russia's Success Story," *Foreign Affairs*, Vol. 73, No. 5, September/October 1994.

foreign policy. A strong and liberal parliament could push Russian foreign policy toward the political left by renewing Atlanticism or isolationism. An authoritarian dictatorship could push foreign policy far to the right, replacing statism with ultranationalism and imperialism. Dramatic foreign-policy switches of this sort are feasible; however, they are not inevitable. A strong, conservative parliament might favor statism over Atlanticism and isolationism—as the Duma does today. Much would depend on public opinion and the mood across the country. Likewise, an authoritarian dictator might not favor nationalism and imperialism. A dictator that gains power on a wave of xenophobic nationalism might adopt an imperial foreign policy. Yet not all dictators come to power by this route; much would depend upon his ideology and the political forces supporting him. Over the past decades, most of Asia's authoritarian governments have had statist foreign policies, as did that of Chile's Augusto Pincohet. If presidential-style government falls by the wayside, foreign-policy statism will not necessarily fall along with it.

Domestic Trends

In the long term, domestic trends in Russia clearly will determine the climate of opinion on foreign policy. In an optimistic climate, Russia will make fast strides toward democracy, market capitalism, a prosperous economy, and a tranquil society, in which case it may become more relaxed about its strategic situation, less inclined to heavy-handed conduct, and more forthcoming in its relations with the West. Conversely, in a pessimistic climate, market democracy will fail and Russia will emerge with an authoritarian government presiding over a command economy, an unsettled society, and rampant nationalism. Consequently, its foreign-policy stance likely will shift toward hostility, militarism, imperial assertiveness, and a new imperialism. Between these two extremes lies a large gray area dominated by an amorphous centrist scenario: a quasi-democracy making a slow and uneven transition to market capitalism, restored prosperity, and a stable society. This outcome is likely to create a domestic setting favorable to foreign-policy statism. As of late 1995, Russia seems headed in this direction.

External Challenges

Russia's national security stance will also be influenced by the external setting, how it evolves in the coming era, and how Russia chooses to react to it.

During the Cold War, the Soviet Union enjoyed superpower status and a huge empire that provided a massive geographical buffer around its border. The Cold War's end spelled the loss of these advantages, as well as the loss of the continuing strategic nightmare of global encirclement by a hostile military bloc and nuclear war. When the new Russia emerged, a new worry came into being: steady deterioration of the current environment from encirclement by widespread chaotic instability and many regional rivals poised to capitalize on the situation at Russia's expense.

Worrisome or not, a new security environment has emerged, and the disruption done to Russia's overall geostrategic situation undeniably has been profound. The domination of the Eurasian landmass attained over several hundred years by czarist Russia was honored by the communist regime. On the whole, the effort was successful, although Russia and the Soviet Union bankrupted themselves in the process. Almost overnight, these more than three centuries of costly efforts were lost as the new era dawned. Russia was left internally weak, its government shaky, military power in decline, economy in collapse, and a society fractious at best. Moreover, the new Russia was now physically much smaller than the old Russia. Indeed, its borders had shrunk to those of the mid-1600s, before Ukraine, White Russia, the Baltic region, the Caucasus, and Central Asia were absorbed. Gone not only were these long-sought geographical regions but also dominating control of the Baltic approaches, the Black Sea, and the Caspian Sea. Also lost was the old buffer, brought about by the collapse of the Warsaw Pact and the Soviet Union's empire to the south and west. Finally, the new Russia was no longer a global superpower. In contrast to the Soviet Union, it no longer enjoyed the advantage of being able to project influence and power far beyond its borders, even in the regions of greatest interest to it: Central Asia, Northeast Asia, and East Central Europe.

Regions of Greatest Interest. Although Russia's security experts seem divided on the meaning of these losses, a sense of great strategic reversal is a common theme in most of their writings, especially those of the political center and right. A related theme is deep concern about what the new era has bequeathed around Russia's borders and nervousness about where the future is headed. The principal worry seemingly is not only that Russia has been left with new strategic problems, but that it now faces weighty problems in all three regions of greatest interest, owing to their separate dynamics.

In Central Asia, where the Soviet empire has been replaced by newly independent states, the principal worry is that the region will steadily sink into local instability and will align with Russia's strategic rivals—both damaging to Russia's enduring interests. In Northeast Asia, the dominating worry is over the strategic intentions of China and Japan, and that a newly unstable system of balance-of-power rivalries will erupt as Cold War bipolarity gives way to multipolarity among the four great powers and Korea. In East Central Europe, the main worry is that Ukraine's departure will be followed by loss of the entire neutral zone, as countries there either forge their own defense strategies and security alignments or collapse into internal instability and rivalries with each other, or steadily move into the West's orbit.[9]

Many Russian analysts judge that all three regions of greatest interest may be headed in negative directions if left to their own devices,

---

[9]For Russian analyses of the issues addressed in this section, see the following articles, all from the monthly Moscow journal *International Affairs*: Elgiz Pozdnyakov, "Russia Is a Great Power," January 1993; Konstantin Pleshakov, "Russia's Mission: The Third Epoch," January 1993; Andrei Zagorsky, "Russia and Europe," January 1993; Elgiz Pozdnyakov, "Russia Today and Tomorrow," February 1993; Andrei Zagorsky, "The Commonwealth: One Year On," February 1993; Alexander Alexeyev, "Security from the Atlantic to the Urals and Beyond," February 1993; Valeri Gorski and Yelena Chebotareya, "Maastricht and Russia," March, 1993; Vladimir Kozin, "New Dimensions of NATO," March 1993; Mahmut Gareyev, "Russia's Priority Interests," June 1993; Viktor Mizir and Sergei Oznobishchev, "Security After the Cold War," August 1993; Mahmut Gareyev, "Some Problems of the Russian Military Doctrine," August 1993; Yevgeny Shaposhnikov, "A Security Concept for Russia," October 1993; Andrei Lipisky, "The Community of Central Asia," October 1993; Sergei Solodobvnik, "The Community of Central Asia," October 1993; Boris Pichnigiv, "The EC and Russia in the All-Europe Context," March 1994; Andrei Zagorsky, "Tilting from the CSCE to NATO?" March 1994; Sergei Stankevich, "A Sphere of Russia's Vital Interests," March 1994; Alexander Itskhoki, "National Interests and National Dignity," July 1994; Anatoly Kasatkin, "Will the Middle East Become a Russian Priority?" July 1994; Oleg Bozmolov, "Russia and Eastern Europe," August 1994; "Russian Interests in the CIS," Conference Report, November 1994; Boris Kozantsev, "First Steps Toward Russia's Partnership with NATO," December 1994.

creating powerful incentives for bringing a sense of Russian grand strategy back to life to manage the current external situation and be prepared for stronger actions if events take a further downhill course. From Russia's perspective, a coordinated and influence-seeking, but resource-husbanding, statist policy—a policy aimed at rebuilding a measure of national strength and attaining greater control over external events—evidently makes sense. This policy appears to offer the best way for a weak and internally preoccupied country to arrest negative trends in all three regions and craft outcomes more conducive to Russia's security requirements.[10]

Alternatives to Statism. Statism is far from the only option available to Russia. But as their writings suggest, Russia's security experts have weighed the alternatives, and most evidently judge statism as being better than the other three options most obviously at Russia's disposal. Isolationism is unattractive. It would enable Russia to focus on its domestic agenda, but it would leave Russia hostage to external events taking their own course. It makes sense only if the international environment is deemed likely to evolve in satisfactory directions on its own; in today's world, this is not likely. Atlanticism offers the promise of close relations with the West. But in Moscow today, hopes have faded that the West will provide huge amounts of aid to support Russia's economic recovery or that the West is sympathetic to Russia's strategic agenda in the three regions. Indeed, a key drawback of Atlanticism is that partnership with the West can be purchased only at the expense of Russia's accepting major constraints on freedom to pursue its geopolitical interests in both Central Asia and East Central Europe. The remaining alternative is that of a new imperialism aimed at restoring lost lands and rebuilding a strategic buffer. Yet Russia's current strategic predicament is not so bad as to make imperialism necessary for security. Moreover, imperialism would be too costly for Russia's weak economy to bear,

---

[10]For analysis, see Allen Lynch, "After Empire: Russia and Its Western Neighbors," *RFE/RL Research Report*, March 1994. For a lengthy Russian analysis of Russian policy in the CIS, including a critique of Kozyrev's approach, see Andranik Migranyan, "Presidential Council Member Migranyan Assesses Policy Toward FSU," *Nezavisimaya Gazeta*, January 12, 1994. For a rebuttal, see Galina Sidorova, "Kozyrev's Policy Adviser Responds to Migranyan on FSU Policy," *Nezavisimaya Gazeta*, January 19, 1994.

and it could backfire by arraying powerful foes against Russia's designs.

Statism itself is not free of troubling risks and costs. It requires attention to foreign affairs even when domestic affairs are paramount, and, although it is far less expensive than imperialism, it can consume at least modest amounts of scarce political, economic, and military resources, and sometimes more. It also can engender controversy among other nations, and it risks becoming entangled in external events that can turn for the worst. Yet, statism provides a strategic bearing and a way to manage multiple security dilemmas at once by addressing interests that are deemed vital while setting aside those that are peripheral. It establishes a coherent set of priorities. It calls on Russia to rebuild its internal strength while focusing on a limited near-term agenda abroad: reintegration of the CIS, not a new empire; a stable balance of power in Asia, not intimidation of old rivals; preservation of a neutral zone in East Central Europe, not restoration of Russian presence and control. To the extent that these goals can be achieved, statism offers not a perfect external setting, but one that will give Russia a sense of strategic comfort as it rebuilds its internal order.

Strategic Requirements: The Interplay of Domestic Politics and External Setting

Over the long term, statism's endurance could be compromised if the outside environment changes significantly. Emergence of a more stable and favorable environment could lead Russia to downgrade statism or to replace it with Atlanticism or isolationism. Conversely, emergence of a less stable and more menacing (or more enticing) setting could lead Russia to forge a more assertive and malevolent version of statism or to embrace imperialism. Much therefore depends not only on Russia's domestic politics but also on the evolution of its external setting, and on the interplay between them.

Table 4.1 illustrates potential outcomes of this interplay for Russian strategic requirements and policy. The three types of Russian government are displayed against a spectrum of alternative external settings, ranging from highly stable to unstable, with subvariations measuring the degree of challenge to Russia's interests and suscep-

Table 4.1

**The Interplay of Russia's Internal Politics and External Setting:
Consequences for Strategic Policy**

External Setting	Domestic Setting		
	Liberal Parliamentary Democracy	Presidential-Style System	Authoritarian Dictatorship
Stable and favorable to Russia	Atlanticism or isolationism	Atlanticism or isolationism	Mild statism
Mildly unstable and unfavorable	Atlanticism or mild statism	Mild statism	Heavy statism
Highly unstable, unfavorable, and unpliant	Mild statism	Mild or heavy statism	Imperialism
Highly unstable, unfavorable, and pliant	Mild or heavy statism	Heavy statism	Imperialism
Highly polarized and confrontational	Heavy statism	Heavy statism or imperialism	Imperialism

NOTE: "Mild" statism means a policy with limited ends and constrained means. "Heavy" statism means a policy of ambitious ends and unconstrained means.

tibility to Russian influence. Each cell of the matrix displays the likely strategic policy adopted by Russia.

The table suggests that a presidential-style system will pursue a statist policy, except for extreme external settings. A liberal parliamentary democracy is more prone to Atlanticism or isolationism, but can revert to statism in dealing with highly troubled external settings. A dictatorship will be prone to statism if the setting is stable, but will pursue imperialism if the external setting is troubled.

The main implication is that statism dominates the interplay. Short of extreme conditions, statism thus is likely to show considerable staying power, because it will be shored up by the internal or external situations, or by both.

STATISM'S UNCERTAIN CHARACTER

Although statism may show staying power over the long term, history shows it to be a flexible policy that can be manifested in different ways, with ends and means having varying degrees of assertiveness. Table 4.1 displays two different types of statism: mild and heavy. In reality, the alternatives are more complex, embodying ascending levels of ambition, effort, and coercion. For example, statism can use diplomacy to persuade a neighbor to sign an economic accord that serves the interests of both countries, or it can use economic coercion (e.g., denial of electrical power unless Russia's political agenda is served) to compel the signing of a one-sided agreement, or it can use military power to compel the neighbor into yielding valuable economic assets. These differences obviously are crucial not only for defining the strategic character of statism itself but also for determining the future of regional security in Eurasia and Europe.

During its long history, the old Russia exhibited the full spectrum of behaviors, as did most other European powers. Today, the new Russia is displaying a moderate form of statist and geopolitical conduct: Outside its borders, its ends are limited and its means are constrained. The key issue is whether, and under what conditions, this version of statism could give way to something more assertive in both goals and the instruments employed to attain them. Table 4.1 implies that, provided Russia does not fall under the spell of a dictatorial regime with a predetermined agenda of imperialism, it likely will craft a statism that responds to the external setting confronting it: a mild form of statism in a mildly unstable setting, and heavier forms in more turbulent settings. Yet, owing to its size and importance, Russia will be more than a reactive power; it will shape the terms of reference for statist conduct in the new era, not merely respond to terms set by others.

Russia's conduct within the CIS and toward East Central Europe will determine largely how statism is defined and carried out. Today, Russia is pursuing an agenda of limited reintegration with the CIS and perpetuation of East Central Europe as a neutral zone. Its primary instruments are diplomacy and economics, supplemented by the limited use of military forces in the CIS for peacekeeping and crisis management. The issues facing its neighbors and the West are as follows: If Russia becomes frustrated in attaining its current goals, will it resort to cruder and more forceful forms of coercion, including the widespread use of military power? If it succeeds in attaining its current goals, will it be satisfied with the accomplishment or will it then embrace larger ambitions? Within the CIS, will it be content with a limited reintegration, or will it aim for something greater, perhaps hierarchical control or even reabsorption into Russia? If Russia succeeds in reestablishing domination over key parts of the CIS (i.e., Belarus and Ukraine), will it be content to see Eastern Europe remain as a neutral zone if the West does not enlarge, or will it seek to again control this region as well? If the West does enlarge, will Russia peacefully accommodate itself to the development or will it resort to confrontation?

Russia's responses inevitably will be shaped by a complex calculus. The nature of its interests in each case will be key. Whereas Palmerston was right in saying that interests tend to endure even as friends and enemies change, interests are not cast in stone, and they do not give rise to a single, immutable blueprint of goals and actions. Because they are relative to the country and the situation at hand, they must be defined and interpreted by the government pursuing them. As history shows, sometimes governments change their interpretations as time passes. The importance attached to their interests also matters hugely. Interests deemed vital are normally considered worth fighting to protect. Less-important interests may merit some efforts, but not war, or even other actions that bring high costs and risks. Sometimes, moreover, governments choose not to be clear about how they appraise their interests, for leaving them cloudy can have advantages.

Interests

Russia's responses will be shaped by its interests, but those interests in the coming era will be known only when the government spells them out with words and through concrete actions.[11]

---

[11]See angry comments by Andranik Migranyan, in "Chechnya as Turning Point for Russian State," *Nezavisimaya Gazeta*, January 17, 1995. See also Sergei Karaganov, "After the USSR: Search for a Strategy," *Krasnaya Zvezda*, February 19, 1993. See Paul Goble, "Russia and Its Neighbors," *Foreign Policy*, Spring 1993; Charles King, "Moldova with a Russian Race," *Foreign Policy*, Winter 1994–95; William Kincade and Natalie Melsiyczak, "Unneighborly Neighbors," *Foreign Policy*, Spring 1994.

Social Interests. Russia doubtless will bring a multitude of social and ethnic interests to the shaping of its conduct within the CIS. As its government and security experts already have made clear, protection of the 22 million Russian citizens now living on "foreign" CIS soil will be one of those interests. About 11 million Russians live in Ukraine, 1 million live in the Caucasus, and 10 million live in Central Asia. In Moscow's view, the rights of many were called into question when the Soviet Union dissolved and the new states came into being.

Economic Interests. Russia also will continue to have powerful economic interests in the CIS. Owing to the interdependent economy fashioned during the Soviet era, Russia already has major economic entanglements with nearly every CIS country, and these entanglements are likely to grow as capitalism develops, markets emerge, trade takes place, currency practices are established, financial relationships are forged, and investments flow back and forth.[12]

Russia's economic interests within the CIS will be influenced by the region's structural features. Russia dwarfs each CIS state individually. But the other eleven states collectively are a near match for Russia. Whereas Russia has 150 million people and a gross domestic product (GDP) of $1.2 trillion, the other eleven states number 132 million people and $1.0 trillion of GDP. They provide important markets for Russia's goods and send Russia natural resources, raw materials, and some manufactured products. They will also be natural targets for Russian investments and acquisitions as they privatize and operate in the emerging regional economy. Ukraine will be especially important, owing to its size (52 million and $63 billion), agriculture, industrial capacity, complex arrangements with Russian industry, and dependence on Russia for energy. Apart from Azerbaijan's oil fields and the region's potential role in providing a new pipeline to ship oil from the Caspian Sea, the Caucasus region is less important. The five Central Asian states rank higher. Together they are about the size of Ukraine, albeit poorer. Kazakhstan (17 million people) is by far the most important; its Tenzig oil field has

---

[12]For analysis, see relevant chapters in Robert D. Blackwill and Sergei A. Karaganov, *Damage Limitation or Crisis? Russia and the Outside World*, Washington, D.C.: Brassey's Inc., 1994. See also Martha Brill Olcott, "Central Asian Independence," *Foreign Affairs*, Vol. 71, No. 3, 1992; and Dimitri Simes, "America and the Post-Soviet Republics," *Foreign Affairs*, Vol. 71, No. 3, 1992.

the potential to be one of the ten largest in the world. It also ships natural gas and minerals to Russia, and is a big grain producer. Uzbekistan, with 22 million people, has large stores of gold, petroleum, and cotton. Turkmenistan has vast natural gas and oil fields on its Caspian Sea coast. Only impoverished Tajikistan and mountainous Kyrgyzstan make minor contributions. The Central Asian states all rely heavily on Russia for trade, subsidies, and technical help—which makes them vulnerable to coercion from Moscow.

An issue of great importance will be whether Russia chooses to seek its profits for itself through mercantilist conduct, conduct that is self-serving and exploitative of others, or, instead, participates in efforts to increase prosperity across the entire CIS on the premise that a rising tide lifts all ships. Economic theory postulates that a rising tide will emerge if trade and other economic relationships operate according to the market principles of comparative advantage. Yet mercantilism can have short-term attractions for countries able to manipulate and exploit. Mercantilism can also be a vehicle for gaining political domination: History shows that, like many other powers, Russia has practiced mercantilism and coercive exploitation in its neighborhood, a practice also carried on by the Soviet Union. The new Russia, moreover, is an economically besieged country with little experience in the benefits of free and fair trade—a judgment that applies for the entire CIS region. How Russia defines its policies on this issue will have a major bearing on how the CIS region evolves—not only in economics but in politics as well.

Strategic Interests. Notwithstanding the growing importance of economics, Russia also has strategic interests in the CIS. As they have for centuries, Ukraine and Belarus will rank especially high strategically, because they form part of the old but still-sensitive invasion corridors to Russia and determine Russia's ability to gain ready access to Eastern Europe. If allied to Russia, their manpower and economic assets would increase Russia's strategic resources by one-third or more. The three small Caucasian countries count for less in the power equation, but they are important to Russia for specific reasons: They are adjacent to a long-turbulent area of Russia, immigration flows and ethnic strife from which could be destabilizing. Located on the Black Sea, Georgia has important military bases and port facilities. All three states form a strategic buffer to Turkey, Iran, and Islamic fundamentalism. In Central Asia, Kazakhstan, Uzbekistan, and Turkmenistan perform similar functions. Again, only Tajikistan and Kyrgyzstan seem mostly peripheral to Russia's strategic interests.

In the old Russia, total subjugation of the entire CIS region reflected the importance placed on these strategic interests by the czars. Russian security experts today, lacking an equivalent defensiveness, have not sought to reestablish similar controls. Yet they agree that the CIS region not only must be kept out of the hands of Russia's adversaries but should also be a sphere of influence for Russia, with Moscow calling the major shots on strategic planning.

These social, economic, and strategic interests will give Russia powerful incentives for orchestrating the CIS's political future. Russia can be expected to favor political structures and values similar to its own in the CIS countries. Hence, if Russia emerges with a presidential-style system, it likely will seek to foster this outcome in the CIS states as well. Within this framework, it can be expected to continue promoting political parties and leaders who want close relations with Russia on terms acceptable to Russia.

Options for Reintegration

For the near term, Russia faces the prospect of working hard to keep its minimalist objectives intact while making slow progress toward its maximalist objectives of drawing these countries into closer bilateral and multilateral relations with Russia. For the mid- to long-term, some Western observers fear that Russia will try to reabsorb the CIS states into a new Russian empire, especially if Russia's internal politics again become authoritarian, although it seems a remote concern that would require an improbable combination of Russian ambition, Russian capability, and widespread acceptance or vulnerability among the CIS states. A more probable issue is how Russia will seek to bring about significant CIS multilateral reintegration, a goal that appears to be inherent in Russia's statist policy today.

Logic and the writings of Russian security experts suggest a spectrum of four reintegration options that could be pursued, ranging from modest to comprehensive: (1) variable geometry, (2) confederation, (3) federation, and (4) hierarchical federation. A discussion of these options is merited here because these options have important implications not only for the CIS but also for Western policy toward enlargement and relations with Russia. In some Western quarters, the commonly held expectation is that CIS integration will yield a new Russian empire. While this outcome could occur, it need not do so automatically. Of these four options, the first two would not result in Russia gaining control of the CIS. Indeed, they might yield the kind of CIS that would enjoy a measure of democracy and could live in tranquility with an enlarged West. The danger feared by many observers is that an enlarged West will stimulate a new Russian empire and then collide with it—but not if the CIS itself develops democratic institutions that buffer against a Russian takeover.

At the modest end is incrementalist "variable geometry" reintegration, whereby CIS would be recombined in small steps that respond to specific opportunities rather than an overarching plan. The CIS thus would grow slowly from the bottom up, in areas where a consensus exists for multilateralism. The exact nature of multilateralism would vary from issue to issue. For example, whereas environmental planning might involve five nations, industrial planning might draw seven, and the two groups might have very different membership bodies. The design concept for the CIS would not be a central-authority structure but a forum for creating loose associations of nations working together in limited but enduring business arrangements. In all likelihood, the enterprise would deal mostly with economic issues rather than creating common foreign policies and security strategies. To the extent that reintegration builds a formal multilateral superstructure, the process would be evolutionary, much like Western Europe's move from the European Coal and Steel Community, to a Common Market, and only later to the European Economic Community and beyond.[13]

---

[13]For an insightful warning of how Eurasian reintegration can take the wrong path of Russian domination, see Sherman Garnett, "The Integrationist Temptation," *The Washington Quarterly*, Winter 1995. In the Russian literature of today, various models of reintegration are being considered, ranging from the model put forth here to more-hierarchical versions aimed at bringing the CIS to life through top-down management. Interestingly, Kozyrev, speaking at a 1994 Moscow Conference, remarked that when the CIS was first created, thought was given to calling it a "community," not a "commonwealth." The latter term, he said, was chosen because it implied a warmer association than a mere community. One can only remark that the definition of "warmth" lies in the eyes of the beholder and the embraced. The West Europeans

The second option, "confederation," would create, at the outset, an overarching plan for building an institutionalized but lightly empowered authority structure. The CIS's existing governing bodies would be given larger responsibilities than they have now, and administrative structures might be fashioned to achieve stronger multilateral coordination in agreed policy areas. The CIS, nonetheless, would remain a league of equal states. Each would retain substantial sovereignty over its domestic arrangements and the freedom to resign easily. The norm thus would be "states' rights," decisions would be made by unanimous vote, and only the minimum-necessary authority would be granted to central organs having limited charters. As with the first model, this confederation would focus primarily on economic issues, not foreign policy, security, and defense.

The third option, "federation," would have an overarching plan to create a central governing body with elaborate executive, legislative, and judicial organs served by professionalized institutions. The norm of states' rights would give way to enhanced federal authority, the federal body would be able to intrude in national practices, and member states could not resign easily. Members would still have equal status, but policy decisions would be made by majority rule, not unanimously. The CIS federation would forge not only common economic policies but also common foreign, security, and defense policies. Such a highly integrated CIS could take two different forms. The first, a limited federation, might join Russia with Belarus and the Central Asian states, whereas Ukraine and the Caucasian states—those least sympathetic to any close integration—would remain outside. The second form, a comprehensive federation, would include Ukraine and the Caucasian countries as well, thereby erecting a tight bond across the entire CIS.

The fourth reintegration option, "hierarchical federation," would be similar to federation in its institutions and scope. A key difference would be that the equal status for member states would be replaced by a scheme for determining relative national importance by size and strength. Thus, the larger states would have greater influence over

---

have found plenty of warmth, yet enough distance, in their community. Judging from the academic literature, the idea of trying to follow the EU's gradualist path was evidently taking hold in some Russian quarters as of late 1994. But it does not yet command a consensus within either Russia or the CIS at large.

policy decisions than the smaller states. Because Russia's size and importance exceeds those of the other CIS states combined, Russia would acquire the capacity to make policy decisions unilaterally or with the support of only a few other countries. In essence, Russia would dominate this hierarchical federation. This option would forge not only common defense policies but would also bring the military forces of the states into a tightly integrated alliance structure controlled by the federation. In essence, the CIS would become roughly equivalent to the old Warsaw Pact and Comecon. Although Russia would not possess totalitarian control over the internal affairs of the CIS states, it would call the shots on all the vital strategic decisions.

What does the future hold for these options? At the moment, Russia realistically can expect progress only toward variable-geometry reintegration. Its own lack of leverage, coupled with widespread disinterest among most CIS countries, prevents anything more ambitious for the foreseeable future. Yet there are plausible conditions under which one or more of the other three options might become feasible. Confederation is the most plausible. It could come to life if Russia's influence grows moderately or if the CIS members come to see greater opportunities in strengthening multilateralism without yielding a great deal of their own sovereignty. Federation could arise if Russia's strength grows to the point where other CIS states are compelled—owing to Russia's power or their own weakness—to yield greater sovereignty while still holding onto majority rule to help inhibit Russia from dictating to them. A hierarchical federation would, of course, require virtually complete Russian domination and the widespread inability of the other CIS members to perform normal governing functions in the international arena. Both forms of federation seem improbable from today's standpoint, but they are not beyond imagining, owing to Russia's dominating position on CIS soil and the uncertain status of several CIS countries.

If the future depends on what Russia wants, what will it seek, and what resources will it be willing to commit? Yeltsin and Kozyrev have spoken of following the EU model, but they are unclear whether this means building from the ground up, or forging a post-Maastricht model, or creating something in between. The writings of statist-inclined Russian security experts express general support for reintegration, but they reflect no consensus on what should be created.

Those treatises preoccupied with practicality focus on incremental steps, à la variable geometry, with only a select group of countries deemed important to Russia and willing to cooperate. The more ambitious treaties, which take into account Russia's limited resources and requirements, seem to endorse confederation as the art of the possible, even if regarding it as less than ideal. The visionary treaties, which ignore impediments, contemplate federation as a desirable outgrowth of Russia's rebirth but deny ruling ambitions by Russia. Although ultranationalists view reintegration as a stepping stone to a new imperialism, few statists argue in these terms. Statists assert that Western enlargement may provoke Russia into adopting more-ambitious goals than it would otherwise, but few argue that compelling security requirements in today's world are a reason for advanced forms of integration.

Statism views reintegration as a means, not an end in itself; therefore, it does not *automatically* embrace the more ambitious options. Moreover, the calculus of costs and benefits will be made by Russians, not by an impartial jury. If the full spectrum of options becomes feasible and affordable, self-restraint by Russia may be needed to resist.

Multilateral Military Reintegration

Irrespective of the CIS's overall future, the West's concern is whether multilateral military reintegration occurs, either as part of CIS planning or as a separate endeavor. The CIS has a Defense Council but not a General Staff or a combined-force posture—an arrangement commonly associated with broad policy development but not multinational operations. Russia favors military reintegration, well-armed Ukraine opposes it, and the weakly armed Central Asian countries have shown a willingness to participate in limited forms of it. Functional categories of such integration could include nonwarfighting tasks—e.g., peacekeeping, hostage rescue, search and rescue, counterdrugs, logistics, industrial planning, maintenance, engineering, and medical support—as well as inherently defensive combat operations—e.g., civil defense, air defense, radar warning, coastal patrol, mining, border patrol, and counterterrorism.

Both Russia and the CIS proclaim a defensive doctrine. The desire to husband limited military resources could readily lead to integrative steps to enhance their capability to carry out such a doctrine. Today, Russian and Tajik forces are integrated to protect Tajikistan's border against guerrilla raids from Afghanistan. A desire by other Central Asian states to gain Russian help in training and maintaining their small forces could lead to similar operations on their own soil.

Projecting its air defenses over Central Asia is another means by which Russia would gain an important buffer against air attack from the south. In exchange, the Central Asian states would gain better defense of their own airspace. The potential scope for mutually advantageous cooperation of a purely defensive nature seems quite broad and could lead to a fair amount of military integration in the coming years.

Nonetheless, national military planning is not limited to defensive preparations, nor is multilateral integration. If a common agreement is reached, CIS reintegration might lead to preparations for power projection, crisis management, and offensive operations. The strategic implications of such a step would depend on the exact nature and level of capabilities created. For this step to occur, however, Russia would have to judge itself as requiring the capability of and benefiting from the help of allies. This step could take place in Central Asia and the Caucasus, but East Central Europe is more immediate to the West, and the principal collaborators presumably would be Russia, Belarus, and Ukraine. If these three countries were to combine their sizable military assets, their capabilities to defend common borders against major attack from Europe would be greatly enhanced. But if their forces were equipped with power-projection capabilities, they would pose a potential military threat to Poland and other East European states. This politically provocative step would require the consent of Belarus and Ukraine, but it could unfold only if Russia elects to lead the effort. Russia thus may have a strategic choice to make for the long term—a choice that could be dictated by the strategic image Russia wants to project not only to the East Europeans but also to NATO and the EU as they enter this region.

STATISM'S STRATEGIC RESPONSES TO ENLARGEMENT

Russia's statist policy toward East Central Europe in the coming years will, of course, be shaped by strategic considerations far broader than military planning. The key issue facing Russia is deciding how it will react to Western enlargement into the region. We see Russia as having three options: (1) normal relations, (2) Cold Peace, and (3) Cold War. These options, and the reasons supporting them, merit appriasal because the one selected will influence the West's choices as it enlarges. The principal worry for the West is that Russia may choose Cold Peace or Cold War. But for the powerful reasons cited below, Russia will face incentives to pursue a policy of normal relations if its vital interests can be protected in this way. If so, the door will be opened to a cooperative diplomatic engagement with Russia as the West enlarges eastward, making possible a serious discussion of Western strategic end games aimed at a stable outcome.[14]

Under the first option, Russia would accommodate itself to the situation and, in return, seek concessions that include enduring Western economic help. It would continue with market democracy reforms at home, and it might step up its efforts to better integrate the CIS. But it would have no incentive deriving solely from Western enlargement to fashion a federation led by Moscow, or any other kind of galvanized security response. It would pursue constructive relations between a moderately integrated CIS and the enlarged West, including free trade. It would keep any new CIS defense arrangements in East Central Europe both modest in scope and transparently defensive. Russia's policy thus would be one of "normal relations."

Under the second option, Russia would react resentfully to enlargement by establishing cool, distant relations in the aftermath. It might slow or halt democratic reforms at home. Unlike in the normal relations option, it would face far stronger incentives to fashion a federal CIS run by Moscow, anchored in Eurasia, and with a standoffish attitude toward the West. In addition, it likely would seek to form a tightly knit military bloc among Russia, Belarus, and Ukraine, which would array strong military forces near the borders of the en-

---

[14]Concern about being pushed out and isolated from Europe is expressed, for example, in a report of the Foreign and Defense Policy Council, "Document Presents Theses of Council," *Nezavisimaya Gazeta*, August 19, 1992. See Andrei Kozyrev, "What Is to Be Done with NATO?" *Moscow News*, No. 39, September 24, 1993; Alexei Pushkov, "Building a New NATO at Russia's Expense," *Moscow News*, No. 39, September 24, 1993; and Sergei Karaganov, "Expanding NATO Means the Isolation of Russia," *Moskovskiye Novosti*, September 19, 1993.

larged West, intended primarily for defense against attack. Such forces would be large and powerful enough—with the capacity for at least limited offensive actions—to be politically intimidating. In essence, Russia's policy would be one of "Cold Peace."

Under the third option, Russia would label the enlarged West as an "enemy," and would embrace a policy of enduring strategic confrontation with it. Internally, Russia might abandon democracy by becoming a dictatorship embodying fascist nationalism, but a more authoritarian presidential-style system with a statist policy could meet Russia's strategic requirements. Regardless of its internal order, Russia would press—at a minimum—for a hierarchical federation within the CIS. It also would seek to fashion a CIS military bloc to conduct major offensive warfare aimed at seizing and holding large parts of Eastern Europe. Its policy thus would be one of a statist and malevolent "New Cold War."

Which of these three policies will a statist Russia likely choose? The answer is unclear and involves making complex trade-offs. A policy of normal relations would make sense if Russia's dominating goal is to continue market democracy reforms at home, avoid substantial new military expenses, and leave the door open to further integration of Europe and Eurasia. Cold Peace would make sense if the goal is to weaken the West's resolve, slam the door on further Western enlargement beyond the Visegrad Four, and restore unquestioned Russian domination of Eurasia—even at the expense of higher defense spending, slower democratic reforms at home, slower economic recovery, and a future of standing outside the Western community and the world economy. New Cold War would be the preferred choice if the goal is not only to slam the door and subjugate Eurasia, but also to give Russia the option of waging offensive warfare in order to reverse the Westernization of Eastern Europe. The trade-off would be to plunge Russia and Eurasia into an era of militarism, authoritarian politics, bleak economic prospects, and confrontational relations with the wealthier West.

President Yeltsin has said that Russia might choose Cold Peace rather than accept Western enlargement gracefully. His comment must be taken not only as an emotional reaction but as a strategic signal that has been echoed repeatedly by Kozyrev and others. At a minimum, the signals coming from Moscow mean that Russia will be willing to maintain constructive relations with the enlarging West only if Russia's own vital interests are respected. Assuming that Russia can maintain control over its own destiny, however, the complex trade-offs illustrate that while it plausibly might elect Cold Peace or Cold War, the choice would not come easily or without painful consequences for Europe and Eurasia, as well as for Russia. A policy of normal relations would compel Russia to accept Eastern Europe's movement into the Western camp while allowing Russia to continue renewal at home, thereby avoiding the heavy costs of alienating the West and trying to restore control over the CIS against stiff opposition. Cold Peace and Cold War would sacrifice these advantages in exchange for the opportunity to contest enlargement, with no guarantees of a successful outcome. They also would mandate a successful Russian effort to impose control over the CIS—alone, a daunting proposition.

Which option Russia might select is impossible to predict, but the West will have a clear incentive to carry out enlargement in ways that elicit a response that serves its own interests and the health of the Continent as a whole.

SUMMARY

In summary, statism is likely to endure for many powerful strategic reasons. But it can be manifested in a variety of different ways in Eurasia and East Central Europe. Much depends on the specific goals Russia embraces for both regions. But much also depends on the resources that Russia will have available to pursue its goals. Irrespective of what Russian statism might want to accomplish, limited resources could compel it to lower its hopes. Conversely, ample resources could lead Russia to elevate them. Answers must be found to the following resource questions: What resources will Russia be able to apply to a statist foreign policy? What military power will Russia have at its disposal? What strategic responses will be permitted by this military power? These questions pertain not only to Russia's aspirations within the CIS but also to its reaction to Western enlargement. Their answers might spell the difference between normal relations, Cold Peace, and Cold War. The following chapter turns to them.

Chapter Five

RESOURCES FOR STATISM

An axiom of geopolitics is that statism requires a strong state. National strength is based on several factors—a stable government, a cohesive society, an outward-looking vision, a vibrant economy, and a strong military—factors that depend on the resources available to the state. The absolute level of resources available to a state is not as critical to evaluate as is their relative level—the level that enables national goals to be achieved and the outside world to be influenced. Because this power is not constant, a country that is weak today may be stronger tomorrow, and just *how much stronger* is an issue that requires close scrutiny.

Russia no longer has the resources to be a global superpower. Not only can it not match the United States in military power or the EU in economic power, but it is afflicted with serious internal troubles—a weak government, a divided society, an inward-looking mentality, a shattered economy struggling to adopt market capitalism, and a large but unready military—troubles that both prevent superpower status and inhibit Russia's ability to act within its own region. These troubles have *not*, however, prevented Russia from carrying out the initial phases of a statist policy, again because the troubles are relative: Although Russia suffers from debilitating problems, it remains far stronger than its immediate neighbors, making a modest rejuvenation probable.

Rejuvenation may permit a more assertive Russian agenda in Eurasia and East Central Europe—but not crude imperialism or creation of large numbers of powerful rivals. However, any effort to gauge Russia's strategic power or associated mind-set should acknowledge the precarious nature of the enterprise. Bismarck once remarked that Russia is never as strong nor as weak as it seems. His observation was accurate then, and it may be accurate still.

In this chapter, we begin with a brief discussion of Russia's economy. We then focus on Russia's military power. We conclude with a composite evaluation of the economy and military. The guiding theme is that Russia will remain a regional power to be reckoned with, becoming a power better able to carry out statism but still constrained from engaging in any wholesale ambitiousness or recklessness. This situation will shape how it appraises its options for dealing with Western enlargement into East Central Europe.

RUSSIA'S ECONOMY

Owing to its large size and smaller neighbors, Russia will remain the premier geopolitical power on the Eurasian landmass. Nonetheless, Russia is near the nadir of its political, social, and economic strength. Barring a complete collapse of the Russian state—which cannot be ruled out—it is hard to imagine Russia becoming any weaker than it is today. A key factor in the rejuvenation hypothesis is that the Russian government may gradually establish legitimacy, and the society may settle down. If so, Russia will be able to pay more attention to foreign policy. Russia's economy will have a critical bearing on establishing that legitimacy and concomitant social stability.

When Russia was reborn in 1991, it inherited impressive economic assets: huge land, vast natural resources, a well-educated workforce, good science, heavy industry, and manufacturing capacity. It also inherited monstrous problems: a command economy, a moribund infrastructure, a lack of modern information technology, a defense-dominated industrial sector, and a lack of consumer goods. During the Soviet Union's last days, its economy was headed downhill, a process that accelerated when Russia came to life and embarked on economic reform in order to create market capitalism. The exact downward trends are unclear, but during 1992–1994, GDP dropped by about 30 percent and production fell accordingly. Rampant unemployment was averted by keeping unproductive plants open, and the welfare safety net was kept intact, but only through heavy government subsidies. The consequence was spiraling inflation: about 1,500 percent in 1992, 900 percent in 1993, and 500 percent in 1994.

During these years, Russia made important strides toward reform. Over half of the economy was privatized. Policies were adopted to shift away from heavy defense industry to civil-sector industry and consumer goods. Market mechanisms and institutions began to appear, setting the stage for a governmental effort in 1995 to tighten spending, thereby slowing inflation and reducing deficits. By mid-1995, the results were encouraging.[1] Inflation had slowed to 7 percent per month. The government's target for late 1995 was an annual rate of only 12–24 percent. A budget plan had been adopted to keep deficits at a manageable 7.8 percent of GDP. Money-supply growth had slowed to 1–2 percent annually. The government had announced a plan to stabilize the ruble's exchange rate at 4,300–4,900 rubles per dollar.[2] The foreign-investment rate had grown from almost zero in late 1994 to nearly $1 billion annually. Unemployment had crept upward to 2–3 percent of the workforce, but the number of people classified below the poverty line had dropped from 31 percent in 1993 to 20 percent in 1995. The downward slide in the economy had also slowed. Indeed, signs of slow growth were appearing: 1 percent annually.[3]

Despite these positive trends, Russia remains a poor country by Western standards. Its GDP of $1.2 trillion is about 20 percent that of the United States and 66 percent that of Germany, a country with 50 percent fewer people. Only 30–40 percent that of wealthy Western economies, Russia's per capita income (PCI) is similar to that of Portugal and Greece: less than midway between the poor Islamic countries of the Middle East and the prosperous economies of Northern Europe. The combination of a weak economy and high deficits prevents ambitious domestic investments, much less costly foreign endeavors.

---

[1] Margaret Shapiro, "Russia's Parliament Passes Tough Budget," *Washington Post*, June 24, 1995. Fred Hiatt, "IMF Flunks Russia's 1995 Budget," *Washington Post*, December 6, 1994.

[2] David Ottaway, "Russia Pledges to Back Ruble on World Currency Markets," *Washington Post*, July 5, 1995.

[3] See Fred Hiatt, "Yeltsin's New Cabinet: Reformers' In-Out, Out-In Ideology Unclear," *Washington Post*, November 21, 1994; Lee Hockstader, "Yeltsin Backs Stringent Budget and Predicts Economic Turnaround in 1995," November 26, 1994; Hiatt, "IMF Flunks," 1994.

The future will be affected by how much Russia's economy rebounds.[4] Table 5.1 lists four growth scenarios for the coming decade that help bound the range of uncertainty.

A 1 percent rate reflects quite slow growth, leaving Russia in the economic doldrums because the population may grow this fast and the economy will still be well below Cold War levels. Rates of 2.5 and 5.0 percent reflect rates for healthy Western economies. They will restore the lost output but will not allow Russia to close the gap with the West by large amounts. A 7.5 percent rate amounts to a capitalist revival: major, sustained improvements caused by market mechanisms that work. Even in the event of a capitalist revival, Russia will remain far less wealthy than the United States and Western Europe. Its PCI will rise from 40 percent of those countries' PCI today to about 60 percent of their PCI tomorrow.

New public-investment funds, which are unlikely to be great, may be an equally important indicator of economic improvement. Defense downsizing will not yield any fiscal bonanza; instead, it will create a smaller force posture that can be funded with the current budget.

Table 5.1

Alternative Russian Economic Scenarios
(10 years)

Average Annual Growth Rate (%)	GDP in 10 Years[a] (billion $)	Annual Available for New Investments[b] (billion $)
1.0	1,300	0
2.5	1,500	10
5.0	1,800	40
7.5	2,100	85

[a]Measured in purchasing-power parity based on IISS data. See IISS, *Military Balance*, 1994–1995.

[b]Author's estimate based on projections for federal budget, deficit policy, and fixed expenditures.

---

[4]"Foreign, Defense Policy Council Revises Strategy for Russia," *Nezavisimaya Gazeta*, May 27, 1994. Sergei Karaganov, "Post Economic Boom, Balanced Conservative Image," *Segodnya*, January 4, 1994.

Domestic priorities will lay claim to any new funds deriving from economic growth. If new funds are available for national security, they may be needed to keep existing programs intact. Russia's national security programs today cost about $110 billion: 75 percent is devoted to defense and the rest to domestic programs, intelligence, diplomacy, foreign operations, and security assistance. For these programs to be continued, annual spending increases of 1–2 percent will be needed to purchase new technology and upgrade infrastructure and capital assets. This requirement is likely to absorb most additional funds deriving from economic growth. New programs thus will be possible only if higher GDP growth rates—in the 5–7.5 percent annual range—are achieved.

Even today, Russia has sizable resources for national security. Only one-third what the United States is spending, Russia's expenditures exceed those of Germany, Japan, and China by a factor of 3. It is still the world's second-strongest military power, and it likely will remain so. The scope for new initiatives could be broadened if secondary, public-sector programs are pared away. By applying its resources this way, Russia may be able to pursue additional national security goals beyond those sought today. Russia, moreover, might be able to pursue its goals sequentially, thus magnifying the effectiveness of its resources over time, as other nations in Europe have often parlayed wise strategy into cascading achievements. Nonetheless, Russia faces a decade of making the best out of constrained national security resources.

Over the longer term, Russia's resources could enlarge, but only if its economy grows at a sustained high rate. For example, a 2.5 percent growth rate for two decades would achieve a GDP of only $2 trillion. A 5 percent annual rate—a difficult feat—could elevate the GDP to $3 trillion. Even then, Russia's PCI would reach the level of an average West European economy today. The sheer size of the economy could permit a large national security effort, but only if the government and society are prepared to accept sacrifices to the domestic agenda. Short of this, Russia may not be free to anticipate a budgetary cornucopia that permits sweeping new strategic departures even two decades from now.

DEFENSE POLICY: GETTING SMALLER WHILE REMAINING A REGIONAL POWER

Russia's economic situation is having a marked effect on the country's defense policy. The major military downsizing Russia is undergoing is aimed at stripping away the bloated defense establishment inherited from the Soviet Union. In so doing, it is greatly reducing the overpowering military threat to Europe posed by the Soviet Union during the Cold War.[5] At the same time, Russia has begun crafting a defense strategy and force posture for the future that will retain its status as a regional power. Russian military power is not disappearing from the Eurasian and European security equation, and it may be able to play a role in buttressing a statist foreign policy.

The historic transformation now under way encompasses major reductions in forces and military spending, withdrawals from territory outside Russia's borders, and internal reorganization of remaining forces. It began in 1989, when Gorbachev announced cutbacks in Russian forces in Eastern Europe, and accelerated when the Soviet Union collapsed in 1991. As of this writing, the reduction campaign is about two-thirds complete and will continue over the next several years, coming to a halt about the year 2000. Only at that time will it be possible to know the extent to which Russia will cast off the legacy of the past. Even then, the picture will be incomplete, because Russia will only be midway in rebuilding for the future. Any effort to forecast the future thus is a tentative exercise.

Nuclear Forces

Developments in Russia's nuclear forces illustrate the importance of keeping the impact of downsizing in perspective. Owing to 40 years of Cold War, the Soviet Union emerged with a huge, three-legged strategic nuclear posture of over 2,000 launchers and 12,000 warheads—enough to absorb a surprise attack and retaliate with devastating force against large target systems in the United States and

---

[5]For an analysis of civil-military relations, see Brian A. Davenport, "Civil-Military Relations in the Post-Soviet State: Loose Coupling, Uncoupled?" *Armed Forces and Society*, Winter 1995. See also Alexei Arbatov, "Arbatov Urges Civilian Control Over Armed Forces," *Nezavisimaya Gazeta*, March 18, 1995.

Western Europe. This posture included nearly 1,400 ICBMs, 175 long-range bombers, and 62 missile-launching nuclear submarines (SSBNs) with 942 submarine-launched ballistic missiles (SLBMs). Also important, the Soviet Union fielded an imposing theater nuclear posture of 608 intermediate-range ballistic missiles/medium-range ballistic missiles (IRBMs/MRBMs) and 570 medium bombers, all capable of striking targets across Europe and Northeast Asia. In addition, the Soviet Union's tactical air forces had hundreds of combat aircraft capable of nuclear strike missions, and its ground forces were equipped with 1,700 short-range nuclear missile launchers and thousands of nuclear artillery rounds. This overall posture could wage an intercontinental war, a theater war, and a battlefield campaign—all at the same time.

Owing to START, the INF Treaty, other agreements, and unilateral downsizing, major parts of this massive posture have already vanished or are now being disassembled. The IRBMs/MRBMs are completely gone. As of late 1995, Russia's strategic posture was down to about 928 ICBMs, 95 strategic bombers, 46 SSBNs with 684 SLBMs, and 130 medium bombers. Once START drawdowns are completed, by 2003, Russia's posture will be further reduced to about 900 launchers and 3,100 warheads, a level that will remain stable unless further drawdowns are agreed upon. START II has provisions limiting the number of SLBMs, banning heavy ICBMs and MIRVed warheads for ICBMs, and constraining the downloading and retention of ICBMs now armed with more than five MIRV warheads. Russia, therefore, seems likely to end up with a post–START II posture of about 525 ICBMs (one warhead apiece), 264 SLBMs with 1,744 warheads, and 128 bombers with 892 air-launched cruise missiles (ALCMs)—a posture that can yield about 2,000 megatons in explosive power.[6]

Thus, Russia may retain only 25–50 percent of the Soviet Union's strategic nuclear forces. Yet Russia will remain a nuclear superpower by any measure. Its intercontinental forces will remain equal to those of the United States and superior to any other nuclear power, including Britain, France, and China. These forces will be capable of

---

[6]See Lt. Gen. Lev Volkov, "STARTII and the Topol Mobile Intercontinental Missiles," *Segodnya*, June 1, 1994.

deterring a U.S. nuclear attack while providing a broad range of options for use against military and civilian targets of any other nation. Russia also will retain sizable theater nuclear options in the form of medium-range bombers and a still-large inventory of tactical nuclear weapons.

All of these forces enable Russia still to cast a large nuclear shadow over Europe and Eurasia, affecting the evolution of the security system there. Both the United States and Russia seem agreed upon the idea that, whereas nuclear weapons were at the forefront of security diplomacy during the Cold War, they should now be retired to the backwaters. These two countries no longer target nuclear forces against each other. Even so, nuclear power will still matter, even if only indirectly. Russia's regional dominance is magnified because, apart from China, none of its immediate neighbors will have its own nuclear arsenal. Even if Russia refrains from trying to translate its dominance into a coercive diplomatic leverage, this dominance still influences how a large number of countries assess their long-range security requirements and options.

Conventional Forces

Russia's conventional forces will play a major role in national military strategy as well—perhaps the dominant role. Russia inherited a Cold War posture that was too expensive and vastly exceeded requirements of the new era. Faced with the task of deciding not only what should be retired but also what should be retained, Russia now confronts determining what is to be sought from its future conventional forces. The decision is important, and it will be anything but easy.

The Soviet Union began the Cold War with a huge conventional establishment, then laid a large nuclear posture atop it, thereby creating a redundant deterrent. Russia evidently intends to preserve a similar redundancy, but with smaller nuclear and conventional legs. Just as it is fashioning a new nuclear strategy, it must also forge a new conventional strategy. The Cold War posture was based on a coherent, if expensive, strategy aimed at making the Soviet Union an intimidating power in several different theaters at once. Because

Russia's future posture will be much smaller, the old concept is now outmoded. But what is to be the new concept? Russia no longer faces an enemy, so it must plan for generic dangers and geography (e.g., sizes of countries to be defended). The task confronting the Russian Ministry of Defense (MOD) is to maintain security over long borders and in several far-flung regions, but with far fewer forces than before. The manner in which Russia addresses this dilemma will determine its conventional defense strategy and posture for the future.

The downsizing effort now under way will help shape the strategy options at Russia's disposal. Although the magnitude of Russia's conventional-force reductions is equally as impressive as that of its nuclear forces, sizable combat forces remained as of early 1995. At the time the Cold War ended, the Soviet Union fielded a mammoth conventional establishment of over 200 mobilizable Army divisions, 7,700 combat aircraft, and 615 major naval combatants (Table 5.2). Russia's ground forces in 1995 were 64 percent smaller, its air forces were 51 percent smaller, and its naval forces were 46 percent smaller. Many divisions and combat aircraft were lost to the breakaway republics when the Soviet Union dissolved. The rest of the reductions, primarily in ground forces and naval combatants, have come from drawdowns to forces inherited by Russia.[7]

The reduction process is by no means complete. As we discuss below, Russia's posture seems likely to decline by the early 2000s to about 45 mobilizable divisions, 3,000 combat aircraft, and 300 naval combatants. Yet this huge reduction should not be allowed to obscure the fact that Russia will remain well-armed. A drawdown of 75 percent in ground forces, 45 percent in air power, and 50 percent in naval forces is a major transformation. But it does not equate to disarmament, because the Soviet Union was a military leviathan to begin with. Russia will still be the best-armed country in Europe. Yet it also will confront problems because of maldeployments and eroded readiness in its conventional posture.

---

[7]Data taken from IISS, *The Military Balance*, London: Brassey's Inc., annual editions 1989–1995.

Table 5.2

Downsizing of Russia's Conventional Forces

	Soviet Union Posture, 1989	Russian Posture 1995
Active Manpower (million)	5.1	1.5–2.0
Percentage of GNP on Defense	13–17	6–10
Ground Forces (number)		
• Divisions	214	77
• Separate Brigades in Division-Equivalents	11	7
• Artillery Divisions	18	15
• Attack Helicopter Regiments	20	21
• Tanks	58,300	20,000
• Infantry Fighting Vehicle/Armored Personnel Carriers	64,000	36,000
• Artillery Tubes/Mobile Rocket Launchers	38,000	21,000
• Attack Helos	1,500	1,000
Air Forces (number of aircraft)		
• Homeland Air Defense	2,300	1,400
• Tactical Fighters	1,900	600
• Ground Attack/Reconnaissance	2,900	1,400
• Strategic Airlift	600	350
Naval Forces (number)		
• Small Carriers	4	2
• Submarines	263	138
• Surface Combatants	268	145
• Amphibious Ships	80	49

MALDEPLOYMENTS

The reductions have left a maldeployed posture that constrains Russia from quickly bringing major power to bear against neighbors on its western or southern flanks. During the Cold War, about 75 percent of the Soviet Union's conventional forces was based in the western Soviet Union or Eastern Europe. The remaining 25 percent was stationed in the eastern Soviet Union, mostly opposite China. What exists today is a remarkable reversal of this strategic pattern. Owing to differential reduction patterns, only 33 percent of the existing posture is now deployed in western Russia; 66 percent is deployed in the east. To a degree not commonly realized, Russia has been stripped of its Europe-oriented strength even as it has preserved its traditional Asian presence. Thus, Russia's posture today is geographically out of balance.

During the Cold War, Soviet forces arrayed against NATO were primarily deployed in either the forward areas or in the Soviet Union's western military districts: the territory occupied by the Baltic states, Belarus, and Ukraine today. These forces, about 60 divisions and 2,500 combat aircraft, were the cream of the Soviet Army and Air Force. They have been the units most directly affected by the withdrawals, drawdowns, and political upheavals now under way. About 30 divisions and 1,200 aircraft were lost to Ukraine and Belarus. An equal number of forces has been withdrawn to Russia from Germany, Poland, Czechoslovakia, Hungary, and the Baltic states. However, the military districts in western Russia, zones where large forces were not stationed during the Cold War, lack the bases, facilities, and other infrastructure to absorb these returning units. Consequently, many of these units have been disbanded, and their equipment has been redistributed throughout the Russian military establishment.

As a result, Russia's western military districts—Kaliningrad, Northern, Moscow, Volga, North Caucasus, and Urals—today house about one-third of Russia's conventional posture: 27 divisions and 2,000 combat aircraft. Most of the remainder, 42 divisions and 1,600 combat aircraft, are based in eastern Russia, in the Siberian, Transbaykal, and Far Eastern military districts. In this situation, Russia can still defend its borders but is limited in quickly projecting operations with large forces in and around Europe. Enough forces would be available—provided they are adequately ready—to launch modest operations (e.g., a few divisions) in western Russia. But taking into account the need to withhold reserves, insufficient forces would be located nearby to launch a powerful, offensive major regional contingency (MRC; i.e., 25 divisions or more). Russia could rectify the problem by redeploying forces from its eastern districts via railroads, but the movement process would be time-consuming.

Over the long term, this unbalanced distribution will be reduced because the next drawdowns are likely to be made in the eastern military districts. A few additional units might be based in the western districts as new facilities are constructed but will not amount to a massive redeployment westward. Strategic requirements and basing realities likely will leave a conventional posture equally divided between west and east. Therefore, Russia will be left in the position of having to redeploy at least some forces from east to west—or vice versa—if it is to launch a large offensive in either zone.

Another constraint is that Russian forces are no longer based in large numbers on the territory of foreign states. During the Cold War, the presence of 31 divisions and 1,300 combat aircraft in Eastern Europe gave the Soviet Union a commanding position for coercively pressuring NATO or even, with the help of Warsaw Pact allies, for launching a short-warning attack on West Germany. Today, Russian forces have been withdrawn (except roughly four divisions and one air regiment in Kaliningrad, which borders Poland), and the Warsaw Pact has been abolished. As a result, Russia can no longer gain direct access to Eastern Europe. Russia would have to gain transit rights across Belarus and/or Ukraine to attack Poland or the other East European states.

Military withdrawal from the Baltic states has sharply reduced Russia's once-impressive ability to bring coercive pressure against these countries short of outright invasion. Within the CIS, Russian troops are present on the soil of neighboring states in relatively modest numbers. As of 1995, Russia had one division and some surface-to-air (SAM) units based in Moldova. In the Caucasus, Russia had two divisions and an air regiment based in Georgia, and one division based in Armenia. In Central Asia, Russia had one division stationed in Tajikistan, three divisions and an air regiment under joint Russian-national command in Turkmenistan, and three air regiments along with SAM forces scattered among Kazakhstan, Kyrgyzstan, and Uzbekistan. As events in several of these states have shown, these force levels allow the Russian government to play influential roles in the turbulent domestic scenes. However, short of invasion from Russia itself,[8] they do not pose the threat of military conquest to these nations.

---

[8]See Stephen Foye, "Russian Security Council Discusses Border Regions," *RFE/RL,* July 14, 1994.

COLLAPSE OF READINESS

Owing to inadequate budgets and dwindling manpower, Russia's forces also have experienced a sharp decline in readiness that has further eroded their strength.[9]

Inadequate Budgets

Senior Russian military officers complained about inadequate budgets in 1992 and 1993, but an especially strong public debate broke out in spring 1994 over the coming year's budget. The finance ministry had decided to allocate 5 percent of GNP to defense spending and, in a manner reflecting its efforts to control inflation, earmarked 37 trillion rubles for the MOD. The military, in turn, asserted that nearly 80 trillion rubles were needed to meet legitimate requirements. When the finance ministry and the Duma blanched, the MOD countered with a demand for 55 trillion rubles, which it portrayed as a bare minimum. The Federation Council endorsed the MOD figure, but the Duma held firm, and the final allocation was 40 trillion rubles.[10] The early-1995 debate saw a similar pattern of the MOD asking for more than it got.

IISS reports an estimated Russian defense budget of $63 billion in 1995 and $76 billion in 1996, using purchasing-power parity as the basis for converting rubles to dollars. In addition, defense-related spending of $10–$20 billion is funded elsewhere in Russia's federal budget (e.g., science and technology, security services, and border troops). The total amount is far less than the Soviet Union's defense spending during the Cold War, but it is still more than that of

---

[9]See Fred Hiatt, "Russia's Military Machine Bares Rust," *Washington Post*, January 17, 1995.

[10]Details on Russia's downsizing and loss of readiness have been reported in the Russian press. For example, see, "Lopatin Analyzes History, Results of Military Reductions," *Novaya Vezhednevnaya*, Moscow, May 26, 1994; "Grachev: Strapped Army at Minimum Level," *Trud*, Moscow, June 7, 1994; "Summing Up the Results of the Past Year and Looking to Next Year," *Mocskoy Sbornik*, Moscow, December 28, 1993; "Shirshov: R55 Trillion Is Subsistence Minimum for Defense Budget," *Krasnaya Zvezda*, Moscow, June 4, 1994; Vladimir Vernolin, "Army Needs Worthy Budget," *Krasnaya Zvezda*, Moscow, June 9, 1994; "Results of Winter Training Period," *Krasnaya Zvezda*, Moscow, June 2, 1994; and "START II Impact on Strategic Forces Viewed," *Segodnya*, Moscow, June 1, 1994.

Germany and France combined. Russia thus remains Europe's leading purchaser of military power. Of Russia's defense budget for 1995, IISS reports that 45 percent was spent on personnel, 21 percent on procurement, 10 percent on research and development, and the remainder on other items. Although the procurement slice is not disastrously low by NATO standards, it leaves sufficient funds for only normal acquisition and, thereby, inhibits large-scale buying of major, new end-items (e.g., ships). Russia's R&D budget of $7–$8 billion is not enough for a robust effort, but it is sufficient to fund high-priority efforts.[11]

For the fourth year in a row, the effect of reduced spending has been a large shortage of funds spread across MOD activities. Because Russian defense spending evidently is divided evenly between acquisition and operations, the need to avoid a wholesale cutback in either is forcing sharp belt-tightening in both.[12] The relatively modern inventory inherited from the Cold War has provided some flexibility for a slowdown in procurement. Even so, Russia in 1992 and 1993 procured no more than 20–25 percent of the new tanks, artillery, and aircraft needed to offset normal obsolescence. At the height of the Cold War, the Soviet Union was producing 700 combat aircraft, 3,500 tanks, and 2,000 artillery tubes per year. In 1992, Russia produced only 170 aircraft, 500 tanks, and 750 infantry fighting vehicles. Production in 1993 was no better. In 1994, only 40 tanks, 400 infantry fighting vehicles, and 50 combat aircraft were produced. Even for a downsized defense posture, this dropoff is large.[13]

In the long run, the consequence could be an aging inventory that itself could compel reductions in the posture. More immediately serious have been the deleterious effects on operations. The MOD has been unable to build nearly enough of the new living quarters needed to house thousands of soldiers returning to Russia. Training funds have been sharply reduced for all three services, maintenance

---

[11]IISS, *The Military Balance, 1995–1996*, London: Brassey's Inc., 1995.

[12]Keith Bush, "Aspects of Military Conversion in Russia," *RFE/RL*, April 8, 1994.

[13]Sergey Leshkov, "Defense Industry's Future," *Izvestiya*, December 30, 1995. Mikhail Maley, "Future Role of Defense Industry in Economy," *Delovoy Mir*, April 11, 1994. D. Belyayev, "Statistics on Deepening Crisis in Defense Industry," *Rossiyskiye Vesti*, June 1, 1994.

has seriously eroded, and purchase of supplies and spare parts has declined. The entire defense establishment now finds itself in the embarrassing position of being a debtor to its suppliers of energy, raw materials, and industrial products. The consequence has been the rapid emergence of a still-large but hollow military.[14]

Lower Manpower Levels

Indeed, the Russian MOD has encountered serious trouble in keeping up adequate manpower levels. Although civilian authorities have set an eventual target for military manpower of 1.2–1.5 million (1 percent of total population), the current authorized level is 2.1 million, and Marshal Grachev has stated his belief that this level should be retained. Of this level, about 1 million are conscripts who serve 18–24 months. Liberal deferment policies and widespread public distaste for serving in the military have resulted in only about 120,000–150,000 conscripts being inducted in 1993: not nearly enough to meet requirements. The MOD has tried to offset the deficiency by enlisting 100,000–150,000 "contract" soldiers for each of the past three years. Even so, total manpower has dropped to a level well below authorized strength[15]—a decline that has been accelerated by major departures of officers and NCOs who have tired of their low pay and primitive living standards. Actual manning levels are a matter of dispute, but as of late 1994, some observers were claiming that the number is as low as 1.5 million: a 30 percent shortfall.[16]

A Triage Philosophy

The MOD has tried to cope with these multiple problems by adopting what amounts to a triage philosophy. First priority is ensuring that the strategic nuclear forces and critical air defense forces are maintained at high readiness. Second priority is preserving a select

---

[14]Vladimir Yermolin, "Army Needs Worthy Budget," *Krasnaya Zvezda*, June 6, 1994.

[15]Marshal Pavel Grachev, "Defense Minister Says Army of 2 Million Needed," *ITAR-TASS*, February 4, 1994; See also Oleg Falichev, "Building Up the Armed Forces to the Proper Strength Is Our Common Cause," *Krasnaya Zvezda*, March 23, 1995.

[16]Stephen Foye, "Latest Figures on Contract-Military Service," *RFE/RL*, April 5, 1994.

cadre of ground, air, and naval units to ensure that immediate small-scale emergencies can be met. With these two priorities consuming a large amount of the available funds, the bulk of the conventional posture has borne the brunt of the funding shortfalls, with not only a consequent decline in training and readiness but also a steep decline in morale that has left senior officers worried about the long-term cohesion of their institution.[17]

These declines should be put in perspective, however. Even during the Cold War, the Soviet Army maintained a staggered readiness profile. Only about one-third of its divisions received high active-duty manning levels (i.e., 75 percent of personnel or more). The remaining units were kept at far lower levels, many at only 25 percent of active manpower, which prevented a serious training regimen. A staggered-readiness profile thus would be natural today even if adequate funds and manpower were available, but the current profile seemingly dips well below the historical norm. Evidently ten or fewer divisions (airborne units and select armored and mechanized divisions) are today combat-ready: 12 percent or less of the posture. These units are scattered across the country: One per military district apparently is the norm. They are capable of small operations and missions, but not the sweeping offensive campaigns of history.

The status of the remaining units has not been revealed, but reports cite chronic shortages in officers and enlisted personnel (up to 40 percent), serious maintenance problems, a lack of spare parts, insufficient training, and grossly inadequate housing. Grachev himself has acknowledged that only about 50 percent of Army personnel are adequately trained, and that only 20 percent of Army tanks are combat-ready. Reports indicate that about 70 percent of planned training exercises were conducted in 1994. Budgetary constraints, however, have led to scalebacks in the large-unit field exercises that influence an army's ability to conduct major combat operations. Division-sized operations have become a thing of the past.[18]

---

[17]Sergei Ianin, "Factors of Tension in the Army Environment," *Russian Social Science Review,* January 1995.

[18]For example, see General Alexander Lebed, "Senior Officer on Army's Problems," *Komsomal Saya Pravda,* February 3, 1994.

Remarks made by senior Russian officers suggest that, whereas 1993 was a calamitous year that raised questions about the survival of the Russian state and Army, 1994 brought a greater sense of calm.[19] Chechnya aside, the Russian Army has commenced recrafting itself for the coming era, and is slowly reorganizing itself and setting future goals. The principal problem now is a lack of manpower and budgetary resources: a difficult problem, but not fatal to the survival of the Russian Army as an institution. Yet, today's problems *are* serious: The Russian Army would have trouble marching off to war in large formations, much less fighting effectively.[20]

The situation with Russia's air and naval forces is similar. Whereas ground forces are especially susceptible to a loss in readiness if their funds are cut, because 50–66 percent of their budgetary costs derive from operations and personnel, air and naval forces are more dependent upon the quality of their technology. But even for them, inadequate budgets for operations can erode readiness. And although complaints about problems facing the Russian Air Force have been less prominent in the public domain than those for ground forces, at many air bases the flying hours for training have been reduced so that not only combat proficiency has been lost but minimum standards for safety are not being met. One report held that Russian pilots were receiving only 50–60 flying hours of training per year; the U.S. Air Force's standard for minimum proficiency is about 220 hours. Lack of aviation fuel, spare parts, and special equipment has also eaten into readiness.[21] Even during the Cold War, when funding was ample, the Russian Air Force was deemed behind its Western rivals in doctrine, training, and all-around flexibility. Since then, the quality gap doubtless has widened.[22]

The Russian Navy has been especially hard hit, and the public clamor by senior Navy officers has been quite loud. The Cold War brought about a huge transition in the Soviet Navy, which went from per-

---

[19]See Pavel Felgengauer, "Year of Military Reform," *Current Digest of the Post-Soviet Press*, March 22, 1995.

[20]See Fred Hiatt, "Russia's Army: A Crumbling Giant," *Washington Post*, October 21, 1993.

[21]See Gen. Mikhail Soroka, "Air Force Commander: No New Combat Aircraft Expected," Foreign Broadcast Information Service (FBIS)-translated text, April 1, 1995.

[22]Public statements by Russian Air Force officers in Russian press, multiple sources.

forming coastal defense missions to acquiring a blue-water capability. By the end of the conflict, it had built the capacity to conduct strike and sealane interdiction operations far from the Soviet coast, and it even had deployed four small carriers. Today, the Russian Navy retains its traditional four fleets: the Northern, Baltic, Black Sea, and Pacific Fleets (the Black Sea Fleet is jointly administered with Ukraine). These four fleets still retain large numbers of vessels, but funding shortfalls have kept many of those vessels unseaworthy.

Reports in Russian military journals and newspapers indicate major reductions in at-sea training, overhaul requirements that go unfulfilled, and sharp increases in accidents resulting from equipment failures. Major shortages have occurred in fuel, spare parts, and other stocks. Serious problems have cropped up in disposal of worn-out nuclear reactors and related equipment. Morale troubles have spiraled, bringing about a rise in criminal behavior among enlisted personnel. Naval bases, shipyards, and repair facilities are also deteriorating.

The case of the Northern Fleet—the pride of the Russian Navy—illustrates the general trend. Official reports indicate that overall manning is 40 percent below desired levels, and civilian personnel—who perform critical support functions—are 30 percent fewer than needed. Liquid fuel is at only 50 percent of desired capacity, food is at 30 percent, and dry freight is at 20 percent.[23] The effect is to leave the Northern Fleet partly crippled. In 1993, 322 ships of this fleet needed repair, but only 27 percent was serviced. Another 70 foreign-made ships were due for overall, but none was sent to places where they could be repaired. On the ships that are still serviceable, training time is severely limited. Some still put to sea, but only 1–2 times per year, and they are not accompanied by adequate support vessels. Large-scale maneuvers and complex exercises have become luxuries of the past.

The Baltic Fleet faces even more serious problems: The Russian government is considering downgrading it to a flotilla or some other

---

[23]Dmitriy Kholodov, "Admiral Chernovin's Submarines?" *Moskovskiye Komsomoletsi*, March 26, 1994; Stephen Foye, "On Budget, Baltic Fleet and Kaliningrad," *RFE/RL*, March 24, 1994.

sublevel. The Black Sea Fleet's problems have become so notorious that they are contributing to a willingness to sell some of its assets to Ukraine. As of 1995, speculation held that only two fleets would be maintained: the Northern and the Pacific.

The overall picture thus is one of a Russian defense establishment in deep crisis, hard-pressed to maintain peacetime norms, much less fight a major war. Yet caution should be exercised before dismissing the entire posture as a rusting relic. Military establishments always face shortfalls; senior Russian officers may be beating the wardrums in order to get larger budgets. Awareness should not be lost that, for all its troubles, the Russian military still possesses many of the assets needed to be a serious fighting force: a large and well-trained officer corps; a large infrastructure of bases and facilities; a very large, if underutilized, supporting industry; a substantial and fairly modern inventory of weapons; and technology that, although not highly sophisticated by U.S. standards, is basically sound.

Chechnya as an Example of Collapse of Readiness

Regardless of its ultimate political consequences, the Chechnya intervention at first was a military disaster. Russian ground units displayed poor morale, weak training and operational skill, and dubious leadership. The result was a serious fight with a poorly equipped opposition that should have been overwhelmed quickly. Yet too much should not be made of this single case. The units committed to Chechnya were hardly the cream of the Russian Army, and reserve-component forces of other countries have often shown weak performance in trying to quell civil disturbances, especially when the operation does not enjoy widespread public support. As the conflict dragged on, the performance of Russian forces improved markedly. In all likelihood, the Chechnya episode will serve as a wake-up call for the Russian Army, not a model for the future.[24]

---

[24]See Lee Hockstader, "Russia Absorbs High Price of Victory," *Washington Post*, July 9, 1995.

the new doctrine also asserts that Russia exists in a still-turbulent world of dangerous threats, and that it will need to remain militarily powerful if its interests are to be protected. These interests include defense of Russian borders and internal order, but they do not end there. The statement points out that Russia will have important interests beyond its borders.[28]

The new doctrine highlights the continuing role that nuclear weapons are to play in Russian military strategy, not only in deterring intercontinental attack on the homeland but also in prosecuting battlefield campaigns. It asserts that Russia will refrain from using nuclear weapons against states not possessing those weapons, but it also makes an important exception to this rule: It allows for nuclear use against an armed attack by any country joined in an alliance with a nuclear-armed state, if that country advances onto Russian territory or merely attacks Russian forces. The obvious implication is that Russia reserves the right to be the first to cross the nuclear threshold if it is attacked, especially if the attacker has direct or indirect access to nuclear weapons.[29]

When queried about this provocative statement, Russian spokesmen asserted that it means nothing more than an endorsement of the flexible-response doctrine long embraced by NATO. Even so, it implies that Russia is not carrying the idea of denuclearization to the point of stripping nuclear weapons out of its military strategy for battlefield campaigns, or even embracing a "no first use" or "last resort" stance. At its summit of 1990, NATO, flush with confidence in its conventional defenses, downgraded any major reliance on the tactical nuclear component of flexible response. Whether the Russian military shares the same view is unclear. Indeed, Russian strategy may be coming to view tactical nuclear weapons as a potential substitute for the loss of its once-overpowering conventional posture. If so, this viewpoint indicates less willingness than in U.S. doctrine to part with the psychological comfort provided by these weapons.

---

[28]See Russian Government, *Main Provisions of the Military Doctrine of the Russian Federation*, Moscow, 1993. For an appraisal of an earlier version, see Scott McMichael, "Russia's New Military Doctrine," *Military Affairs*, October 1992.

[29]For an appraisal, see Col. Gen. Mikhail Kolesnikov, "Army: Problems, Solutions," *Armeyskiy Sbornik*, January 1995.

Nuclear deterrence aside, the new doctrine points to conventional forces as the centerpiece of future Russian military strategy. It lays down no guidelines on the size and configuration of the conventional posture, but it does mandate that the posture be mobile, well-armed, and sufficiently large to meet the requirements of the day. Recognizing the important role played by qualitative factors in determining defense adequacy, it calls for a sizable industrial base capable of manufacturing modern weapon systems for the Russian military. It also calls for a strong research and development program aimed at maintaining a high level of military science and technology. In its view, Russia is to remain an independent military power, beholden to no country for its weapons and technology.[30]

The new doctrine lays down important guidelines regarding the strategic purposes to be served by Russia's conventional forces. It highlights the need to defend Russia's borders from attack, but it also addresses external efforts—for example, by ethnic nationalists—to foment domestic discord within Russia, as well as territorial claims on Russian land, local conflicts near Russian borders, and nuclear proliferation as serious dangers that could mandate military counteraction. Conveying an obvious warning to NATO and China, it signals that any military buildup near Russia's borders by a hostile state or alliance will be regarded as a threat to Russia's security. In doing so, it implicitly lays claim to a zone of security around Russia's periphery: not abnormal for powerful states, but geopolitical all the same. It is silent on whether Russia's own forces might prove menacing to neighboring states for the same reason, although in reverse.

While disavowing aggressive intent, the new doctrine proclaims Russia's legitimate right to employ military force either within Russia or beyond its borders if necessary. Participating in U.N.–sponsored peacekeeping is but one mission in a spectrum of potential activities. The new doctrine asserts that Russia can rightfully station forces on the territory of friendly countries and allies, implying a willingness to project military power to disrupt efforts by unfriendly countries or alliance blocs aimed at assembling direct threats to Russia's security.

---

[30]Anatoliy Dokuchayev, "The Russian Army: Footnote to Assets and Conclusions," *Krasnaya Zvezda,* May 6, 1994; Andrei Kozyrev, "Russia's Interests: Country's Military Doctrine and International Security," *Krasnaya Zvezda,* June 14, 1994.

It also asserts that Russian forces can be used to protect the lives and safety of Russian citizens living abroad. The overarching rationale is that of protecting not only Russia's physical security but also its vital interests, some of which lie outside Russia's territorial boundaries. None of these proclamations is inconsistent with the views of many other countries, but taken together, they reflect an attitude that Russia's use of military power will be dictated by traditional reasons of state.[31]

The new doctrine also lays down broad guidelines governing the use of military power in wartime. When Russian forces are committed to battle, it asserts, they are to be used in militarily decisive ways. Adequate forces are to be quickly mobilized and deployed to the scene of conflict. Their main objective, the new doctrine says, is to localize tensions and to quickly end hostilities on terms beneficial to Russia. The battlefield goal is to repel hostile strikes and to defeat enemy forces through a combination of firepower and maneuver by air, land, and sea units. The new doctrine points out that some conflicts might lead to escalation, and it calls on Russian forces to be capable of carrying out their missions in this event. This stance is not different from the military doctrines of many states, but its blunt terms reflect professional military thinking. The implication is that any country foolish enough to tangle with Russian military forces will be treated firmly, in a manner consistent with sound military strategy focused on victory.

The new doctrine says that Russian forces should be prepared for military operations in any direction and in many places. Yet it says nothing specific about how Russia will confront the strategy dilemmas brought about by force downsizing. During the Cold War, the Soviet Union carried the logic of being prepared for simultaneous contingencies to its ultimate conclusion. With an army of over 200 mobilizable divisions, the Soviet Union was prepared for conflict anywhere on its periphery and did not face the prospect of moving large forces across long distances so that they could be concentrated in a single region. Downsizing puts a permanent end to this strategy of being everywhere at once, and in large quantity to boot.

---

[31]Vitaliy Tsygichko, "What Kind of Army Do We Need? The Political Context of Russian Military Doctrine," *Nezavisimaya Gazeta*, April 13, 1994.

Downsizing means that Russia will no longer be able to blanket multiple different regions with large forces in peacetime. If faced with a major war in a single region, Russia *will* be compelled to move forces across the country for concentration. Even then, it will not be able to assemble the huge masses of forces that marked Soviet strategy in the past: enough to saturate the terrain, meet all plausible operational needs, and outnumber the enemy. Its ability to mass large forces will especially be constrained if two or more conflicts occur at once.

A More Selective, Adaptive Strategy

A smaller posture means that Russian strategy will have to learn how to be selective and adaptive. The new strategy will be required to use a smaller pool of forces in flexible ways that allow for responsive but not continuous coverage of a wide geographic area in peacetime. It also will be required to avoid fighting multiple large wars at once and to rely on quality to make up for a lack of quantity when large combat missions must be undertaken in wartime. The manner in which Russia responds to these mandates will define how its new conventional strategy is to be shaped.

During the Cold War, the Soviet Union seemed capable of massing 60 divisions in Central Europe as the major contribution to a 90-division Warsaw Pact attack on NATO while also dispatching 25 divisions to attack the Persian Gulf oil fields. Meanwhile, the Red Army had sufficient additional forces to commit about 30 divisions to support offensives directed at NATO's northern and southern flanks. Even if these campaigns were in progress, enough forces were left over to maintain 45 divisions in the Far East to ensure stability there, and to hold back a strategic reserve of nearly 50 divisions. Meanwhile, Russia's naval forces were large enough to launch concurrent offensives in the North Atlantic and nearby waters, in the Baltic and Mediterranean Seas, and in the Pacific. Seldom before, apart from World War II, has equivalent military largesse been seen. Whether the Soviet Union had any intention of launching the worldwide war feared by Western strategists is open to question, given the aversion to multiple-front wars normally shown by the Soviet government during its history. But the Soviet Union assembled enough military power to *contemplate* such a task. To put matters mildly, it was amply insured.

The drawdown now under way means that Russia's new military strategy will not be able to embrace multiple insurance policies and mass in similarly robust ways. Just as the United States abandoned its "2-1/2"–war strategy of the 1960s in favor of "1-1/2" major wars during the 1970s and beyond, Russia will have to make a similar choice. The United States was aided because rapprochement with China made unnecessary further efforts to plan for concurrent major wars in Europe and Asia. Russia today faces no comparable strategic luxury. Its southern flank seems likely to permanently fester with local discord. Although the Russian government claims to perceive no threats from major powers, it evidently continues to cast a wary eye on both its western and eastern flanks, apparently regarding neither Europe nor the Far East and Asia as permanently stable. War with either NATO or China, or with both at the same time, may seem beyond the pale to diplomats and other observers. Yet this prospect is unlikely to be dismissed as fanciful by Russian military planners, whose reputation for conservatism is well-established.

In all likelihood, future Russian military strategy will continue to contemplate the prospect of wars being fought in three zones: on Russia's western, southern, and eastern flanks. Fear of more than one conflict occurring at the same time is likely to be a major barrier to any Russian military strategy limited to the capability to fight only one war. Perhaps Russia will prepare for two medium-sized conflicts, but conservative planning easily could give rise to a three-conflict standard: one for each threatened region. Regardless, Russia will not again be able to apply the principle of relying on locally available forces in the lavish terms of the past. Owing to budget constraints, it will be hard-pressed to assemble enough forces in each region during peacetime to handle a sizable conflict with local forces alone. In a crisis, it most likely will have to adopt a practice of relying on rapid cross-country mobilization and reinforcement in order to concentrate enough forces to deal with the contingency of the moment.

If so, this greater reliance on strategic mobility will bring about a major new departure in Russian military strategy. Russia will have to become like the United States: a country that relies on mobility and flexibility at the heart of its strategic concept.

Perhaps a reliance on mobility will enable Russia to concentrate enough forces for any single major contingency. But if the requirement proves large, the need to also withhold sufficient forces for other regions and missions will likely stretch thin the smaller Russian posture of tomorrow. This development seems likely to bring about a second revolutionary departure in Russian military strategy. Most probably, Russia will no longer be able to assemble the huge forces for any single contingency that dominated Soviet doctrine during the Cold War.

A Second Revolutionary Departure: Qualitative Rather Than Quantitative Superiority

The Soviet strategy—to commit enough ground forces and combat aircraft to saturate the terrain and battlefield airspace, to overpower the enemy with sheer numbers of tanks, mechanized formations, and artillery, and, if the initial contingent failed, to commit a second and third echelon of reserves until the enemy finally collapsed from sheer exhaustion—will no longer be possible in the military world of tomorrow. Indeed, Russian forces may find themselves matched in numbers or even outnumbered. As a result, Russian military strategy will face powerful incentives to replace the old reliance on mass with a greater emphasis on qualitative dominance and the operational art. If so, this development will reinforce trends already under way in modern military doctrine, weapons, and tactics—all of which seemingly are grasped by Russian military officers. These trends originated in the unfolding of the NATO–Warsaw Pact military competition in the Cold War's final years, and the evolution of the U.S. and Soviet militaries in response. A brief discussion of these interacting trends will help illuminate the pressures now confronting the Russian military and how it may respond.

Throughout most of the Cold War, NATO endeavored to carry out its forward linear defense of West Germany through an old-style doctrine that never attempted to match the Warsaw Pact in numbers of ground forces. It did rely on its high-quality logistics units and tactical air forces to achieve equality in firepower on the battlefield. The idea was to offset NATO's deficiency in mass with firepower sufficiently intense to destroy invading Warsaw Pact forces as fast—or faster—than NATO's forces were destroyed in return. By attempting to fight and win an attrition battle in these ways, NATO endeavored to bottle up a Warsaw Pact attack in the forward areas and exhaust it before NATO's forces themselves became exhausted. In reaction, Soviet commanders adopted a doctrine aimed at concentrating their forces at select points, quickly punching through NATO's forward defenses, and fighting a victorious battle of maneuver in the rear areas.

In the early 1980s, NATO departed from this old approach by fashioning new doctrine for modern warfare. Three factors contributed to this change: fear of vulnerability to enemy breakthroughs; reawakened interest in battlefield maneuver and the operational art as developed by the German Wehrmacht in World War II; emerging technological breakthroughs. NATO strategists came to conclude that by shifting from forward linear arrays to nonlinear formations, they could generate sizable operational reserves. These forces, in turn, could be used to launch devastating flanking attacks on advancing enemy columns, thereby inflicting far more attrition than by simply firing at the enemy with NATO units lined up abreast of each other. The appearance of high-speed tanks and infantry fighting vehicles (IFVs; e.g., the Abrams tank and Bradley IFV), coupled with the development of accurate guidance systems for directing artillery fires, made this nonlinear doctrine possible. Equally important, the development of AWACS, ATACMS, and improved aircraft avionics opened up the prospect for directing lethal fires deep into the enemy's rear areas, against second-echelon forces. Whereas NATO's tactical air and missile forces were once largely irrelevant to the battle being waged on the ground, now they were offered the prospect of becoming quite relevant, especially if a greater capacity for joint, ground-air operations could be developed.

Pursued during the 1980s, these innovations in doctrine and technology coalesced in the years prior to Desert Storm. When that conflict began, the U.S.–led coalition force enjoyed numerical superiority in the air, but it was matched on the ground by the huge and well-entrenched Iraqi Army. The coalition forces, however, arrived on the Kuwaiti battlefield with a well-honed capacity for joint operations. They were also armed with highly lethal weapons and C3I systems having a revolutionary capacity to see the battlefield and direct strikes against enemy forces in the rear areas. Employing these assets in ways new to modern warfare, the coalition's ground, air, and naval forces worked together far more closely than before.

When the war began, coalition air forces gained air supremacy over the outclassed Iraqi Air Force and Air Defense System, then proceeded to pummel enemy ground targets for a full month. When the coalition ground attack was launched, it was carried out through a coordinated maneuver that skillfully employed the operational art. Iraqi ground forces were fixed with frontal assaults, then U.S., British, and French forces swept around the enemy right flank, descended upon the Iraq rear, and tore apart the Iraqi defense scheme. The result was that the Iraqi Army—which had been designed according to the Soviet model—was crushed in only 100 hours by a ground force no larger than itself but far better prepared. Many factors contributed to the coalition's lightning victory with almost no losses. One thing seemed clear: Almost overnight, the old Soviet model had become archaic.

As many Russian commanders have acknowledged, Desert Storm alone is reason for uprooting outmoded features of their force structure, weapons, and battlefield doctrine. Beyond this, the downsizing now taking place in the Russian Army creates equally compelling reasons for a shift in the direction of Western practices, including relying more heavily on advanced C3I systems, sophisticated reconnaissance platforms, high technology, well-trained troops capable of seizing the initiative, tactical mobility, swift ground maneuvers, responsive logistics systems, deep fires, tight air-ground coordination, and an imaginative use of air power to influence the ground battle. To an important degree, a smaller Russian Army will need to rely on these determinants of qualitative superiority to ensure success in future wars.

How far will the Russian military go?[32] Russian officers have ideas and preferences of their own, and many may attribute the Desert

---

[32]See Pavel Felgengauer, "Expert Appraisal: The Russian Army Employs New Tactics," *Current Digest of the Post-Soviet Press*, February 8, 1995.

Storm fiasco to Iraqi incompetence rather than to their own flawed concepts. Their force structures and logistics systems are so different from the U.S. model that a complete conversion might be impossible, even if deemed desirable. For example, U.S. Army divisions are 25 percent larger than traditional Russian divisions. The difference lies not in heavy weapons but in the infantry and support assets that give U.S. units their diversity. The average U.S. division, moreover, receives logistics support from higher echelons (e.g., corps and theater) that is four times greater than that given to Russian divisions. The differences in air forces are even greater. Not only are U.S. aircraft and munitions of higher quality, but pilots receive far more training and enjoy greater latitude in carrying out combat operations. Moreover, U.S. air units place far greater emphasis on being able to perform multiple types of missions, including ground attack.

During the Cold War, the Soviet Army emphasized mass rather than unit quality, and the Soviet Air Force was primarily responsible for keeping the sky clear of enemy aircraft, not helping out the ground troops. The U.S. philosophy is the opposite. These dissimilar philosophies have given rise to polar-opposite force structures whose differences go far beyond surface appearances. The Russian military has inherited the legacy of the Cold War and, indeed, the whole military history of the Czarist era. Uprooting this legacy in order to adopt Western practices will require far more than a minor face-lift for the Russian Army's organizational structure.

The Russian military lacks the technology and money to duplicate sophisticated U.S. forces anytime soon. Yet some movement toward the U.S. model seems likely and evidently is already under way. For example, greater emphasis is being placed on reconnaissance strike platforms, brigade formations, and beefed-up ground logistics. The Russian Army and Air Force will remain distinctly Russian. Yet the years ahead probably will witness a slow but steady evolution in the Western direction. To the extent success is achieved, the Russian military may reacquire some of its legendary reputation for professional competence that was lost by its Iraqi surrogates in the Kuwaiti desert.

FORCE POSTURE FOR THE FUTURE

A Three-Tiered Structure

Regardless of the progress the Russian Army makes toward acquiring higher quality, it will still face the worrisome strategy dilemma of defending a large geographic space with a force posture far smaller than that during the Cold War. In reaction, the prevailing concept now evidently being adopted is to create a three-tiered structure: territorial forces, mobile forces, and strategic reserve components. The territorial forces are to be lightly equipped units charged with day-to-day guarding of Russia's borders and key installations. The mobile forces are to provide a cluster of highly ready units, with differing types of armaments, that can quickly converge on a threatened zone and conduct medium-sized combat operations. The strategic reserves are to be less-ready, heavy ground formations that can be mobilized over a period of weeks and deployed to conduct large-scale missions. The Russian Army's apparent hope is that this three-tiered system can handle the emerging situation. Because the entire Russian landscape will not be guarded at all times, a responsive mobilization system will ensure prompt dispatch of sufficient forces to quell troubles wherever they might crop up.[33]

Mobile Force

The mobile force is the most interesting part of the new Russian defense posture, because it will provide the combat forces that deal with most crises.[34] Although plans are still fluid, evidently the MOD is thinking in terms of two different categories of forces—Immediate Reaction Forces (IRF) and Rapid Deployment Forces (RDF)—both of which may be under a new Mobile Forces Command that will report to the General Staff. The two categories are identical to those adopted by NATO for shaping its own mobile forces capable of

---

[33]General Vadim Makarevskiy, "Military Reform Is Proceeding," *Obshchaya Gazeta*, April 1994.

[34]Stephen Foye, "Plans for Mobile Force Outlined," *RFE/RL*, March 3, 1993.

reacting quickly and deploying responsively to crisis areas far removed from their peacetime bases.[35]

Immediate Reaction Forces. The IRF will be able to deploy within 1–3 days of callup. Current models suggest that the IRF will be made up of about 5 airborne divisions—composed of 6 airborne brigades, 8 light motorized rifle brigades, and a "Spetznaz" (special forces) brigade—as well as 12 helicopter regiments and associated support units. Also attached will be several naval infantry and assault landing battalions. Air support is to be provided by 5–7 air regiments, 5 bomber regiments, and 4 air transport divisions. If these models are realized, the IRF will principally be an airborne force supported by air units, both of which can be moved quickly to distant areas. Total strength will be about 60,000 ground troops and 300–400 combat aircraft. It will be capable of intervening quickly in a crisis in Russia and around its periphery. Although it will have some IFVs and artillery, an Immediate Reaction Force will not have the heavy weaponry needed for intense armored combat.

Rapid Deployment Forces. The RDF will be larger and heavier than the IRF, and will be expected to be ready within 3–7 days of callup. Current public writings suggest that the ground component will include 3 corps, 2 traditional heavy divisions, 3 helicopter regiments, 5 Multiple-Launch Rocket System (MLRS) brigades, and support forces. The "corps" is a new formation of about 35,000 troops that will include 5–6 heavy brigades: tank, mechanized, and motorized rifle units. The "brigade" also is a new formation, similar to a U.S. Army brigade in total manpower but more heavily armed. The corps will deploy about 600 tanks, 1,500 IFVs, and 900 artillery tubes: equivalent to 4 or more traditional Soviet heavy divisions. The total RDF ground posture amounts to about 200,000 troops and the equivalent of 15 heavy divisions, armed with 2,200 tanks, 5,100 IFVs, and 3,000 artillery tubes, along with sizable numbers of helicopters and MLRS. The air component is to include an air army of 300–400 combat aircraft and 3 bomber divisions of 270 aircraft. If it does, this posture will be similar in size to an old-style Soviet "front," but with a ground structure reflecting the Western model.

---

[35]William O'Malley and Edward McDonald have written an in-depth analysis of these forces in "Russia's New Mobile Forces," Santa Monica, Calif.: RAND, unpublished draft.

Thought was originally given to basing the new Mobile Command in central Russia, in the Volga and Ural military districts, but lack of adequate bases has led to the judgment that the Command's forces will have to remain scattered across Russia in several different locations. Regardless, the Mobile Command amounts to an imposing posture in the aggregate: 20 combat division-equivalents, sizable combat support units, mobility assets, and up to 1,200 combat aircraft. It also is a diverse posture that includes a mix of light airborne and heavy armored/mechanized formations, plus specialized units, that are aligned with a broad spectrum of missions and contingencies. Its air component, composed of fighters, fighter bombers, and bombers, provides a range of assets for the full set of air missions. The posture evidently is intended to provide a grab bag of assets from which specific capabilities can be tailored for individual missions. But if ever assembled in one location and given adequate support, it would provide an overall capability similar to that of the Desert Storm force deployed by the U.S.–led coalition in 1991.

The RDF's structure of three corps suggests that the Mobile Command may be sized to conduct three concurrent combat operations, either together or in separate places. If the Mobile Command is arbitrarily divided into three parts, each segment would be composed of 6.6 divisions and 400 aircraft. The Mobile Command is similar to U.S. plans for its own rapid-reaction and -projection force: The U.S. active-duty "building-block" posture for a combined MRC operation (one including allied forces) is 6.5 divisions and 700 combat aircraft. Although the number of divisions is equivalent to Russia's, the difference in air allocation reflects a long-standing U.S. tendency to assign more combat aircraft to ground operations than do the Russians.

If the Mobile Command is brought to life, it will leave Russia well-armed for most contingencies, without having to mobilize unready reserve-component forces. But whereas the United States possesses the naval forces and airlift/sealift mobility assets to project its rapid-reaction forces across the Atlantic and Pacific Oceans, to almost any point along the periphery of the Eurasian landmass, Russia will not be able to intervene in crises far from its borders—especially when large bodies of water stand in the way. Yet Russia does possess a well-developed rail system and a large force of cargo aircraft for limited-range missions. As a result, it will have sufficient projection power to deploy large forces anywhere along its periphery—including somewhat beyond its borders, if necessary.

The Russian Army will not be defined by the mobile forces alone; strategic reserve components will also be retained. Divisions will have a cadre of active troops and full sets of equipment, but will include 50–75 percent reservists. They will be mobilizable over a period of weeks and months. In their main capacity, they will provide an affordable reservoir of forces that can be called upon to greatly enlarge the Army in a national emergency. The combination of these reserve units and the mobile forces, plus other active units not assigned to the Mobile Command, will determine the total size of the Russian Army.

Posture Estimates

As yet, final plans for how many total divisions the future Russian Army is to possess have not been formulated. That the Army will have less than there are in today's posture is clear, but the final number is uncertain. What can be done is to offer estimates based on aggregate manpower data and related factors. Surface inspection suggests that if an authorized MOD end strength of 2.1 million allows for today's posture, then a future level of 1.5 million should allow for about 60 divisions, assuming the Army is reduced by a proportional amount (30 percent). In all likelihood, however, the Army will take more than an equal share of cuts, because other MOD elements— headquarters staffs, the strategic rocket forces, the air force and navy, and infrastructure organizations—will be reduced by less than the overall 30 percent cut. If none of these elements is reduced below today's level, then only 400,000 slots will be available to the Army: 40 percent of today's total. Ceteris paribus, an Army of about 34 divisions will be permitted.

Given a range of 34–60 divisions as the region of uncertainty, the actual number of divisions will probably fall somewhere in the middle. If the other MOD elements are reduced by 20 percent, an Army of 52 divisions will be the outcome. If those elements are reduced by only 10 percent, then 43 divisions will result. The number could be somewhat higher if the MOD wins its battle to preserve an overall manpower level higher than 1.5 million. Conversely, lack of acquisition funds needed to buy new equipment, spares, and other stocks for a large force structure could drive the number downward. With all these factors taken into account, it seems likely that the MOD will strive to keep a posture of 40–50 mobilizable divisions, with about one-half of these maintained as less-ready core units.

This posture appears quite large at first glance, but it is no bigger than the ground forces being kept by the United States. At the moment, the U.S. plan calls for only 13 active Army and Marine divisions; when reserve-component forces are included, the count rises to 28 division-equivalents. Because U.S. divisions and logistics support assets are larger than their Russian counterparts, 28 U.S. divisions equates to 45 Russian divisions. Affordable resources may permit this many units, and a posture about this size seems sufficient to meet Russia's diverse strategic needs.

A posture of 40–50 divisions will not fulfill all of the requirements that might be identified in a conservative analysis emanating from the Russian MOD. Above all, it will not enable Russia to wage large offensive campaigns in several theaters at once, or to fight both NATO and China at the same time. But it will allow Russia to meet its far-flung peacetime needs and to cope with a variety of small crises and disturbances. It also will permit the MOD to assemble sufficient forces to wage a single regional campaign of limited offensive purpose without exposing the rest of the country to other threats. If this proves to be the outcome, the result might be a convenient, if not altogether happy, marriage between Russia's emerging defense strategy and budgetary realities.

If the MOD strives to maintain a hedge to enlarge the Army beyond the level of 40–50 divisions in a crisis, it may configure division-sized sets of equipment that can be kept in storage and quickly broken out if a decision is made to increase the manpower pool. Evidently this practice—which was followed during the Cold War—is already being pursued: Reports in the Russian press suggest that 5 mobilization depots were formed in 1994. Precisely how many division sets will be retained is uncertain; constraints on acquisition and maintenance costs will place an upper limit on what is possible. A reasonable estimate is between 10 and 15 sets, which will increase equipment holdings to a level 20–33 percent above those of the manned posture. The United States keeps extra equipment stocks of this magnitude as "war reserves," which are intended to serve as individual replacements for weapons lost in combat. A similar practice is followed by most other Western countries. Taking into account that about one-half of the Russian Army will be based east of the Urals, the equipment inventories envisioned here are consistent with the CFE Treaty.

A similar future of making a virtue of necessity and meeting new-era defense needs lies in store for Russian air and naval forces. Owing to worry about air attack, Russia will retain a homeland air defense force based throughout the entire country. It also will deploy a tactical air force oriented to normal missions. Russia places less emphasis on tactical air power than does the United States: Its air regiments have about 40 aircraft as opposed to 72 in the U.S. Air Force. Even so, it likely will have about 1,400 aircraft in its inventory, divided among air intercept, ground attack, and reconnaissance roles. The Russian Navy will retain its Northern and Pacific Fleets, and some forces in the Baltic Sea and in the Black Sea. Its mission will continue to be protecting the Russian coast and nearby waters while providing assets for blue-water missions and modest projection operations.

AFFORDABILITY

Taking into account strategy requirements and budgetary realities, where is the future headed? Recognizing the uncertainty in any projection, this study offers a "best estimate" of a post-2000 Russian military that will be composed of about 45 mobilizable divisions, 3,000 tactical combat aircraft, and 300 principal naval combatants.

What the Russian Economy Will Bear

A major issue, of course, is whether the Russian economy and federal budget will permit a military establishment this large. The current debate in Moscow suggests that 5.0 percent of current GNP will be adequate for a military of 1.5 million troops. Although Grachev has demanded 6–7 percent of GNP for defense, this estimate appears to be linked to a posture of 2.1 million troops. Yet there are reasons to doubt that 5 percent will be enough even at the 1.5-million level. The reason is that today's Russian defense budget has modest acquisition plans. An adequate procurement effort would drive the defense budget higher, and the share of GNP along with it. If equipment procurement were to be accelerated to the level claimed necessary by MOD officials, the defense share would rise to about 6.25 percent of GNP. A higher tempo of construction for personnel quarters and new bases could elevate spending to 7.0 percent of GNP.

A level of 6–7 percent of GNP is well above the 2–3 percent standard being set by the West Europeans, and it is 20–40 percent more than Russia's Duma evidently is willing to tolerate. Opposition to this spending could compel the MOD to lower its plans for the future posture. Conversely, a Russian economic recovery could somewhat alter the equation. If the Russian economy rebounds to the level of 1989, then a fully funded MOD budget for a 1.5-million-troop posture might be possible at 5 percent of GNP. An economic recovery beyond this level could permit an allocation of only 4 percent of GNP to defense. Even so, it is hard to see how Grachev's plan for 2.1 million troops can be afforded, short of an economic miracle. This posture not only would consume 6–7 percent of GNP in the best of circumstances, it would require that more than 1 percent of the total population serve in the defense ministry—a large number if the demand for skilled workers in other sectors is high.

Procurement Requirements

Future procurement requirements will also have an impact on the size of the defense budget and posture. Like the United States, the Soviet Union pursued an intense modernization campaign during the 1980s, its defense industry producing a wealth of new-model ground weapons, aircraft, and ships that were bought by the MOD in large quantities. The Soviet military entered the 1990s with a gleaming new inventory of weapons, even if the national economy was bankrupt and the government tottering. This situation has allowed Russia to take a procurement holiday in the 1990s, because most of its weapons were new and years away from the end of their normal life cycles. The ability to view procurement requirements in a leisurely manner is destined to come to an end in the coming five years.

Obsolescence will compel modernization. Most immediately affected will be the Russian Air Force, whose turnover cycle begins a few years before that of the U.S. Air Force, which itself faces a mounting obsolescence problem from the year 2000 onward. Even today, several new aircraft models are progressing through the development cycle and will be ready for procurement soon: the MiG-33, the Su-35, the Type 701, and the L-42. In a similar vein, the T-90 tank, IFVs, helicopters, and other equipment for the Army will eventually have to be procured. New ships will also have to be bought, even if Russia's Navy continues to shrink. If Russia can succeed in its campaign to sell its new equipment abroad, the MOD's procurement burden will be reduced, because the marginal cost of each item will be lowered somewhat by economies of scale and amortization of R&D costs. Even so, procurement demands loom as a potential issue in Russian defense management, and as with the United States, could compel adoption of a smaller posture.

Because Russia inherited most of the Soviet Union's huge defense industry, it will possess the industrial capacity to produce the required weapons even after defense conversion is carried out. The issue is whether enough money will be available to keep the production lines running fast enough. Today, Russia is buying enough new weapons to meet only about 25 percent of inventory-turnover requirements. If inadequate funding forces this practice to continue, then Russia's military will suffer a slow but steady decline in modernization and combat effectiveness. It doubtless will attempt to compensate through mid-life upgrades and enhanced maintenance of aging equipment. But even this practice can be expensive, and, in the final analysis, it buys only a few extra years of life cycle. To stay modern and ready, Western military establishments are required to devote 25–30 percent of their budgets to research, development, and procurement. Russia is unlikely to escape this iron law of military preparedness.

If economic recovery is not attained in ways allowing for a sustained modernization effort, the Russian military establishment may suffer the fate of Turkey. It will have a large army and air force of aging, unserviced, and rusting weapons. It will have the appearance of impressive combat power, but not the reality. If the economy rebounds and adequate funds can be made available for the defense effort, a different future will await the Russian military. Even in the best of circumstances, it will face a difficult juggling act in attempting to preserve a defense posture that is large, modern, and ready. But a steady stream of adequate defense budgets would make this task far easier. The future of Russia's military power is coming to rest on whether the conversion to market capitalism can be accomplished.

All-Volunteer Force

Another issue will be whether Russia moves toward an all-volunteer force and a professional military. The advantage of conscription is that it keeps manpower slots full and permits a large posture at affordable cost because draftees can be paid low salaries. If conscription is ended or even scaled back, the Russian military will have to compete in the open market for talented volunteers. In 1994, the MOD was required to recruit over 100,000 contract soldiers. If conscription is abandoned, the number will increase at least threefold. This situation, in turn, will compel salary increases, which could elevate spending on personnel in demanding ways that lead to a smaller posture or a slower modernization rate. As in many West European countries, fear of this result may impede Russia's willingness to abandon conscription, even though the draft will remain unpopular in the country.[36]

Summary

In summary, the MOD's emerging plans for a new strategy and force posture will create burdens for the national economy and pressures for a higher level of spending than is now acceptable in the Western democracies. Yet the Russian public may be more willing to tolerate higher defense spending than are its counterparts in the West. Perhaps most important, the financial burden being proposed by the MOD today is far smaller than that proposed by the Soviet MOD during the Cold War, when the mammoth MOD and bloated defense industry consumed 15 percent of GNP. Even though Russia is far smaller than the Soviet Union in total population and resources, Russia's emerging defense posture will be only one-fourth the size of that fielded by the Soviet Union. Defense spending levels of 4–7 percent of GNP are not trivial for an economy attempting to recover

---

[36]See Irina Khristolyerbova, "Hearings: Chief of the General Staff Considers Professional Army an Unaffordable Luxury," *Current Digest of Post-Soviet Press,* May 10, 1995; Pavel Felgengauer, "Call-Up: No Professional Army Yet in Sight in Russia," *Current Digest of Post-Soviet Press,* May 31, 1995.

while converting to market capitalism. Yet the U.S. economy tolerated these levels through forty years of Cold War and showed sustained growth as well as considerable domestic prosperity during
that period. If the Russian public is willing to accept the sacrifice in
exchange for gaining a still-large and -effective defense posture,
these spending levels may prove to be tolerable.

COMBAT CAPABILITY

How effective will the future Russian posture be in carrying out military operations? Senior Russian officers understand that innovation
in doctrine, organization, and weapons is needed to upgrade the
performance of their forces. As a result, Russian forces likely will become more capable in time. Judgments about the implications will
depend upon the measurement standard employed: whether
Russian forces are evaluated in relation to U.S. and NATO forces or in
relation to less-capable forces along Russia's periphery.

Technology

Russian forces are unlikely to close the wide technology gap that exists in relation to U.S. and NATO forces. During the Cold War, U.S.
equipment was commonly rated as 10–20 percent better than
Russian models of equivalent generation. Desert Storm showed that
the current U.S. advantage is more than this marginal amount. Yet
the competitive process is dynamic and subject to a back-and-forth
flow. The U.S. advantage over Iraq in Desert Storm was owed heavily
to a few areas of technological superiority: ability to penetrate ar-
mor, to suppress air defense, and to deliver accurate counterbattery
artillery fire; navigational aids; smart munitions; and C3I systems.
Having witnessed Desert Storm, the Russian military doubtless is
trying to remedy its deficiencies in these critical areas. Because minor changes in technology can have huge operational effects, modest
advances by the Russians could partly erode the U.S. advantages
shown in Desert Storm.

Russian equipment may improve in the years ahead, but so will U.S.
equipment. Indeed, the quality gap may widen if current U.S. hopes
for dramatic new technological breakthroughs in C3I and munitions
are realized. Even so, Russian equipment is not so far behind

Western models that it is uncompetitive if handled by skilled troops. Equally important, the Russian Army may be fighting not Western-equipped forces but military establishments equipped with weapons originally made in Russia itself: weapons that are one or two generations behind current top-of-the-line Russian equipment. Fighting the United States and NATO is one thing; something else again is fighting Ukraine, or Poland, or China, or any other country on Russia's periphery.

Skills and Doctrine

Moreover, force quality is determined not only by weapons but also by the skills of the officer corps and enlisted ranks, by doctrine, and by the capacity for joint operations. If the Russian military wisely uses the equipment that will be available, and makes the most of opportunities in these other areas, it could regain the status of being a serious fighting force. The relevant issue is not whether Russian forces are qualitatively equal to U.S. units, but whether they are equal or superior to the adversaries they actually may confront in combat. In this arena, the Russian military's prospects are far from dim, because many of its opponents may be less than stellar on the battlefield.

Missions

Russia's forces also can be judged in relation to the military missions they will be called upon to carry out. They will be able to perform military missions at the low end of the spectrum, including limited crisis interventions. An issue that will affect Russia's overall strategic power on the Eurasian landmass and elsewhere is whether it will be able to mount an MRC-sized offensive equivalent to those posed by Iraq and North Korea. The Russian Army will not be able to wage a 90-division campaign of Cold War lore, but will be able to mount small operations (e.g., a limited regional contingency [LRC] of 4–5 divisions). An MRC campaign falls into the gray area between these two extremes: It implies an offensive carried out by 25–35 divisions and 400–700 combat aircraft. A best estimate is that, if the Russian Army is composed of 45 mobilizable divisions, it probably could generate 25 divisions for a single campaign. A Russian Air Force of 3,000 airplanes could also generate the 1,000 tactical combat aircraft and

300 bombers that normally would accompany 25 divisions. Hence, the capacity to conduct an MRC-style offensive will be one arrow in the quiver of Soviet military strategy.

If equipped with these forces, an MRC campaign launched by Russia could be conducted with greater strength than MRC campaigns by either Iraq or North Korea. One reason is the professionalism of the Russian officer corps and the steadiness of its troops. Whether Russia's soldiers are better than North Korea's may be a matter of debate, but they are better than Iraq's. Another reason is that the Russian Army will be better armed and equipped than either the Iraqi or North Korean armies. Iraq's equipment is one or two generations behind the most-modern Russian models, and the North Korean Army is largely an infantry force with even less-modern weapons. A third reason is the Russian Air Force. MRC land campaigns by Iraq and North Korea would be backed up by a few hundred aircraft apiece, most of them old models flown by pilots lacking top-notch skills. The Russian Air Force may not match U.S. standards, but it is far better in qualitative terms than either the Iraqi or North Korean Air Force. Moreover, it is larger. A Russian MRC campaign likely would be conducted with 2-3 times the amount of aircraft flown by Iraq or North Korea. For all these reasons, a Russian MRC campaign could be more swift, lethal, and imposing than similar operations by Iraq and North Korea.

Deploying a Russian posture of MRC dimensions, however, would not be accomplished easily. Several weeks—or even months—could be required to conduct the necessary mobilization, training, and movement of forces across the vast Russian landmass. Russia's mobile forces might be ready within a few days, but the strategic reserves would have to be committed, and some of them would be used in the MRC campaign. These units likely will require several weeks of refresher training before being combat-ready. An appropriate military infrastructure would have to be built. But, given the huge infrastructure inherited from the Cold War, this task might be accomplished, in the coming years, in the course of normal improvements. Equally important, the mounting of an MRC operation in either the west or east would require a cross-country movement of sizable forces. For example, about 10 divisions might have to be moved from the eastern military districts to the western districts to take part in an MRC campaign in East Central Europe or to backfill for other units contributing to this effort. Russia owns the rail capacity to contemplate a movement of this magnitude; in the future, it may improve its rail system specifically to enable speedier movement of forces back and forth across the country. Even with an efficient rail system, several weeks or months could be required.

The Russian military's poor readiness today means that an MRC campaign could not be undertaken in the current setting. An MRC is an operation that will become feasible only some years from now and will be mountable only if the Russian Army reestablishes its coherence. If coherence is regained, the military effectiveness of a Russian MRC campaign will depend on the *quality* of Russian forces.

The Russian military thus faces the challenge of building a first-class MRC fighting force—if this, in fact, is a goal—through qualitative means: modern doctrine, joint operations, high technology, skilled leadership, and sophisticated training. By meeting these challenges, the U.S. military showed in Desert Storm that a relatively modest force can carry out a crushing campaign even against a large opponent. It also showed that ambitious strategic goals—once thought the sole province of much larger postures—can be achieved.

Even if Russia does acquire the capability to assemble enough forces for a regional operation against serious opposition, this posture will not allow Russia to contemplate conquest of all of Europe in a sweeping campaign reminiscent of Cold War planning. But it would be capable of launching a limited but potent offensive on a single axis 200–300 kilometers wide. It could defeat less-powerful forces in the way, advance 200–300 kilometers before pausing to regroup, and occupy this territory in the aftermath. This capability would enable Russia to again menace Eurasian and European countries near its own borders. It also would give Russia options for a localized advance into China, perhaps a punitive border campaign. As with its future in Europe, however, Russia will not possess the military strength to threaten a conquest of all of China, or even major parts of it. Indeed, an MRC campaign might become the vehicle by which Russia endeavors to deter attack by a large Chinese army that may well modernize in the coming years.

Thus, Russia may rebuild the capacity to conduct a single MRC offensive in Europe, Asia, or Central Asia if it is willing to take the time and effort to assemble the large forces needed for such an operation. An equally important conclusion is that, even if Russia becomes capable of mounting one MRC offensive, it will not reacquire the capacity to launch more than one. For the years ahead, Russia will be a single-MRC power, not a country able to mount multiple large offensives as was the Soviet Union.

Lack of forces will be the main reason for this new reality. A critical constraint on even a single-MRC operation will be the need to withhold sizable forces for other duties. For example, if Russia was to mount an MRC operation in one of its three sectors, it would need to withhold some forces for internal security and others for deterrence in the remaining two sectors. These requirements easily could consume the remaining 20 divisions of a 45-division posture, as well as the additional air forces. Hence, an MRC campaign might be possible with the posture envisioned here, but it would stretch this posture thin; it therefore is not something that could be contemplated lightly. Above all, this posture will necessitate that Russia avoid two-front wars or even two-front political clashes. Thus, Russia will no longer be able to menace Europe at the same time it faces trouble with China, or vice versa. Regardless of its political preferences, Russia will have ample military incentives to remain on the good side of either NATO or China, if not both. If Russia does find itself in political conflict with both NATO and China at a time when an MRC campaign must be launched against one, it will have an incentive to rely on nuclear weapons to deter the other.

This judgment of imposing constraints applies only if Russia's posture is no larger than envisioned here. If the Russian MOD somehow succeeds in preserving a posture larger than 45 divisions and 4,000 combat aircraft, it will have greater military flexibility. A similar outcome will prevail if Russia succeeds in bringing other CIS countries into its security orbit in ways that could make their forces available to Russia. For example, Belarus and Ukraine together will field about 17 divisions and 700 combat aircraft, forces that, together with their proximity to Eastern Europe, could enable Russia to again pose a military threat that goes beyond the province of a single 25-division MRC operation undertaken in the face of troublesome constraints. Whether Russia could acquire the capacity to mount attacks on multiple strategic axes is moot. But at a minimum, it could apply larger forces to a single MRC.

THE COMPOSITE PICTURE

Russian Rejuvenation

If the rejuvenation hypothesis proves correct, three interacting developments will cause Russia to experience a slow but steady growth of its strategic power over the coming decade and beyond. Russia's government may become more stable and its society more settled, thereby permitting less preoccupation with domestic affairs and emergence of a more outward-looking vision. Russia's economy may experience sustained, if unspectacular, growth rates that will yield a slowly increasing GDP and perhaps some growth in funds for national security programs. Russia's military posture will be smaller than today's, but it will be reorganized, more ready, and more capable of carrying out a new strategy. This picture of gradual rejuvenation qualifies as a best estimate of what the future holds.

If gradual rejuvenation occurs, Russia will not spring back to life as a world-class superpower but will be better able to exert influence within its region. It can better pursue its current external agenda, perhaps gradually enlarging it. Russia will be in no position to hit the imperial trail, but it may become a country able to seek more-ambitious goals and to employ more-assertive means. Yet Russia will also remain subject to powerful constraints, one being that Russia's assets will have many demands placed upon them, stretching them thin. Another constraint is that the external environment may not be pliant to the assertion of Russia's powers. The CIS region, the zone most susceptible to growing Russian influence, likely will not be such an unstable power vacuum that it invites any easy and wholesale rebuilding of a new Russian empire. Farther out, Russia will face a host of great powers in Europe and Asia with strategic agendas of their own. Even if Russia becomes more able to assert itself, these powers will set limits on how far Russia *can* assert itself.

Russia in Eurasia

In Eurasia, the strategic power balance—brought about by Russia's dominating position over its immediate neighbors—will delimit how far Russia can pursue its statist agenda. Russia will remain far larger than its CIS neighbors in population and economic strength. It will be about three times larger than Ukraine, the only other CIS country large enough to become a medium-sized power. The other countries will all be small powers, ranging from one-seventh to one-fortieth of Russia's size. These facts ensure Russia's continuing influence throughout Eurasia.

How much Russia will remain a military colossus in Eurasia is illustrated by Table 5.3, which presents Russia's future military assets with those of its immediate neighbors, for comparison. The intent of the table is to portray the main elements of combat power for each country; Russian postures are displayed to illuminate the portion of its total posture that will be available for European operations. Judgments about stability can be made by employing the old standard of a 1.25:1 ratio in the overall index. That is, two countries are judged to be in military balance with each other if one does not enjoy

Table 5.3

Future Conventional Military Balance in Eurasia (2000–2010)

	Population (millions)	Division- Equivalents	Combat Aircraft	Combined Index[a]
Russia	150			
• Local (Peacetime) Mobile Command		6.6	400	9
• MRC Posture		25	1,300	34
• Total Posture		45	4,000	69
Baltic States	13	3	135	4
Belarus	10	4	172	5
Ukraine	52	13	500	16
Moldova	4	1	45	1.3
Georgia	6	2	106	2.6
Armenia	4	2	45	2.3
Azerbaijan	7	2	45	2.3
Kazakhstan	17	4	140	5
Kyrgyzstan	5	2	90	2.6
Turkmenistan	4	1	45	1.3
Tajikistan	6	2	90	2.6
Uzbekistan	22	3	130	3.8

[a]Combat index assigns a score of 1.0 for each ground division and 162 combat aircraft.

a numerical advantage over the other of greater than 1.25:1. If the ratio exceeds 1.25:1, then a situation of imbalance exists.[37]

What stands out from this chart is Russia's overwhelming dominance of all the Eurasian states taken individually. Indeed, readily available Russian forces of the Mobile Command, without any reinforcement, would have more than a 1.25:1 advantage over every state except Ukraine.[38] Russia would need to assemble a larger posture—20 divisions and 750 combat aircraft: well within Russia's capability—to gain dominance over Ukraine's 13 divisions and 500 combat aircraft. Indeed, Russia would enjoy an MRC posture with about a 2:1 advantage—normally a decisive amount if a war is fought—that none of these states acting on its own could hope to defend against.

Nor would their prospects be good if these states joined together in regional alliances. The Baltic states, already displayed here as a group, are hopelessly outgunned. If Belarus, Ukraine, and Moldova were to join together, they could achieve a combined combat index of 21.3 to yield a 1.6:1 ratio in Russia's favor against an MRC Russia force: too high for safety, and politically improbable because Belarus has close relationships with Russia. If the Caucasian states overcome their rivalries, they could achieve a combat index of 7.2: enough to balance local Russian mobile forces, but not nearly adequate against a Russian MRC posture. The five Central Asian states could attain a combat index of 15.3: again, not nearly enough for balancing against an MRC posture.

These data suggest how future security affairs are likely to take shape in Eurasia and the CIS region. Quite apart from Russia's nuclear dominance, no single state or group of states will possess the military power to seriously threaten Russia's borders. Ukraine could assemble enough forces for a local advantage, but Russia could mobilize enough combat power to rectify the imbalance. Conversely, Russia will enjoy an immense military advantage over all CIS countries so that little purpose would be served by their banding together in an alliance aimed at counterbalancing Russia. Ukraine is the only ex-

---

[37]Data for current forces are provided in International Institute for Strategic Studies, *The Military Balance, 1993–1994*, London: Brassey's, Inc., 1994.

[38]Arguably, the stability ratio may be as low as 1:1. A ratio of 1.25:1 implies that the defense enjoys inherent advantages that reduce its requirements.

ception, but if it is to achieve alliance security, the connection will have to come from countries to the west, not from CIS neighbors.

Although these resource advantages will place a great deal of political influence in Russia's hands, if these states build their own internal strength and desire for independence, Russia may still not possess the assets to easily overrun the region and reabsorb it into a new empire. Ukraine is well-situated to keep itself out of Russia's orbit. In the Caucasus, the small states of Georgia, Armenia, and Azerbaijan are vulnerable to Russia's power. In Central Asia, both Kazakhstan and Uzbekistan are large enough to put up serious resistance, and they provide a geographic screen for the three small states to the south. The CIS region thus is far from a zone lying open to Russia's power.

Plausibly, Russia could coerce a small number of countries or even invade them. Yet Chechnya has shown the difficulties that can be encountered even in a small country if a significant portion of the population resists. Russia cannot afford a steady stream of Chechnyas if it wants to rebuild an empire that may not want to be reestablished. Consequently, full-scale Russian takeovers are not likely to occur, unless the governments of the CIS countries collapse and widespread turmoil erupts, threatening critical Russian interests. Provided these countries maintain their internal cohesion and do not flout Russia's vital interests, their relationships with Russia likely will be marked by the give-and-take typical of normal diplomacy in a region where one big power dominates the rest but cannot afford the effort to conquer them, or even control them.

East Central Europe and Asia

Russia's ability to project power into East Central Europe will be influenced by its overall geostrategic setting and the situation in Eurasia. Even if Russia undergoes rejuvenation, it will face the prospect of a stronger China and Japan. Its requirement to maintain adequate strength in Asia will inhibit its ability to turn its attentions and resources westward, and, in turn, its freedom to act provocatively toward adversaries there. Plausibly, success at achieving CIS reintegration could give Russia greater freedom to act in East Central Europe, and place greater resources at its disposal to do so. Equally as likely, local instability will prevail within the CIS for some time.

Russia could find a considerable portion of its army bogged down in local strife and peacekeeping duties. Its CIS agenda thus could curtail Russia's freedom to pursue its agenda in East Central Europe.

Western Enlargement and Policy Choices

The constraints imposed by its dealings with Asia and Eurasia may similarly affect Russia's strategic response to Western enlargement into East Central Europe. Although the availability of power assets will be only one factor in Russia's policymaking, it likely will be an influential one, because it will set upper limits on the options that can be safely embraced. In the coming years, Russia will not be militarily impotent, but neither will it enjoy a situation of largesse. It will have to pick and choose its military involvements, and take care to avoid being inundated by unmanageable requirements. Given its defense posture and budget, it may find itself challenged merely to counterbalance China in Asia and to keep its southern flank stable at the same time. If so, it will not be in a position of strength for enforcing restoration of empire within the CIS, much less for carrying out a renewed military confrontation with NATO in East Central Europe. A great deal will depend on how the Eurasian situation evolves. In all likelihood, however, Russia will be driven by powerful military incentives to pursue a policy of normal relations with the West to free up resources for dealing with many demands close to its southern and eastern borders.

To the degree that its southern and eastern situations can be brought under control, Russia will have greater flexibility for addressing new military requirements on its western flank. At a minimum, it will be far from militarily impotent in Europe if it develops a flexible posture that can be moved back and forth across its landmass as the situation demands. Yet the strategic implication of being a regional power, as opposed to a superpower, is that Russia will be capable of stretching flexible military assets only so far. At some point, even a flexible posture will become overwhelmed because it will not be large enough to handle simultaneous requirements arising in several different regions. Throughout its history, Russia has tried to reduce this problem by maintaining a large army; the Soviet Union tried to eliminate the problem entirely by maintaining a *huge* army. Present-day budgetary and manpower constraints mandate that the new

Russia limit the military missions to be performed and, therefore, the geopolitical aims to be pursued.

All factors considered, it is difficult to see how Russia could conclude that its strategic assets will be large enough to permit a policy of New Cold War toward the West. It will lack the military posture for this policy. If large commitments must be made in Asia and Eurasia, the Russian Army will have only 15–25 divisions available for western missions—not nearly enough to pose the kind of sweeping offensive threat needed to menace all of Eastern Europe in the face of a militarily prepared NATO. Russia could aspire to assemble this threat only by regathering the CIS countries under its control and creating what amounts to a new Warsaw Pact on CIS soil. Even then, it could muster only about 50–60 divisions for western missions—far less than the 90 divisions assembled by the Warsaw Pact during the Cold War in Central Europe alone. Quite apart from these military constraints, Russia will lack the economic wherewithal for a New Cold War that could endure for years and decades, as did the first one. Renewed Cold War would cut Russia off from the Western economy while imposing immense defense burdens, thereby bringing about the bankruptcy that destroyed the Soviet Union.

As for Cold Peace, Russia may have the military latitude for this policy if Asia and Europe are stable, because the military requirements for this policy are less than those of renewed Cold War. Whether Russia could afford the negative economic and political consequences of Cold Peace is a separate and more-complex issue, but one filled with imposing constraints of its own.

The strategic implications are clear. The geopolitical imperatives flowing from its new statist foreign policy mean that Russia regards itself as having important interests in East Central Europe. It wants to keep NATO out of East Central Europe and to preserve this region as a geopolitical neutral zone. Russia may also aspire, over the long term, to rebuild its economic, political, and military influence over this region, provided its influence within the CIS can first be reestablished. But for the coming years or decades, it must deal with strategic realities, including its own limited resources for national security endeavors, its domestic turmoil, and the weighty challenges confronting it in Eurasia and Asia.

As a result, the features of a policy of normal relations will appeal to Russia, provided that Russia can negotiate with the West so that its core interests are protected even as the West, and NATO, enlarges eastward. This strategic calculus does not mean that Russia will be indifferent to the security arrangements that take shape in East Central Europe; however, it does help explain why Russia, despite complaining angrily about NATO enlargement, is also voicing willingness to participate in a diplomatic dialogue for finding a mutually acceptable solution.

Whether a solution can be found will depend on the manner in which strategic affairs and security policies unfold in East Central Europe. Where is this region headed, and what do the trends imply for the West's ability to advance its interests while reaching an accommodation with Russia? This question is addressed in the next chapter.

Chapter Six

RUSSIA AND THE WEST IN THE NEW GEOPOLITICS OF EAST CENTRAL EUROPE

To assess the implications of a slowly rejuvenating Russia seeking to put an imprint not only on its Eurasia neighborhood but on East Central Europe as well, we must begin by viewing Russia not in isolation but as one important actor in a larger setting of many states. Russia will be trying to promote its own interests; at the same time, the other countries will be working hard to safeguard their own destinies.

Where is East Central Europe headed and what does it mean for the West? No single-point forecast can be offered, because the region could evolve in a variety of ways. A stable, peaceful outcome is possible if all goes well. Nonetheless, this chapter's thesis is that the future provides cause for concern, because the existing system is neither stable nor static, and some of the trends taking shape are pointed in unhealthy directions. Several different unstable security systems could emerge if the West does not enlarge into the region. Yet if the West *does* enlarge and the associated changes are mishandled, the outcome could be a different kind of instability: a confrontation with Russia. The proper conclusion is that the West has ample incentives to enlarge in order to help make the region stable, but it needs to act wisely to ensure that the effort produces a successful outcome, not the reverse.

To stave off such a confrontation, the West will need a clear understanding of the complex setting that awaits it. Accordingly, we begin this chapter with a discussion of the region's structural characteristics. We then appraise how a stable outcome could evolve. Next, we discuss how alternative, negative scenarios could emerge if the West does not enlarge. We conclude with a discussion of how an unstable future could evolve if the West does enlarge but the effort backfires.

STRUCTURAL CHARACTERISTICS

As Russia acts to carry out its statist agenda with more vigor than it is now, greater pressure and stress will be brought to bear on the East Central European security system. The other countries of this region are already conscious of the opportunities and problems posed by the new era. They can be expected to respond to Russia, and to other challenges, by stepping up their own activities in ways that safeguard their interests. The political temperature across this region will rise as the future unfolds. Relations with Russia will matter, but so will relations that each of these countries has with the other or others. Absent Western enlargement, a pattern of geopolitical interactions will ensue and will be heavily affected by this region's structural characteristics: the building blocks that determine its nature. We analyze four such building blocks, or characteristics, here: the region's anarchical foundations, its diverse politics and economics, its imbalance of military power, and its propensity for change.

Anarchical Foundations

A dominant characteristic is this region's sheer anarchy stemming from the way the Cold War ended. During the Cold War, the region was dominated by the collectivism imposed by the Soviet Union, the Warsaw Pact, and communist ideology. The collapse of communism resulted not in a new collectivism but in a large group of nations left free to pursue their national identities—and determined to do so. Most sought to distance themselves from Russia, with whom they no longer shared a common ideology or strategic interests. Most viewed themselves as European countries in quest of rejoining Europe after being left on the outside for over forty years. Most aspired to embrace Western political and economic values. All recognized the importance of having normal relations with their neighbors, but none wanted any repetition of the recent past, which had submerged their self-respect. As they pursued their separate identities by tearing apart any lingering vestiges of the Warsaw Pact and substituting nothing similar in its place, regional anarchy in security policies was the outcome.

As used here, the term *anarchy* does not imply mob rule or runaway chaos. *Anarchy* means a lack of central government or ordering principles to govern fundamental political relations. It especially means a lack of guaranteed security arrangements and assurances about the future. East Central Europe is bordered by two major powers long active in the region: Germany on the west and Russia in the east. Located in between are eight smaller powers that lack membership in a powerful alliance. Their primary security guarantees come from bilateral treaties with each other. Apart from the countries that belong to the CIS, their only multilateral institution is OSCE: a Europe-wide pact that provides a forum for political consultation and other cooperative activities, but no firm guarantees of military help in a crisis.

Anarchy does not itself always beget instability. If the overall political setting is harmonious, i.e., there are no serious conflicts, then stability can be the outcome. But anarchy can magnify already-existing conflicts. Moreover, anarchy can create a climate of uncertainty about the future that leads countries to think in fearful terms and to contemplate actions aimed at buying security, even at the cost of producing tense relations with neighbors. Anarchy thus can act as an independent agent, causing political conflict in the form of rivalries born of the quest for long-term security. Ceteris paribus, anarchy is a natural breeding ground for instability—an enduring lesson from history, and one that could apply to East Central Europe. The situation there is one of almost pure anarchy: Not only is a collective-defense structure lacking, but there are no powerful sub-alliances. Every country is left on its own, and many have neighbors that plausibly could become enemies.

Diverse Politics and Economics

Another key structural characteristic is this region's diverse politics and economics. Although beset with potential problems and fault lines, several stabilizing factors are present. The countries of East Central Europe enjoy acknowledged sovereignty over their terrain. All of them are trying to establish their identities in the new era, and, in varying ways, they are pursuing market democracy. None is pursuing an expansionist agenda abroad. All are downsizing their military forces. Many have signed accords of friendship and cooperation with each other. Virtually all want close relations with the West and to avoid animosity with Russia. Yet the region is afflicted with destabilizing factors. Most important, the domestic situation in every country is tenuous: Market democracy and economic recovery are far from ensured. Reformist parties are pitted against anti-reform parties in a struggle for power. And with social anxiety mounting because of economic strife, ex-communists have been gaining office by wearing the mantle of social democrats who favor slow reforms and continuing welfare-state policies. Some countries seem vulnerable to demagoguery, authoritarianism, and nationalism. Several countries are wary about their immediate neighbors. Disputes have arisen over historical issues such as fuzzy borders and ethnic groups living abroad. Virtually every country has a deep fear of Russia, yet remembers the times Germany was a menace. The reaction is diplomacy aimed at maintaining calm relations with Russia while drawing closer to the West. The common fear is that this diplomacy may fail, leaving small and vulnerable powers to a troubled fate. The result is chronic worry about domestic affairs, security, and foreign policy. In essence, this region, while far less a powder keg than the Balkans, contains many explosive ingredients.[1]

Germany and Russia's Interaction Within the Region. The future will be affected by how two powerful outside states, Germany and Russia, interact within the region.[2] In many ways, Germany is becoming Europe's most important country. With a strong democratic government, a stable society of 81 million people, and a GDP of $1.8 trillion, its overall size and power dwarf those of its eastern neighbors. Germany today is a member of the EU and NATO, but it has many traditional interests to the east. As it emerges from its inward-looking preoccupation with unification, it is beginning to craft a policy for the East primarily of growing political and economic ties: German investments are pouring heavily into the Czech Republic and Hungary. An outward-looking security agenda is

---

[1]Chronological material for this chapter is compiled from IISS's *Strategic Survey*, 1992–1994, and from *RFE/RL Daily Digest* during these years; multiple authors.

[2]For a background analysis of U.S.–German relations, see Wolfram F. Haneider, *Germany, America, Europe: Forty Years of German Foreign Policy*, New Haven, Conn.: Yale University Press, 1989. An appraisal of German-Russian relations in Europe's geopolitical history is provided in Henry S. Kissinger, *Diplomacy*, New York: Simon and Schuster, 1994.

also starting to unfold. The Kohl government has been overcoming domestic opposition to move Germany closer to involvement in NATO peacekeeping, and it is refashioning a small pool of forces (2 divisions) for external security missions. From the outset, Germany has been an active promoter of EU enlargement. In mid-1995, Chancellor Kohl abandoned his earlier low profile by advocating NATO enlargement by the year 2000. Part of Germany's agenda for NATO enlargement is to promote democracy, but another motive is to secure its potentially vulnerable eastern flank. In all likelihood, Germany's involvements in East Central Europe will be growing a great deal in the coming years.[3]

As its eastward involvements grow, Germany will encounter a Russia struggling to maintain influence in a region trying to slip out of Moscow's grasp. Since the mid-1700s, these two major powers have jockeyed for influence in East Central Europe. At times their relationship has been peaceful, owing to their ability to divide the region into spheres of influence. At other times, equilibrium broke down and war erupted. Prussia and Russia fought during the eighteenth century, were allies most of the nineteenth century, and engaged in titanic struggles during World Wars I and II. The centerpiece of the Cold War was the Soviet Union's attempt to keep Germany divided and occupied. When the Cold War ended, Russia and Germany collaborated as Germany unified and Soviet troops withdrew. Germany and Russia have since enjoyed stable relations. The future will depend on whether these two great powers continue to perceive their agendas as being harmonious. Antagonism by no means is inevitable, but if Russia rejuvenates and tries to assert its influence westward, the result could be strained relations.

If trouble lies ahead, it will amount to a reversal of what exists today. Germany is supporting Russia's efforts to reform by providing it with economic aid and technical advice. It is Russia's largest trading partner and a potential source of major investments in Russia. Germany is showing sensitivity to Russia's diplomatic concerns in Europe by backing the trade agreement signed between the EU and Russia, and it has played an influential role in granting Russia a voice

---

[3]Rick Atkinson, "Germans Invest in East Europe, but Curb Image of Empire," *Washington Post*, April 17, 1994.

in G-7 deliberations. Aware of its need for Germany's help, Russia is showing no signs of regarding Germany as a strategic menace; nor is Russia making threatening gestures to Germany. Nonetheless, the long-term worry for their relations is that the two countries may be shaping incompatible strategic agendas for major parts of East Central Europe. Germany wants the heart of this region brought into the Western community. Russia wants this region to remain a neutral zone, unless it too can get equal membership in Western institutions. Germany does not want Russia brought into these institutions anytime soon. These separate agendas do not add up to strategic harmony in the long run.

A complicating factor is that Germany and Russia rely on different instruments of power. Germany is a great economic power but only a medium-sized military power. Russia has large military forces but lacks economic strength. This situation may allow for Germany's economic power to expand eastward, whereas Russia will lack the economic strength to influence the trade and commerce of East Central Europe. Apart from political protests, Russia's only access to strategic influence may be military power and the coercive threats that come from it. Concern about Russia's military power, in turn, plausibly could give Germany incentives to enlarge its own arsenal and develop a better capacity to project forces eastward. Without implying that militarization lies ahead for Germany, we need to emphasize that this power relationship offers no natural equilibrium and may create incentives for an escalating rivalry. Much will depend on the overall political setting, but if these countries fall apart in their diplomatic agendas, the stage could be set for trouble between them.[4]

Ukraine and Poland. The two most important countries lying between Russia and Germany are Ukraine and Poland. We addressed Ukraine's complex relations with Russia in Chapter Three. Suffice it to say that the Ukrainian government feels acute anxiety about its status and security. To little effect, it has argued in favor of cooperation among the East Central European powers, but its western neighbors are themselves looking west, not toward Kiev. Ukraine has

---

[4]For an appraisal of Germany's current defense strategy and force posture, see Federal Ministry of Defense, *White Paper, 1994*, Bonn, Germany, 1994.

voiced appeals for a closer relationship with NATO; at the moment, however, PFP is the primary vehicle open to it. The current geopolitical structure leaves Ukraine as a neutral country with no security allies—a situation that, in the eyes of President Leonid Kuchma, cannot be tolerated forever.

Poland also suffers from chronic anxiety about its neutral status. A country of 40 million people with a Western culture, it has a GDP of only $90 billion. The combination of poorness and notoriously fragmented politics leaves it more vulnerable than is suggested by its size. As with other East Central European countries, it has been pursuing market democracy. Its adoption of shock therapy is starting to have a beneficial effect on its economy: Annual growth rates averaging 4 percent were achieved in 1993–1995, and annual inflation rates slowed from 40 percent in 1993 to 6 percent by mid-1995. Yet the accompanying social stress has led to a shift in its politics. As of early 1993, Polish politics encompassed fully 29 different parties, and the number was destined to remain high even after passage of a new law restricting seats in parliament only to parties capturing more that 5 percent of the vote. Parliamentary elections in 1993 resulted in the fall of its reformist government of six parties led by Hanna Suchocka. In its place came a government led by the ex-communist Democratic Left Party and the Peasant Party. Waldemar Pawlak of the Peasant Party became prime minister, but in early 1995 he was replaced by ex-communist Jozef Olesky. The consequence has been a slowing, but not abandoning, of privatization and decentralization of government powers. As of mid-1995, Lech Walesa was still president, but his popularity was fading. He ultimately lost the fall election to an ex-communist. The larger question of Poland's reform efforts was left embroiled in the country's never-ending tussles among its multiple political parties.

Notwithstanding its domestic turbulence, Poland's foreign policy has reflected its geopolitical setting. Poland has stable relations with its southern neighbors: the Czech Republic and Slovakia. Its relations with Ukraine have been cordial but well short of any close security collaboration. Poland's strategic affairs are largely dominated by its vulnerable location between Germany and Russia. Poland's goal has been to engage Germany within the framework of Western institutions. Poland's main nightmare has been that Russia will recover and again threaten it. In 1992, Poland and Russia signed a Treaty of

Friendship and Good Neighborliness. Since then, Polish foreign policy has endeavored to maintain stable relations with Russia, and some cooperative economic endeavors between the two have been launched. The withdrawal of Russian troops from Poland has removed a major thorn in Poland's side, but the continuing presence of large Russian forces in nearby Kaliningrad remains a concern in Warsaw. Likewise, Russia's close relations with Belarus create the prospect that Belarus someday could be used as a highway for Russian troops moving east to menace Poland. As a result, Poland's overwhelming desire has been to join NATO and the EU, thereby gaining protection from Russia and an institutionalized relationship with Germany.

Since 1992, a quadrangular interaction has been taking place among Germany, Poland, Ukraine, and Russia that is shaping the new geopolitics of northern East Central Europe. Acting as a leading member of the Western community, Germany has been pursuing a strong outreach program to Poland. Aided by Germany, Poland is steadily drawing closer to the Western community and away from Russia. Meanwhile, Germany and other Western countries have been establishing closer relations with Ukraine, but stopping well short of inviting it into their charmed circle. These two trends together are stressing Russia's interests, because they threaten permanent loss of Russia's traditional influence over Poland and could even see Ukraine establish itself outside of Russia's orbit. The effect is to draw Russia into a more assertive policy aimed at protecting its geopolitical prerogatives.

The process of Germany and Poland drawing together began in 1991, when the two countries negotiated a treaty confirming the Oder-Neisse line as Poland's western border. Germany thereby renounced any claim on old lands (e.g., Silesia). In early 1992, Walesa visited Germany in search of reconciliation and economic help; in response, the German foreign and defense ministers journeyed to Poland. Germany forgave half the Polish government's $5.5 billion debt. While insistent that Poland adopt market democracy, German officials held out the lure of their support for Poland's eventual admission into the EU. In the spring, Germany and France joined together in establishing a regular high-level dialogue with Poland. In January 1993, Poland and Germany signed a bilateral military agreement calling for cooperation in security policy, arms control, and training.

Although this was one of several similar pacts signed by Poland with Russia, Ukraine, and eight other European states, it sent powerful strategic signals because it marked the onset of Germany's involvement in Eastern security affairs.

Early 1993 saw Poland and Germany quibbling over a treaty regulating joint policies for handling asylum seekers. By June, Poland was participating in its first NATO military exercise: "Baltops 1993," a naval maneuver in the Baltic Sea. In early 1994, Poland and Germany laid out plans for a joint military exercise as part of 77 military activities for that year. In the spring, Kohl told Polish Foreign Minister Waldemar Pawlak that Germany would support Poland's quest for membership in the EU, the WEU, and NATO. In July, the "Weimar Triangle" (Germany, Poland, and France) signed an agreement for joint military training and creation of a joint commission on arms technology, which set the stage for Poland to be the first country to draw up a work program for NATO's PFP program in July. That summer, Germany took over the EU presidency for six months and used its tenure to help promote Poland's future membership. In August, Russia's Yeltsin declined an invitation to attend the fiftieth anniversary of the Warsaw Uprising, but German President Roman Herzog attended and asked Poland's forgiveness for Germany's conduct in World War II. German-Polish relations continued to improve in the following months, thus setting the stage for Kohl's visit to Poland in 1995, when he announced support for Poland entering NATO and the EU as early as 2000.

The process by which Germany and Poland have drawn closer to Ukraine has proceeded at a far slower pace. Ukrainian President Kravchuk visited Germany in early 1992, and although Germany provided assurances of its support for Ukrainian sovereignty, it also stressed the importance of Ukraine becoming a non–nuclear power. A year later, Germany promised financial support for Ukraine's nuclear dismantlement program after Ukraine ratified START I, and Ukraine returned German cultural artifacts taken in World War II and offered to help settle German citizens deported to the Soviet Union after the war. The two countries signed a military cooperation agreement providing for joint visits and consultations. By late 1993, Kravchuk was calling on German support for a new Central European security zone. Germany's reaction was lukewarm for many reasons. During 1994, Germany supported improved EU economic ties with Ukraine and an active Ukrainian role in NACC and PFP. But it ruled out Ukrainian admission to NATO and the EU. Since then, Germany's stance has paralleled that of the United States. Improved relations with Ukraine came in the aftermath of Kuchma's election.

Poland was the first country to recognize Ukraine's independence. In 1992, diplomatic meetings yielded agreement that neither country had territorial claims against the other. Shortly afterward, a quadrilateral border agreement was signed among Poland, Ukraine, Czechoslovakia, and Hungary aimed at increasing trade and tourism. In June, Poland and Ukraine signed an agreement on neighborly relations, friendship, and cooperation. In early June came a joint military cooperation agreement, one that proclaimed the two countries as strategic partners but that denied any military alliance between them. The two countries signed a set of economic and cultural agreements. In 1993, Ukraine's Kravchuk pushed the idea of stronger security cooperation with Poland and the other Visegrad states, but Walesa voiced no special enthusiasm. In the aftermath, economic and cultural ties between the two countries continued to grow, but Poland's horizons were steadily shifting westward toward NATO and the EU. The result is that, as of mid-1995, the two countries are carrying out normal relations but are not showing signs of forming any permanent strategic bond.

Visegrad Four. A similar pattern of closer political and economic relations, but no deep security ties, has marked relations among the Visegrad Four. This group came into existence in early 1991 at a summit meeting in Visegrad, Hungary. Originally composed of three nations, it grew to four when Czechoslovakia broke apart. Its main charter is to harmonize common policies toward other European institutions, to consult on security questions, to promote economic cooperation and trade, and to promote collaboration in such specific areas as ecology, transportation, and information. During 1992–1994, a series of friendship and cooperation agreements were signed among the members. Policies were launched to promote tariff reductions, investments, and cultural exchanges. Military exchange and cooperation programs were started. Talks were also held on establishing a security bloc among them. But the idea gained little momentum. By mid-1994, the attention of Poland and the Czech Republic had shifted westward, toward drawing closer to the EU and

NATO, whereas Hungary and Slovakia were inward-looking and pre-occupied with ethnic problems. By 1995, all four countries were signing economic accords with the EU and joining NATO's PFP. This development diverted attention further away from the concept of a tightly knit Visegrad Four structure as a strategic framework for orchestrating the region's security affairs. At the moment, the Visegrad Four show no signs of becoming an integrated military alliance or even a loose coalition of defense partners.[5]

Within the Visegrad Four, Poland's history and identity are distinctly different from those of the other three countries. Poland has always been a country of northern Europe, caught between Russia and Germany. The other three Visegrad states are countries of central-southern Europe. Indeed, they were originally parts of the old Austro-Hungarian Empire, which worked with Germany and Russia to keep Poland suppressed during the eighteenth and nineteenth centuries. As members of this empire, they were dominated by then-strong Austria and did not enjoy strong communal bonds with each other. Indeed, the lack of strong bonds played a critical role in bringing about this empire's unraveling from within. The independent countries of Czechoslovakia and Hungary emerged from the Versailles Settlement after World War I. The guiding idea was to create nations with distinct cultural identities, thus fostering stability on the basis of national self-determination. Czechoslovakia and Hungary emerged from Versailles seeking not close relations with each other but separate identities born of frustration at living too close together under Austrian hegemony. The flaws in Czechoslovakia were demonstrated when it fell apart shortly after the Cold War ended, thereby yielding the Czech Republic and Slovakia. If the original Czechoslovakian model failed because it tried to create one nation out of two, the Hungarian model was flawed at the outset because it tried to reduce a larger cultural zone into a smaller nation. The small Hungary that emerged from Versailles left large ethnic Hungarian populations living outside the borders of the new nation. Hungary thus has been a frustrated country, and this frustration can become a source of irredentist nationalism.

---

[5]For analysis, see F. Stephen Larrabee, *East European Security After the Cold War*, Santa Monica, Calif.: RAND, MR-254-USDP, 1993; IISS, "Security Concerns in Central Europe," *Strategic Survey, 1993–1994*, London: Brassey's Inc., 1994.

Czech Republic. Of the three southern countries, the Czech Republic is the most secure politically, economically, and strategically. Although small (10 million people), it is a proponent of market democracy and is the wealthiest country in East Central Europe on a per capita basis. Under the leadership of President Vaclav Havel, it is strongly pro-West; indeed, Havel has been a persistent critic of the West's failure to enlarge faster. Although beset by internal debate over the pace of reforms and internal political conflicts, the Czech Republic is experiencing steady economic growth and is benefiting from heavy Western investments. It has stable relations with its neighbors and is less directly threatened by Russia than are other countries. Although nervous that Poland is the apple of the West's eye, it stands to gain entrance to NATO soon.

Slovakia. Paradoxically, the Czech Republic has the least-strategic need for alliance assurances. Smaller Slovakia (5 million people) is beset by more serious internal problems and is more exposed to troubled relations with its neighbors. Slovakia gained independence in early 1993 under the leadership of Vladimir Meciar, its nationalist prime minister. Meciar's tenure was marked by moderate reform policies, but the economy sputtered as GDP fell by 5 percent, inflation rose by 20 percent, and unemployment soared to 15 percent. Meciar fell from power in spring 1994 and was replaced by Jozef Moravcik, who pursued faster privatization and economic reform. Within a few months, government spending was under control, inflation and unemployment had slowed, and GDP was rising by 5 percent annually. In the fall, national elections resulted in Meciar being returned to office, presiding over a parliament deeply divided on internal reform. As of mid-1995, Meciar was taking a pro-West stance by advocating entrance into the EU and maybe NATO, but his government was split between two factions: one supporting Meciar and another advocating closer relations with Russia. The result was a foreign policy seemingly suspended between the two options.

Hungary. Hungary began the 1990s with a healthy economy by regional standards, a long tradition of economic reform, a strong middle class, and a democratically elected government dominated by the centrist Democratic Forum and the liberal Alliance of Free Democrats. This bright picture soon darkened. Despite Hungary's pursuit of privatization and foreign investments, its economy nosedived when it suffered a recession and loss of foreign trade. By 1993,

Hungary's GDP was 20 percent below the 1989 level, and unemployment had risen from 4 to 12 percent. Internal frictions caused the Forum and the Free Democrats to lose their cohesion. Elections in 1993 resulted in a stunning victory for the Socialist Party, which won an absolute majority in parliament: 209 of 386 seats. Ex-communist Gyula Horn became prime minister and entered office promising that economic reform would continue, but in discriminating ways.

A country of 10 million people, Hungary is suspended between Poland and the Czech Republic in per capita income, and has labored under a bloated welfare state. In spring 1995, the government embarked on a radical economic-reform agenda aimed at cutting spending, reducing welfare, and promoting exports. This controversial departure may improve Hungary's economic standing, but would bring social anxiety.

Hungary's most immediate foreign-policy problem derives from its great loss of territory after World War I, causing nearly 3 million ethnic Hungarians to live in adjoining countries: 1.8 million are in Romania. The result is chronic tension with Romania over Transylvania, the border region where most Hungarians live. In more distant terms, Hungary fears Russia in the ways shared by most East European countries.

Romania. Romania is a country of 23 million people with a backward economy, roughly one-half as prosperous as Hungary's on a per capita basis. Slow to reform, its politics have been dominated by a nationalist coalition led by the moderate Social Democrat party, but also composed of the anti-Hungarian National Unity Party. The result has been a stalling of talks with Hungary ostensibly aimed at recognizing borders, renouncing territorial claims, and guaranteeing the rights of ethnic Hungarians in Romania. Although Romania has been trying to draw closer to the West, its slow internal reforms and troubles with Hungary have had a restraining affect. Romania is strategically significant because it is larger in size than its western neighbors and is situated as a border state between East Central Europe and the Balkans. Romania's relations with Russia are strained because Moldovan separatists want to join with Romania. Romania may be inclined to join the West but is not yet taking the steps to qualify for NATO membership, and seems destined to be at the margins of enlargement for some time.

The geopolitics of East Central Europe thus is quite complex and is acquiring growing intensity in response to domestic developments and the interstate diplomacy now appearing. Seemingly none of the outside and inside powers have agendas in mind more malevolent than traditional statism, but, conversely, all are worried about the future and none is satisfied with the status quo. All want to craft a different regional system. The rub is that there is no consensus on how the future regional system should take shape. Indeed, the visions of some countries appear to be in conflict with those of others. Among those who share common goals, there is disagreement on the exact steps to be taken to attain those goals.

Having agreed that they cannot collaborate to shape a strong and stable regional architecture of their own, the East Central European states are individually embarking upon efforts to join the Western community, where they presumably are to receive help from other Western powers in creating satisfactory relations with Germany. The chief propensity for conflict lies in the fact that Russia is opposed to their bonding with the West in ways that would leave it on the outside looking in. Russia aside, the countries of this region view each other in individualist and often-ambivalent terms. As they move to join the West, maintain stable relations with Russia, *and* deal with their own affairs, each is pursuing policies of its own, each with a somewhat different mix of goals and priorities for itself and for each other.

Imbalance of Military Power

The future security affairs of this region will be largely determined by politics and economics, but military factors will play a role as well. Consequently, this region's third structural characteristic is its asymmetric distribution of military power—representing the great disparities among the nations in their overall size, population, and economic strength—coupled with its high armament levels. The two bordering countries, Russia and Germany, are by far the largest and strongest overall. Next to them come Poland and Ukraine, two medium-sized countries that are considerably smaller than their two large neighbors. The remaining countries have less than one-half the strength of Poland and Ukraine, as Table 6.1 shows for the distribution of conventional military assets in estimated force levels in the next decade, after the current downsizing is complete.

As the table shows, a key stabilizing factor is that Germany holds no numerical military advantage over Poland and therefore poses no threat to it. Although Germany's forces are more modern and better armed, the two countries are in rough balance. This picture of stability becomes clearer when the details of Germany's posture are examined. Of Germany's 8 divisions, only 2 or 3 are to be active forces; the rest are reserves that could be mobilized only over a period of weeks. Although 2 active divisions are being prepared for projection missions (e.g., NATO peacekeeping), the rest of the German Army will retain the home-based logistics system designed during the Cold War, which allows German forces to protect their homeland but prevents them from operating in strength beyond those borders. In addition, German forces are assigned to NATO's integrated command and are heavily committed to NATO's multinational corps, which inhibits their ability to act on a national basis. In essence, Germany

Table 6.1

Conventional Military Balance in East Central Europe
(2000–2010)

Country	Population (millions)	Division-Equivalents[a]	Combat Aircraft	Combined Index[b]
Russia	150			
• Local Mobile Command		7	400	9
• MRC Posture		25	1,300	33
• Total Posture		45	4,000	70
Belarus	10	4	172	5
Ukraine	52	13	500	16
Moldova	4	1	45	1
Poland	39	9	350	11
Czech Republic	10	4	172	5
Slovakia	5	1	90	2
Hungary	10	4	90	5
Romania	23	7	220	8
Germany	81	8	450	11

[a]Mobilizable divisions, counting active and reserve units.

[b]The "combined index" is an amalgamation of ground and air forces, assuming that three air wings equal one division in total strength.

is a country without a major expeditionary army, a fact that dissolves any security shadow that it might cast on Eastern Europe.

The CFE Treaty reduced the old Warsaw Pact force levels by roughly one-half, but it fell far short of disarmament and did not fashion equally armed countries. The level of military power in the region is still quite high. Russia aside, the eight countries total 43 divisions and 1,639 combat aircraft. The addition of local Russian forces brings the total to 50 divisions and 2,039 aircraft. If a full Russian MRC posture is counted, the total rises to 68 divisions and 2,939 aircraft—nearly equal to NATO's total force posture in Europe.

NATO's forces are more ready, better trained, and have better weapons. Even so, the forces of East Central Europe have the capacity to mobilize over a period of time. Their weapons and support structures are capable of inflicting immense violence, as has been demonstrated in Bosnia and Chechnya. Of the region's countries, only Moldova and Slovakia lack sufficient forces to contemplate offensive operations. For example, Ukraine will have enough divisions to equal the U.S. ground forces that were deployed in each of three major regional wars: Korea, Vietnam, and the Persian Gulf. Poland's army also will be large—enough for large-scale battlefield maneuvers—as will Romania's army. Belarus, the Czech Republic, and Hungary will have only 4 divisions apiece—about 100,000 combat and support troops—but this number equals the ground forces that Britain can field. As a result, they too will be capable of at least limited offensive operations. These armies may lack the fighting prowess of U.S. and NATO forces, but against lesser opponents—including each other—they have significant capability. Nor should the air forces of these countries be discounted, given that the Persian Gulf War showed the great destruction that modern air power can inflict on industrial targets and economic infrastructure.

These data underscore the strategic significance of the multiple military imbalances in East Central Europe. Russia's local forces likely will be sized for defensive missions and local contingencies. However, with reinforcements, they could rise to dominant levels over those of every country in the region. As Chapter Five explains, Russia's almost 2:1 edge would allow it to overpower Ukraine, its closest competitor, and its military power easily overmatches that of any other nation. Indeed, the four Visegrad states together would not achieve an adequate defensive force ratio. The military-imbalance problem, moreover, does not end with Russia. Ukraine will have a significant advantage over Poland and every other country on its western border. Poland, in turn, dominates the Czech Republic and Slovakia. Hungary dominates Slovakia and is dominated by Romania.

No defense ministry in this region can peer into the future and guarantee national defense on the basis of the strength of homeland forces. Because East Central Europe is a small region with many countries close together and surrounding each other, all these ministries can imagine plausible circumstances of neighbors ganging up and attacking their country. Fear of Russian military power is an especially potent force in their internal calculations: If Russia attacks in strength and they have no strong allies, their cause is hopeless. As a result, Russian military power casts an ever-present shadow over East Central European security planning, even if Russia's current diplomacy is seen as unthreatening.

The upshot is that although Russia is secure, every other country will find itself dominated by one nearby country, and many of them, by more than one country. Ukraine has mainly Russia to fear, but possibly could be threatened by a Visegrad coalition. Poland has reasons to be wary of both Russian and Ukrainian military power. Exposed Slovakia and Hungary face potential military dangers from fully three directions. Hungary's nightmare is a military coalition of Romania, Serbia, and Slovakia arrayed against it. To some degree, these quantitative imbalances can be offset by qualitative edges. Yet, these countries have inherited similar force structures, weapons, and doctrines from their Warsaw Pact membership in the Cold War. Moreover, the biggest countries are likely to possess the best weapons and the most-ready forces because their budgetary and industrial resources are larger.

Imbalances in military power, of course, do not spell war, or even political conflict. Yet in a setting of already-existing conflict, they can exacerbate tensions and even create incentives for aggression. Equally important, they can create an atmosphere of worry in peacetime because vulnerable countries are uncertain about the *distant* political future. This atmosphere, in turn, can breed political tension in itself, thereby rendering the entire region prone to instability and competitive conduct. This problem of military imbalance goes far beyond Russia, for the countries of East Central Europe have something to fear from each other.

Even so, the biggest problem is Russia—and by a wide margin. Table 6.1 illuminates numerically why many East Central European countries are worried about Russia as a potential threat to them if the political climate sours. It also illuminates why so many want to join NATO: Without NATO membership, they have no confident way to defend themselves from Russia—or from each other.

Propensity for Change

The combination of anarchy, a diverse political-economic setting that is leading many countries to seek changes in the strategic status quo, and a prevailing military imbalance of power add up to this region's fourth structural characteristic: its capacity for great change. The current situation, a newly minted outcome of the Cold War, appears to be transitional. The domestic politics of the region are in the midst of a revolutionary upheaval moving toward an uncertain destination. The anarchical interstate setting is an historical anomaly. Every country in the region has a wide range of choices for defining its domestic affairs and foreign policy. No major impediments bar the way to an equally wide range of alternative security orders.

PROSPECTS FOR STABILITY

In the absence of Western enlargement, what do these structural characteristics mean for the pattern of interactions that may ensue in a region where Russia will be asserting itself and where dynamic changes, stresses, and frictions are rife? Even a reformed Russia is likely to be viewed with misgivings, as an alien force, owing to its size, history, and statist agenda. However, there are conditions in which the outcome could be stability, or at least no greater instability than already exists. First, Russia's own stance will be an important contributing factor to stability. If its aims are modest and deemed legitimate, and if its instruments are persuasive, its activities will be unlikely to have a polarizing effect. Second, the potential for a stable outcome will be enhanced if the East European region itself becomes healthy and stable. If these countries all emerge with well-entrenched democratic governments, satisfied societies, prosperous economies, and tranquil relations with each other, then Russia's actions are more likely to be absorbed without deleterious consequences.

Prospects for stability will be enhanced if the interactions ahead produce three key geopolitical outcomes: Russia and Germany agree on their respective roles; Poland and Ukraine emerge as secure countries; and the countries south of Poland and Ukraine become secure from Russia and from each other.

First, if Russia and Germany can reach agreement on their respective roles in East Central Europe, they will be less likely to come to loggerheads as they encounter each other. History suggests that Germany and Russia have gotten along best when they have established spheres of strategic influence that were carefully respected by both countries. Poland's current eastern border has typically been the point where predominant German influence to the west gave way to predominant Russian influence to the east. To the extent that the past is prologue, this practice may establish a model for suggesting how harmonious relations between them can be achieved in the future.

Second, a stable outcome will be more likely if Poland and Ukraine can emerge as secure countries with their sovereign independence intact. If these, East Central Europe's two biggest countries, straddling the geopolitical corridor separating Russia and Germany, are secure, no outside power will be able to shape East Central Europe's geopolitics in ways that are threatening to the stability of Europe as a whole. Moreover, they themselves will be more likely to refrain from any conduct that could unsettle the region. A stable outcome likely will result in Poland being part of the West but friendly with Russia, a westward-leaning Ukraine having constructive relations with Russia, and both countries serving as bridges between Europe and Eurasia.

Third, stability will be more likely if the countries to the south of Poland and Ukraine are rendered secure, not only from Russia but from each other as well. Although the Czech Republic and Slovakia are important, the former will be secure if the entire region is stable, and the latter is a geopolitical sidekick as long as Poland, Ukraine, and Hungary are stable. The relationship between Hungary and

Romania is important, for it is the bridgepoint between East Central Europe and the Balkans. Depending on how well these two countries can settle their disputes over Transylvania and the Hungarian diaspora in Romania, East Central Europe will be rendered more stable, even if the Balkans experience continuing turmoil.

If these are the developments that can lead to a stable outcome, what are the odds that they will occur? Perhaps the best answer is that they are feasible for the future. Yet they are unlikely to occur on their own if the negative forces at work today are left unchecked. East Central Europe is undercut with fault lines, and its integrative dynamics are too fragile to justify any conclusion that a democratic and peaceful future is guaranteed by immutable political laws of the post–Cold War world. A positive outcome can be achieved if a concerted effort is made to bring it about. In the absence of such an effort, quite different developments could take place. Russia might define its agenda in ambitious and coercive terms. It might encounter East Central European countries still afflicted with weak democratic governments, unsettled societies, unprosperous economies, and tense relations with each other. The interaction between Germany and Russia might sour. The integrity of Poland and Ukraine might become an uncertain issue. In the south, Hungary and Romania might be in confrontation, thereby spreading Balkan turmoil northward. Under these conditions, Russia's efforts to promote its statist interests in East Central Europe could touch off a pattern of heightened geopolitical conduct that has serious destabilizing consequences.

DESTABILIZING SCENARIOS IN THE ABSENCE OF WESTERN ENLARGEMENT

Exactly how might these negative forces be manifested if Western enlargement does not occur? In the analysis that follows, we examine four generic models, each of which could have different submanifestations. The first model, "local turmoil," envisions instability growing out of Eastern Europe's internal affairs. The remaining three models all postulate an assertive Russia as a cause of instability. In the second model, "neo-imperial Russian domination," Russia rejuvenates, then proceeds to reestablish control over East Central Europe, including Poland and the other Visegrad states. In the third model, "regional multipolarity," the threat of Russian domination leads East Central European states to take major steps to protect themselves, perhaps amid conflict and turbulence among themselves. In the fourth model, "tripolarity," Germany distances itself from NATO so that it can lead a new security coalition in East Central Europe or, alternatively, reconfigures NATO and the EU to achieve this purpose, in a narrow way serving its own interests. As a result, Europe settles into a new form of its old historical pattern. The following analysis describes these models, assesses their consequences, and judges their feasibility.

Local Turmoil

The local turmoil model calls attention to the possibility that East Central Europe could slide into instability on its own, irrespective of whether Russia becomes more assertive. Postulating that the region's structural characteristics alone could be the cause, the model, begins with the progressive failure of reform across East Central Europe. The result is many countries left with unprosperous economies, frustrated societies, and ineffective governments, conditions setting the stage for a return to authoritarianism and reactionary politics. In this setting, security anarchy could lead several countries to take steps to increase their military power even in the absence of a military threat from Russia. The outcome could be an atmosphere of tension and growing competition among the states, aided and abetted by the asymmetric distribution of power among them. The appearance of authoritarian regimes, in turn, could exacerbate the tensions already present among many countries. One outcome could be domestic turbulence—ethnic clashes, class warfare, anti–status quo rebellions, mass immigrations, and regular upheavals—within several countries, making stable government impossible. Another outcome could be serious interstate frictions erupting across the region. For example, Poland could confront Ukraine or Belarus. Hungary could clash with Romania, Serbia, and Slovakia. The triangular relationship of Romania, Moldova, and Ukraine could deteriorate into open hostility. Out of these frictions could come periodic border clashes and even open warfare.

Of the four models examined here, this model has the highest probability of occurring. The conditions for its occurrence are already present. This model could come to life regardless of how Russia behaves, but its likelihood would increase if a more assertive Russia is on the scene. How destabilizing would this model be for Europe? Minor eruptions of turmoil might not have larger consequences, but major and sustained eruptions would be virulent in all three directions: west, south, and east. Western Europe would be hard-put to insulate itself from a turbulent East Central Europe. At a minimum, Western investments would be threatened, and a deluge of immigration could overwhelm the capacity of West European governments to cope. As has been true in Bosnia, sharp disagreements over how to react could divide the Western community and the transatlantic alliance. To the south, local turmoil in East Central Europe could infect the Balkans, thereby making that region more unstable and violence-prone. To the east, an unstable East Central Europe could damage prospects for stability in Russia and the CIS. In particular, the failure of market democracy in East Central Europe could enhance the likelihood that market democracy will fail in Russia as well. Widespread turmoil in East Central Europe thus spells serious trouble for Europe as a whole.

Neo-Imperial Russian Domination

Neo-imperial Russian domination is the model that next comes to mind when dark scenarios of Europe's future are contemplated. For this model to come to life, Russia would have to commit itself to an ambitious rebuilding of the empire lost by the Soviet Union. To provide the resources for this ambitious form of statism, it would first need to rejuvenate its internal strength. In all likelihood, it would have to abandon democracy at home in favor of a new authoritarianism: probably a right-wing nationalist regime. Externally, it first would have to reestablish firm control over the CIS countries, possibly to the point of absorbing many back into an enlarged Russia. At a minimum, Russia would need to regain control over Belarus and Ukraine, and possibly Kazakhstan and Uzbekistan as well. Following consolidation of this achievement, Russia would have to extend its strategic reach eastward. The core of this model is Russia's success at installing governments in East Central Europe that either tilt heavily toward Russia in strategic affairs or are outright aligned with it in a new security alliance to replace the Warsaw Pact. In an extreme version, Russian troops might again be based in Eastern Europe, where they might menace Western Europe.

How and to what degree would this model be destabilizing? This strategic outcome would spell the death of democracy in Russia, Eurasia, and Eastern Europe. Democracy would be replaced with right-wing authoritarianism and a new ideological confrontation in Central Europe, pitting authoritarianism against democracy. Strategic and military rivalry between NATO and a new Russian-led alliance might also ensue. In the extreme, a new form of the old Cold War could evolve. The problems posed for the West would be formidable. NATO might need to rebuild some of its old Center Region defenses. Again preoccupied with a Central Region danger, NATO would be less able to attend to other strategic problems, including North Africa, the Balkans, and the Persian Gulf. In Central Europe, stability would again come to rest on the old concepts of containment and deterrence.

This model could be realized only as the result of a staggering sequence of improbable events. The most obvious difficulty is that even before setting any sights on Eastern Europe, Russia would have to assemble the resources for a strategic campaign of these dimensions and then reabsorb the CIS. An equally difficult task would be imposing control over Eastern Europe. For this model to transpire, the East Europeans would have to fail to see the danger coming and not take appropriate counteractions. Even after achieving success, Russia would face the task of holding its new empire together. During the Cold War, Communism provided an ideological glue that bonded the Soviet Union and the Warsaw Pact.

What would be the new glue now? A new ideology would be needed, because, in its absence, the governments of reabsorbed countries would derive their power largely from Moscow and, therefore, would lack domestic legitimacy. Domestic legitimacy could come from a common ideology of fascism, but fascism tends to be nationalistic and would eat away at the bonds of a large coalition led by Russia. Beyond this, could fascist regimes or milder authoritarian regimes sustain the market economies needed to make these countries prosperous enough to carry out a sustained rivalry with the West? If not, could they remain in power for long? Indeed, could a Russian authoritarian regime remain in power if it saddled itself with the expensive cost of trying to shore up an empire of these dimensions?

All of these barriers make this model a low-probability outcome. Yet it is not one that can be dismissed as impossible, especially for a lesser version of the model: a volunteer coalition between a rightward-leaning Russia and several similarly inclined states. These regimes might see advantage in associating themselves with a Russia that shares their form of government and strategic perspectives. In essence, this coalition would not be due to Russian coercion from above but from an undergirding consensus. Russia would be the leading power in this coalition, but it would act more as chairman of the board than as a dictator. The feasibility of this version thus hinges on the degree to which a right-wing ideology of authoritarianism, nationalism, and even fascism lies below the surface in East Central Europe, waiting to be born. The widespread appeal of market democracy in East Central Europe makes this birth unlikely. Yet, if greater economic renewal is not experienced in the coming years, the smoldering discontent of today could grow. The history of the 1930s and current events in the Balkans make this model something to be kept in mind—and guarded against.

Regional Multipolarity

Regional multipolarity is based on the premise that the East Central European states will see Russia rejuvenating and asserting itself outward, and will take steps to preempt the danger and protect themselves. One alternative envisions all or most of these states joining together into a tight-knit security bloc. A more likely alternative envisions the bloc-formation process taking place amid disagreement and conflict among these states, so that more than one bloc forms and the strategic alignments are constantly shifting. Both alternatives could highly polarize the region. Both result in less anarchy, but, in different ways, they also set the stage for strategic tension. The consequence is a classical form of multipolar geopolitics, but with modern technology: highly competitive and unstable as a result of its own complexity.

The first alternative could be anchored in a security alliance among the Visegrad Four, with Poland acting as the leader. This bloc would yield a combined population of 64 million people, a GDP of about

$200 billion, and a combined defense posture of 18 divisions and 700 combat aircraft. It would be an impressive strategic alliance, but its combined military assets would leave it still facing an overall numerical disparity against mobilized Russian forces of about 1.5:1. The step that would propel this bloc into conventional military adequacy would be the addition of Ukraine. This bloc would have 112 million people and combined military assets equal to those of available Russian and Belorussian forces together. Thus, the outcome would be rough security equivalence in East Central Europe. Even so, this alliance would remain vulnerable because it lacks nuclear weapons. A great issue would be whether it would determine to cross the nuclear threshold in order to remedy this deficiency.

The second alternative could come in many different varieties, but a common image is of a strategic checkerboard across the region, with one bloc opposed to Russia but the other seeking close relations with Russia. For example, whereas Poland might join with Ukraine, the Czech Republic, and Hungary, Belarus, Slovakia, and Romania, sensing danger to themselves, might seek alignment with Russia. Depending on the politics of the moment, other clusters are possible. The region's current anarchy would give way to a complex new structure reminiscent of earlier centuries, in which alliances formed among countries that were not physically contiguous to each other.

Is this model feasible? In recent years, several countries across the region have explored the option of joining together to create a regional security framework. Discussions among the Visegrad Four have been held, as have discussions between Poland and Ukraine. Thus far, all participants have turned toward PFP and NATO membership as their preferred choice. One reason for their failure to unite is that these countries have little history of cooperating with each other. Indeed, some have seen each other as long-time rivals or at least as coolly distant neighbors. Beyond this, a key barrier is that, in general, alliances are difficult to form among a group of small-to-medium powers facing a major power. A true alliance requires a collective-defense commitment: Assurances of security can be gained only if all members are willing to commit themselves to defense of each other—a commitment that involves serious risks and dangers, and that becomes justifiable only if the gains exceed the costs, all countries have confidence in the intentions of each other, and the risks are manageable. In addition, such alliances typically encounter trouble allocating authority and making decisions, because there is no leader to set the agenda, and decisions come only when unanimity prevails. All of these factors argue against this model coming to life.

Yet, if these countries fail to gain membership in NATO and the EU, they will be confronted with the imposing dangers of enduring neutrality, anarchy, and vulnerability. Their fears could mount if they see Russia reappearing as a potential strategic menace—perhaps, of necessity, enough to motivate them to cross the alliance threshold. As a result, this model is far from a distant longshot. If this model comes to life, the issue will be, Which alternative? Political theory suggests that new alliances will grow large enough, but only large enough, to achieve strategic equilibrium with the major menace. This postulate forecasts the first alternative: an alliance among the Visegrad Four and Ukraine. Yet practical politics enters the equation as well, pointing to a checkerboard pattern.

What will be the consequences for stability if the model of regional multipolarity comes to life? Surface appearances suggest that stability could be the outcome if the first alternative prevails, because an equilibrium of military power would exist between this coalition and Russia. Yet stability is a product of far more than military mathematics. The political outcome likely would be a high degree of polarization and animosity between the coalition and Russia, especially if Ukraine becomes a member of the coalition and Russia perceives a threat to its dominance of the geopolitical terrain around its borders. Moreover, the new coalition might not operate effectively or be guided by wise statesmanship. The result could be a propensity to conflict, crisis, and war. These negative features would be enhanced if checkerboard diplomacy prevails, in which case peacetime affairs likely would witness an unending process of political maneuvering and competition. The bottom line is that, while this model might seem stable in theory, it could be very unstable in practice.

Tripolarity

Of the four models, tripolarity is the least probable and may be deemed fanciful by many observers. However, it calls attention to the geopolitical basics (security affairs and economic relationships) not only in East Central Europe but across all of Europe. This model envisions a process of decay in both East Central Europe and the Western alliance. As a result, Germany is led to distance itself from the Western alliance and to reestablish its old role as a mitteleuropäischen power broker. In this model, Germany acts independently to carry out a strong security policy in East Central Europe, forging a power bloc there to protect its strategic and economic interests and to block Russian reentry into the region. The new bloc would include some or all of the Visegrad Four, along with Austria. This bloc could be a military alliance. It would have a combined force posture or at least national postures whose defense policies are coordinated on behalf of collective defense. It might also have nuclear weapons, and they would be owned by Germany. The result would be a tripolar Europe with this new German-led bloc at its center. To the west would be a truncated NATO, based on a trilateral U.S.–French–British relationship. To the east would be a Eurasian bloc, dominated by Russia. Stability would rest on geopolitical management of this tripolar structure.

This model could come to life only if Germany not only becomes alarmed about an emerging Russian menace to East Central Europe but so loses faith in NATO and the EU that it sees no alternative but to act on its own. Notwithstanding this model's improbability, it offers the key insight that the Western alliance is itself a geopolitical creation, crafted during the Cold War to defend its members from a communist military threat occupying Central Europe. The collapse of that threat removed one of this alliance's most important strategic bonds. The new era's conditions imply that if the alliance is not adjusted to perform new security missions, it will fail to meet the emerging strategic requirements of its key members. They, in turn, will face growing incentives to craft alternative arrangements. If Germany were to become deeply apprehensive about unfolding events in East Central Europe, it would turn first to NATO. If NATO were to falter, it would turn to the EU and try to invigorate the WEU by seeking help from Britain and France. But if both institutions were to fail because they defined East Central Europe as lying beyond their outer strategic perimeter, Germany would be left to its own devices. Under these circumstances, it might turn to some version of the tripolar model, which is exactly what it did in the centuries before the Cold War, when its eastern flank was not protected and it had no security anchor in the west. The tripolar model thus amounts to a rebirth of Europe's history in the nineteenth century and before.

The negative consequences for Europe's stability are obvious. The tripolar model is mainly *why* Europe's history was so unstable and violent. Perhaps modern-era values would soften the hard edges of a new tripolarity. Yet the hard edges of the old model were created partly because of the model itself, not because of any moral weakness and low strategic horizons of statesmen at the time. A new tripolar model, moreover, would be carried out with modern technology. Whereas a century ago, military doctrine for major war relied on the mobilization of huge armies, today's military doctrine calls for much smaller forces armed with immensely destructive weapons, including conventional weapons that have acquired great lethality. The nature of this technology alone could be destabilizing: Modern technology interacting with conflicting political motives could make a new tripolar model competitive in security policies and the surrounding atmosphere poisonous. In the extreme case, the German-led bloc could develop a competitive relationship not only with Russia but with the truncated NATO. If events deteriorated in this extreme way, a new tripolar structure could be unstable owing to the dynamic interactions of the big powers and the small powers. In the nineteenth century, peace came to rest on a fragile balance-of-power system that, if re-created in a new form, would be no more politically stable today.

Tripolarity doubtless is an extreme and highly improbable case. However, a lesser version is more readily imaginable. This is the scenario of Germany remaining inside Western institutions but using its power within those institutions to serve a narrow version of its interests in unhealthy ways: Germany could draw away from the United States, seek to dominate Britain and France, and endeavor to re-create NATO and the EU as bodies led by it on behalf of a Central European order, not Atlanticism or European integration. The consequence would be a muted form of tripolarity. The Western alliance would still exist in form, but less so in substance. Its ability to work together to create a unified Europe would be weakened, and the prospects for troubled relations with Russia would increase.

Summary

In summary, each of these four models provides a different theoretical snapshot of how instability could evolve if the emerging geopolitics of East Central Europe are not handled properly. Russia is part of the problem, but systemic dynamics are the much bigger problem. These models might be dismissed as low-probability events when viewed through the lens of today's situation. But when viewed through the lens of history and structural analysis, their probability rises, because the European security order has a well-demonstrated capability to change in sweeping ways over just a few years and decades. Although, separately, each of these models might be assessed as improbable, their combined probability must be taken into account, because the emergence of only one of them could be enough to undo Europe. If the average individual probability of each model is only 15 percent, the combined probability that one of them might come to life is nearly 50 percent—ample reason for a vigorous Western policy aimed at forging a stable order in East Central Europe.

INSTABILITY IN THE PRESENCE OF WESTERN ENLARGEMENT: FOUR WORRISOME SCENARIOS

A key purpose of Western enlargement is to help prevent all four of these destabilizing scenarios. Implicit in the West's decision to enlarge is the belief that the act can dampen local turmoil in East Central Europe, close the door on any future Russian domination, squelch multipolarity, and remove any incentives for Germany to act on its own—apparently sound strategic judgment. Yet Western enlargement is not a risk-free proposition. It could backfire, thereby bringing about a new form of instability of its own. The challenge facing the West, therefore, is to carry out enlargement in ways that achieve its benefits by avoiding its risks.

Four worrisome scenarios define the ways that enlargement could backfire. First, enlargement might be unsuccessful in East Central Europe. It might be carried out in ways that, while entangling the West in the region, fail to dampen the region's local turmoil and its proclivity for multipolar behavior. Second, enlargement might result in a bipolar standoff with Russia: Cold Peace. Third, enlargement might result in an even worse relationship with Russia: a bipolar confrontation that yields a new Cold War. Fourth, enlargement might result in a combination of dangers: a still-turbulent local setting coupled with either Cold Peace or a new Cold War with Russia.

Unsuccessful Enlargement in East Central Europe

The first scenario is feasible. It could come about if Western enlargement is too weak and ineffective to cure the local ills it is designed to remedy. On the surface, enlargement seems to be an all-powerful remedy—it offers troubled nations membership in the West's two strongest institutions—the EU and NATO. Yet membership in these bodies alone will have no beneficial effect if vigorous actions and positive consequences do not flow from such membership. EU membership will count for little if it does not help reinvigorate the economies of new members and thereby help solve the problem of collapsing prosperity that threatens to wreck market democracy across East Central Europe. NATO membership will count for little if it does not reassure new members of their security, persuade them to forsake provocative defense policies, and lead them to treat each other in a neighborly fashion. If EU and NATO enlargement falls short of these goals, the West could find itself committed and heavily involved in a still-turbulent region. Rather than pull East Central Europe out of the vortex, an ineffective enlargement could cause the West to fall into it.

The negative consequences of this scenario are obvious. Even after enlargement, East Central Europe could remain beset with deep problems: uncertain domestic reforms, a chronic lack of security, worry about Russia, and potential frictions among the region's countries. The difference is that the West would now be heavily entangled. It might find itself dangerously embroiled in the region's troubles, but not influential enough to resolve them. This is the precise reason why Western offers to admit new members are made on the condition that the new members are irreversibly committed to market democracy and are pursuing stability-enhancing security policies. Yet the countries of East Central Europe are pursuing membership because, lacking in both areas, they want a strong infusion of Western economic help and security. Even if they step up their own performance, membership inevitably will be a bridge intended to fill a still-existing gap of significant magnitude. If the act of extending membership fails to fill this gap, the goals of enlargement will not be achieved. East Central Europe will not become a stable region and, in contrast to today, the West will be far less able to insulate itself from its dangers.

Bipolar Standoff and Bipolar Confrontation

The second and third scenarios—bipolar standoff (Cold Peace) and bipolar confrontation (Cold War)—are also feasible. One or the other could result if Western enlargement results in an estranged relationship with a Russia that is capable of mounting a countervailing response on CIS soil. The essence of a standoff is two security coalitions that are well-armed and animated by defensive military strategies. Their political relationship would not be primed for war, but it would be coolly hostile. The enlarged West would enjoy market democracy within its borders, but it would be required to engage in a higher level of defense preparedness than today. In particular, it would need to assemble a well-equipped military posture in Eastern Europe for stalwart defense. The CIS would become a tightly integrated military bloc led by Russia and marked by authoritarian politics. Cooperation between the two blocs might take place, but it would be limited and of a strictly business nature: not systematic, but on a limited, case-by-case basis.

The scenario of confrontation amounts to more than an intensification of standoff. In this scenario, the Russian-led coalition on CIS soil would pose a powerful offensive military threat to Eastern Europe. The remaining vestiges of cooperation would give way to deep animosity and outright strategic conflict. Depending on the exact military balance, Western military strategy would be compelled to reembrace some of the doctrines of the old Cold War: containment, deterrence, forward defense, and flexible response. Stability would rest on deterrence and bipolar security management.

Enlargement as Entanglement

The fourth, backfire, scenario would produce the worst nightmare of all. In it, enlargement would not cure East Central Europe's troubles, and the West would not only become entangled in a still-turbulent setting but would also find itself facing deep trouble with Russia in the form of Cold Peace or Cold War. Strained relations with Russia would magnify the West's difficulties in managing East Central Europe. Meanwhile, the lack of stability among its new Eastern allies would compound the West's problems in dealing with Russia. The West thus would find itself juggling two different security balls, one interfering with the other. Although the odds that this scenario might occur are less than that of either local turmoil or trouble with Russia, an ineffective enlargement that also confronts trouble with the Russians is conceivable.

A New Geopolitical Division in Europe

Any of the scenarios involving trouble with Russia would yield a new geopolitical division of Europe. The new line, presumably, would be drawn along the eastern borders of Poland, Slovakia, Hungary, and Romania. If standoff developed, the new geopolitical line would be firm but not hard-edged. If confrontation developed, it would be quite hard-edged. What would be the consequences for stability? In some quarters, the history of the old Cold War has bred a belief that bipolar systems are stable. Yet, the Cold War was a unique event whose stability rested on fragile foundations. Although the two sides were opposed to each other's political values, their geopolitical designs were sufficiently compatible to avoid war. The Soviet Union enjoyed a dominating position in Eastern Europe and, having achieved a divided Germany, it did not have powerful incentives for further territorial gains that could be purchased only at a heavy price. It assembled an offensive military posture in Eastern Europe that constantly threatened the West, but it was not prepared to use this posture to launch an aggressive war. The West was preoccupied with protecting its own territory and was not prepared to directly challenge the Soviet Union for control of Eastern Europe. Moreover, the West assembled a powerful defense force that denied the Warsaw Pact high confidence of victory and threatened nuclear retaliation in the event of an invasion: a tenuous and dangerous way to preserve peace. Stability resulted because, in the final analysis, both sides showed enough restraint to dampen the always-existing potential for crisis. Even so, the two sides may have been lucky to avoid a conflagration. A new bipolar structure in East Central Europe might not have similarly stabilizing features—or be so lucky.

Whether Russia could muster the resources to sustain a new Cold War is uncertain. If it could, a new Cold War in this region might not benefit from the same mixture of political and military restraints that marked the old Cold War. Sensing a threat to its geopolitical heartland and enjoying the advantage of proximity to its logistics base, Russia might be more prone to risk war. Less committed to defending territory farther removed from its geopolitical heartland, the West might be less willing to constantly maintain the highly primed military posture needed to deter and defend. The new forms of containment, deterrence, and defense thus might not work as well as those of the past. Even if stability is maintained through these mechanisms, the economic and political costs to both sides would be very high. The confrontation could doom Russia and the CIS to a bleak future, but it could also drain away valuable resources from the West and prevent Eastern Europe from becoming a healthy region. A future of Cold Peace might have less deleterious consequences, but serious consequences all the same. At a minimum, hope for a democratic, prosperous, and tranquil Europe stretching from the Atlantic to the Urals would be lost.

THE COMPOSITE PICTURE OF THE NEW GEOPOLITICS

A new geopolitics of East Central Europe is emerging because Russia is now pursuing a statist policy that may affect the region and because other powerful dynamics are emerging from within the region itself and from the West, which is drawing up plans to enter the region. The current situation in this region has integrative features, but it also has worrisome, disintegrative features.

The West has powerful incentives to enlarge into this region, not only to promote market democracy and peaceful conduct, but also to head off a number of negative scenarios that could inflict great damage on Europe as a whole. Indeed, the West will need to avert these negative scenarios so that it can establish the conditions needed for its positive values to flourish. To do so, the West will need to enlarge with vigor and effectiveness; a weak enlargement might achieve little of value while entangling the West in a still-turbulent region. The rub is that a strong enlargement will send signals to Russia, which already has deep misgivings about the basic concept of *enlargement* as defined by the West. The act of enlargement, coupled with the methods of carrying it out, therefore, carries with it some risk of a destabilizing outcome of its own: a bipolar standoff with Russia that produces a Cold Peace or a less-likely new Cold War.

The West thus finds itself confronting a complex strategic dilemma. Enlargement is not only desirable, it is necessary; therefore, it is unavoidable. The act of enlargement raises potential trouble with a statist Russia pointed toward some measure of rejuvenation. The degree of potential trouble with Russia may increase as a function of the vigor with which enlargement is carried out. If enlargement backfires by producing a Cold Peace with Russia, or worse, the West will have traded one strategic problem for another. It will find itself extended farther eastward, facing danger on a new frontier. The trouble will be all the greater if Russia and the CIS region succumb to their own problems, falling into turmoil or restored authoritarianism coupled with hostility toward the West.

The challenge facing the West is to craft an enlargement that will be sufficiently strong to achieve its goals while avoiding trouble with Russia, and preferably fostering a positive outcome in the CIS. How can this complex mission of multiple objectives be accomplished? In the next chapter, we turn to this question and propose strategic end games.

Chapter Seven

STRATEGIC END GAMES FOR ENLARGEMENT

Barring a loss of resolve, the West has made the strategic decision to enlarge, even though the timing, extent, and ways are as yet undecided. The agenda ahead for the West is to guide this process to a positive outcome. Doing so may not be easy, because the West will be pursuing multiple objectives, not all of which are readily achievable or automatically compatible. The task of balancing objectives and crafting policies that support them will require careful planning. A key feature will need to be the fashioning of a *strategic end game*: a final political destination and a plan for getting there. How far is enlargement to go? What is the accompanying theory of stability for the overall regional security system of East Central Europe and Eurasia? What role is Russia to play in this system? These are the questions to be addressed as a strategic end game is designed. Enlargement by the EU and NATO will help the countries brought into the fold. But even if no new rigid geopolitical lines are drawn, a tightly knit economic and security bloc will emerge in East Central Europe with intimate ties to the West, sharpening the distinction between those countries entering the West's fold and those that remain outside it.

This prospect elevates the importance of thinking broadly about where enlargement is headed. Even if an enlarged West is strong and cohesive, it cannot insulate itself from the larger strategic affairs of East Central Europe and Eurasia. A strategic end game is needed to help determine how the outside region is to be rendered stable; otherwise, the trends may begin pointing toward an angry Russia or a turbulent Eurasia—a dangerous new frontier confronting the West. A strategic end game is needed to avoid the pitfalls of muddling through. The West cannot afford to pursue separate strands of activity that work at cross-purposes on behalf of contradictory goals. It cannot be driven by short-term imperatives into embracing a long-term strategic theory that is incoherent. Nor can the West afford to take "wrong roads" in the early stages: It may be unable to reverse course later. The West needs to take the correct roads from the outset, but it will be able to take them only if it knows its destination.

COMPONENTS OF A STRATEGIC END GAME

A strategic end game that determines roads and destinations should have three components. First, it should offer a portrayal of how the entire regional security system is to be structured when the process of enlargement reaches its conclusion. Second, it should offer a credible theory of how this regional system preserves stability and fulfills the West's key objectives. Third, it should offer a broad game plan for achieving the final result: not a detailed blueprint, but a general sense of policy priorities, stages for implementation, and the relationship between means and ends.

The purpose of this chapter is to identity and assess alternative strategic end games for the West. The five end games analyzed here are ideal types. While they draw upon views put forth in the academic literature, they are independent creations of this study. This analysis first examines these five end games in their ideal form to help clarify the options and trade-offs they pose. We address ideas for combining them at the end of this chapter.

These five end games do not exhaust all the permutations and combinations, but they do provide a broad menu of choices to help illuminate the different kinds of strategic reasoning that might guide Western policy:

- The single-community solution

- Collective security

- The institutional web

- Open-door enlargement

- The two-community solution.

Each end game has very different implications for the priorities that should be set, specific outcomes to be created, and actions to be taken. As well, each end game goes further than current plans for enlargement, which do not go beyond admitting the Visegrad Four to NATO and the EU. We specified two criteria for evaluating these end games: feasibility (Are they realistically attainable at acceptable cost and risk?) and desirability (Will they produce beneficial results and thereby enable the West to attain its key objectives?). The following sections describe each end game and evaluate it according to these criteria.

THE SINGLE-COMMUNITY SOLUTION

This strategic end game proposes to solve the dilemmas of enlargement by creating a single, unified community that would stretch from the Atlantic Ocean to the Urals. Enlargement into East Central Europe might be the first step, but it would soon be followed by a further vast extension eastward, leaving no one on the outside looking in. Within a few years, Russia would become a full-fledged member of the Western community, as would Ukraine and most or even all of the other CIS countries.

Theory

The theory behind this end game is that the combination of market democracy and international community-building can achieve great things, thereby overpowering any barriers. These two causal agents are presumed capable of fashioning the conditions needed to bring about this single community and maintain it in the aftermath. As they take hold, conflict presumably would give way to consensus; disintegration would yield to integration and, ultimately, the emergence of a Europe and Eurasia bonded together in common values, harmony, and cooperation.

Institutional Vehicle

The specific institutional vehicle for achieving this end game would need to transcend any of the bodies existing today. The OSCE would not suffice, nor would NATO. The EU/WEU might serve, but it would need to be enlarged beyond recognition. In its most comprehensive form, this end game would replace the EU and NATO with a new transcontinental structure having a very large membership. If an enlarged EU and the CIS are added together, the total would be 38 states. Carried to its logical conclusion, the total could be the same size as that for the OSCE: 53 states. At a minimum, this community would resemble the vision established by the Maastricht Treaty for the EU; in time, it might evolve into a United Nations of Europe and Eurasia.

Regardless of its title and institutional composition, this community would have a far-reaching charter. Its primary mission would be to promote economic integration through common monetary, economic, trade, and customs policies. It would strive for common domestic policies, and for close cooperation in key transnational fields: communications, environment, health, education, scientific research, energy, and immigration. It would also aim for common foreign policies, security policies, and defense strategies. The member countries would retain their national sovereignty, but federal bodies—executive, legislative, and judicial—would be established and given governing powers. Its evolution would follow the EU model, but at a faster pace. An economic community would first be established, then would give way to an ever-larger political union.

Desirability

Because this end game offers not only stability but also enduring peace, it merits high marks for desirability. It would resolve the tension between Western enlargement and stable regional relations with an all-encompassing community that includes Russia and the entire CIS. Hence, no geopolitical lines would be drawn anywhere. Because it would produce a stable Europe and Eurasia, it would allow the United States to attend to other troubled areas of the world.

Feasibility

The drawback of this end game is its lack of feasibility. It fails to provide a credible theory showing how this outcome can be created out of the current vast differences between Europe and Eurasia. Perhaps a single community may be attainable in the distant future.

The single-community solution could become a viable end game if the Continent makes great strides toward democratic integration in the next few years, but in the coming era, it does not seem realistic, irrespective of the efforts the West is prepared to make.

Barriers to Feasibility

Slow-Growing Democracy. A principal problem is that this end game is predicated on the assumption that Western-style democracy is being adopted universally. An all-encompassing community would be almost impossible to build without widespread agreement on basic political values, which is precisely why the EU and NATO are now mandating that new members already have established satisfactory democratic credentials before being admitted into their folds. At the moment, Russia and the CIS countries are all trying to become democracies. But many seem to be settling into a pattern of being "quasi-democracies," combining leftover authoritarianism with representative government. If democracy is the common outcome, it could be many years in coming. Such an outcome is possible, as demonstrated by South Korea and Taiwan, which have followed the path from authoritarian rule to market democracy. In general, they first built market economies under central political rule and only later gradually modified their governments to achieve democratic rule. The process has taken them thirty years. If a similar dynamic applies to Russia and Eurasia, the time when common democratic values arrives may be several decades off. Until it does, the single-community solution will be confronted by a formidable barrier: the failure of Europe and Eurasia to agree on the political foundations of governance.

Economic Barriers. The economic barriers to unity seem equally formidable, owing to the great disparities between Europe and Eurasia. The European Union is able to contemplate its economic unity because its members have quite similar, prosperous economies. Nearly all are post-industrial, have elaborate capitalist structures, enjoy comparative advantages, and are able to compete in the world economy. The EU's 15 nations are composed of 370 million people with a combined GDP of $6.1 trillion, for an average per capita income (PCI) of about $16,500. Eight of the countries have PCIs of $18,000 or more. Only two—Greece and Portugal—fall under

$12,000. The difference between the EU and the CIS is stark. The 12 CIS countries have 282 million people and a GDP of only $1.6 trillion, for an average PCI of only $5,900. None has a PCI reaching $8,000. Six fall under $3,000. None has yet entered the post-industrial information age, has full-fledged market capitalism, or is able to compete with Western economies. In essence, the CIS countries are a generation or two behind the EU in economic prowess.

Owing to this lack of parity, the two economic blocs are far apart in their ability to be integrated—a main reason for the EU to reject calls for any early enlargement into the CIS region. Full economic integration makes sense only if the prosperity of both blocs will be enhanced. EU members would find themselves saddled with enormous financial-assistance burdens if the CIS countries were brought into their midst: Absorbing East Central Europe will be difficult enough, and the CIS has a population and economy nearly three times as large. Whether the CIS would benefit is itself uncertain. Apart from selling natural resources, the CIS countries would lack the competitive capacity to export manufactured goods to Europe. Their own poverty would prevent them from importing European products in large quantities. Their low-wage market would be their chief attraction for European investors, but the consequence could be European ownership of their industrial sectors. These problems are the tip of the iceberg in a process that would mandate massive developments for establishing legal, financial, and business ties between Europe and Eurasia. The vast difference between these two economic blocs may allow for a steady buildup of trade relationships, but not a pell-mell rush to full union.

Interstate Political Barriers. In addition, the contemporary interstate political barriers are so daunting that no amount of institution-building seems likely to overcome them. Institutions cannot work in a vacuum. They require an underlying consensus among the member states on their scope and purposes. The more comprehensive the institution, the greater is the consensus required. The single-community solution would require a sweeping consensus. Western Europe's experience is an example of how a large community can be built, but it has been possible because the countries there have come to embrace common strategic horizons—not the case at the outset 45 years ago. Over these decades, the European countries have resolved most of their status and territorial disputes, and no longer view each other with suspicion or as a competitor. Jostling still takes place over EU policies, but, on the whole, these countries have grown accustomed to working with each other and are confident that established bargaining mechanisms will protect their vital interests. It is this long experience at bargaining and collaborating that has allowed them to build the EU's institutions, not the other way around: Political accord came first, and institutionalization followed. Although institutions played a contributing role in helping the EU evolve, they have mostly been a consequence of growing harmony, not a principal cause of it. Had the EU's institutions been created out of whole cloth four decades ago, they would not have been effective. If the political accord built over these years were to vanish, EU institutions would wither. The key point is that the act of creating political institutions aimed at uniting Europe and Eurasia would not itself be enough to trigger political integration in the absence of an underlying accord on the geopolitical and economic foundations.

At the moment, this accord does not yet exist, and it is likely years away from becoming established. A good deal more is required than democratization of the CIS. European countries as yet have no well-established track record of working with Russia and its Eurasian neighbors in satisfying ways. To a limited degree, the process has been under way since 1992. But Europe is not yet prepared for unity with Russian and Eurasia, and the converse is also true; Russia and its CIS neighbors are preoccupied with their own dilemmas, not with dealing with Europeans. Beyond this, issues governing relative status, strategic roles, and geopolitical agendas have not yet been seriously engaged, much less worked out. The two sides have not yet established the successful bargaining that leads to a willingness to partake of large common endeavors. Neither side is confident that its legitimate interests will be safeguarded if it engages in compromise and accommodation. Until effective working relationships between Europe and Eurasia are established, political union between them will lie beyond the pale.

Role of United States and NATO

Equally problematic is the role to be played by the United States and NATO. Adoption of the single-community solution implies that the need for U.S. security guarantees to its alliance partners will go away.

NATO likely would dissolve or degenerate into a diluted pact that would act as the transcontinental security arm of the new community. Would the new community be cohesive enough to perform the core security functions without U.S. military commitments and NATO's coalition capabilities? The answer is unclear, but, again, the existence of a community in name does not beget the capacity to operate effectively in practice. The risk is that the United States would leave Europe and that NATO would dissolve prematurely, leaving weakened security relationships in their wake.

Summary

The word *community* means something far more encompassing than an atmosphere of cooperation. It means creation of an organic entity capable of making far-reaching policy decisions and carrying them out. It also means the establishing of political authority patterns and an agreement on basic interstate political, economic, and security relationships. The mere act of proclaiming a community and establishing an institutional facade does not mean that an actual community exists or will spring to life. If this end game were adopted, central geopolitical questions would still have to be answered: How will Russia relate to the CIS countries in its Eurasian neighborhood? What will be the status of East Central Europe? How will Russia share influence with Germany and its EU partners? What will be the role of the United States and the transatlantic connection? Until these core questions are answered, the single-community end game will be more rhetoric than reality.

Perhaps the natural course of political and economic evolution will eventually lead to a single community. Far-sighted policies by many countries can contribute to this evolution, as can institutions that work. But as with the EU, the process cannot be rushed. Community-building is the consequence of long and patient efforts to resolve disputes and build consensus. If full-fledged institutions were established in the hope of producing a true community, the consequence almost inevitably would be overload and paralysis borne of the inability of 40–50 countries to work together on an agenda this large.

COLLECTIVE SECURITY

Theory

Collective security has more-modest ambitions than the single-community solution: to regulate conflict and promote peace among states in the world as it exists today, and to lessen the risk that enlargement, by fashioning newly divisive geopolitical lines in East Central Europe, will create trouble with Russia. This end game would endeavor to reduce the enlargement risk by creating a large body in which Russia will be a leading member. It envisions the forging of a diplomatic treaty and an associated institutional framework that would provide countries in East Central Europe and Eurasia with reassurances of their safety while not offending Russia. The dangers of the current anarchical system would be lessened, but not eliminated. Envisioned here is not a formal alliance against an external threat but a looser arrangement aimed at protecting all members from each other. The participants would agree to resist aggression by any of the signatories. OSCE already is a collective-security pact, but with weak powers. Building on OSCE, this end game calls for stronger forms of collaboration and more-powerful guarantees. A modern-day League of Nations for Europe and Eurasia would be required, one with real teeth. In contrast to the single-community solution, collective security seems feasible. Efforts to enhance OSCE make sense as part of any Western policy. The question is whether collective security passes the test of desirability as a stand-alone end game.

Institutional Vehicle

This collective-security pact would include the same membership as OSCE: the Western nations, Eastern Europe, and the CIS countries. Members would agree to promote peace, renounce the use of force, and subordinate their own interests to the common good. They would also agree to support the norms of the new system. Resort to force would be the ultimate sanction, and the safety of each nation would be guaranteed by the entire membership. The pact could be launched by the signing of a transcontinental treaty. In the aftermath would come a formal institution intended to provide adequate enforcement power. This end game envisions an institution composed of a security council, a general assembly, and subsidiary bodies for carrying out common policies. The major powers would have influential voices, but policies would be formed by consensus, and authority would be exercised by the institution as a whole. In all likelihood, a rule that unanimous agreement is not required would be adopted to prevent any single actor—or small group of actors—from blocking action. Nonetheless, widespread agreement would be needed for decisive responses.

This structure would be invested with the authority to make decisions to carry out crisis management and employ military force, including waging major war. Unlike a formal alliance, it would not have an integrated military command or large forces under its control in peacetime. It might be given a small posture for peacekeeping and similar missions, but forces for major combat operations would be kept under national control. Sovereignty would remain the guiding theme: Members would agree to consult in a crisis, but they would make no binding commitments prior to the event. Military operations would be undertaken voluntarily as the need arises rather than as an automatic response prepared in advance.

How would this end game jibe with Western enlargement? The answer is that the EU would enlarge but NATO would not. East European states would receive security guarantees from the collective pact, not from NATO. The CIS would be provided all of the guarantees given to other members. Each country would receive political guarantees of major help if victimized by aggression, but not formal collective-defense commitments. The CIS countries would receive no special help in their internal political and economic reforms. The Western states might continue giving them aid through their own policies and institutions. But apart from ruling out aggressive conduct and formation of any military alliance on CIS soil, the collective-security pact would take no stand on political and economic arrangements within the CIS. Indeed, it would not necessarily mandate market democracy there. It would be color-blind to ideology and to the region's political, economic, and social goals.

Desirability

The attractions of this pact are the same as those of collective-security bodies in general. It clearly is superior to anarchy, could help promote a sense of trust while aspiring to maintain a stable balance of military power, could help underwrite security and peace, and could provide a forum for debate and cooperation. It would provide a legal basis for common action and serve as a partial deterrent to aggression. It would offer its members military aid in a crisis, thereby helping reduce incentives for provocative arms buildups. It could perform security operations at the low end of the spectrum, e.g., peacekeeping and humanitarian aid. In the event of aggression, it would provide a framework for launching military interventions aimed at saving the threatened parties. To the extent this pact is stronger than the relatively weak OSCE, it would make a more powerful contribution to stability. It would reduce the damaging features of systemic anarchy in East Central Europe and Eurasia.

Feasibility

Just as this pact offers the attractions of collective security in general, it also has the same theoretical drawbacks. Its effectiveness is predicated on widespread consensus among its members. In particular, it requires strong agreement among the major powers regarding the underlying political and strategic order. When this consensus exists, a de facto concert is created among the major powers, who can agree to act together and lead the entire pact, thereby enabling decisive action by the collective-security body. But when this consensus is lacking, the capacity for decisiveness can be lost, because one or more major powers may block calls for decisive action.

Barriers to Feasibility

Unique Individual Priorities. Paralysis can also come from other quarters. Collective security, in theory, requires all its members to accept major responsibilities for security management everywhere within its boundaries. The problem is that most countries have unique priorities, and when a security challenge lies outside their vital interests, they tend to be unwilling to commit their military forces. Collective security's responsiveness comes to rest not only on consensus of the vast majority to approve strong action in principle, but also on the willingness and ability of a subcoalition to carry out the agenda. When the willingness and ability of that subcoalition are lacking, decisive military campaigns to enforce security guarantees can become an impossibility.

Components of Conflict Are Unclear. Paralysis especially can result when a gray-area conflict is occurring and the stakes are unclear. Collective security works best in dealing with clear-cut aggression by a single power that is grossly violating common norms. Its capacity is enhanced when the aggressor's conduct poses a major threat to the system as a whole, and when its military strength can be over-powered by the collective entity. Not all wars, however, are clear cut. Sometimes their origins are so murky that perpetrators are difficult to distinguish from victims, and a proper outcome is hard to define. Sometimes the aggressor's conduct is local and sends out few larger ripples. Sometimes the aggressor is not easily beaten, because its forces are strong and it receives help from allies. In such situations, a large collective-security body can be hard-pressed to act.

Military Impediments. Military impediments can also lead to paralysis. Whereas an alliance such as NATO builds a combined command structure and force posture, a collective-security body would not provide for this level of preparedness. Because the forces of its members do not collaborate in advance, they might not be capable of deploying rapidly or operating effectively once on the scene. The need to be better-prepared is the reason why NATO became a full-fledged alliance when the Cold War broke out. A new collective-security body could remedy this preparedness problem by allowing for suballiances to form in its midst. The barrier to this step, however, is that the theory of collective security discourages suballiances because they tend to compete with each other, giving rise to the balance-of-power politics that collective security is intended to dampen.

Feasibility: The Historical Verdict

The historical verdict on collective security is mixed. The theory was first put into practice when the old League of Nations was created after World War I. The League had some successes in handling local conflicts in the 1920s but was ineffective in others. The 1930s brought major deterioration in international relations, and the League failed to rise to the challenge, mainly because major Western powers failed to act: The United States was not a member, Britain had no taste for power-balancing, and France was weak internally. The League failed to halt Italy's invasion of Ethiopia or the Spanish Civil War. It was unable to stop Japan's occupation of Manchuria or Germany's occupation of the Rhineland. As war clouds gathered in Europe and Asia, the League collapsed in ruin. In the aftermath of World War II, the United Nations was established as a worldwide body with a security council and greater enforcement powers. But apart from resisting aggression in Korea, it soon fell into paralysis, playing only a minor role since in managing Cold War security affairs and giving way to the Western alliance system for carrying out containment. After the Cold War ended, the United Nations became the forum for the West's decisive response in the Persian Gulf War, but that action was led by the United States. Both the United Nations and OSCE have encountered trouble in trying to deal with the breakup of Yugoslavia and the war in Bosnia.

Summary

The bottom line is that collective security can work in theory and practice when a widespread consensus exists on the strategic issues of the day, and when the preponderance of its members are not in conflict with each other. But it breaks down when it is handed the job of managing the security affairs of a region undercut with deep strategic troubles. Under these conditions—conditions for which strength is most needed—collective security tends to be a weak instrument for security management. The key question in judging collective security as a strategic end game is this: Will East Central Europe and Eurasia be marked by consensus and stability, or by conflict and instability?

If they are marked by conflict and instability, creation of a new, stand-alone collective-security body able to handle the security challenges of tomorrow is doubtful. In the absence of NATO enlargement, an issue is whether this body could provide sufficiently strong military guarantees to stabilize the situation in East Central Europe. Would these countries be satisfied to the point of forsaking intensified defense preparations of their own or of suballiances? They could be, if they perceive that the major powers are prepared to come to their rescue in an emergency and if they will not use the collective-security body to block each other. Many of these countries, however, are unlikely to invest adequate confidence in Russia; without a NATO guarantee, they might distrust the Western powers as well. Beyond this, many governments might wonder whether a collective-security pact would have the physical capability to help defend them even if the political willpower is present. The risk is that they might come to regard the collective-security pact as a hollow entity with little capacity to ensure their safety.

A collective-security pact would have little to say about strategic affairs in Eurasia. It would establish a norm barring Russian aggression against its neighbors. But could it enforce this norm if it lacks military power and Russia has influence over its conduct? Key issues are whether Russia will be satisfied with its strategic role in Eurasia, whether stable market democracies will evolve, and whether further disintegration or integration takes place in Eurasia. These are geopolitical issues lying outside the scope of collective security. The same judgment applies to Russia's strategic relations with the West in East Central Europe.

A key factor is whether a political equilibrium can be found that allows enlargement to take place in a manner that leads Russia to accept the new status quo. If not, political conflict with Russia will ensue as enlargement unfolds. A new collective-security body might be able to temper the incentives to confrontation, but only if it is widely regarded as a powerful contributor to stability. The interaction in East Central Europe will be influenced by powerful political and economic undercurrents that shape the framework within which defense policies and security horizons are judged. The theory of collective security has little to offer about the management of these undercurrents.

Especially because this collective-security body could not itself manage the region's core political affairs, an issue is whether it could perform its deterrence and defense functions if relations among the big powers did not work out for the better. Could it deter and defend in an unstable setting marked by would-be aggressors eager to upset the status quo and willing to run risks to achieve their goals? If doubt prevails, the consequence would be a destabilizing power and security vacuum. The incentives would be renewed for NATO to enlarge along with the EU, as would the incentives for formation of some kind of multilateral security organization in Eurasia.

THE INSTITUTIONAL WEB

Of the five end games examined here, the institutional web reflects important aspects of current Western policy and has the advantage of being the most flexible, because it can be combined with other end games. The issue here is its ability to function as a stand-alone end game.

Theory

This end game is based on the premise that a full-fledged, but limited, Western enlargement will occur: The EU and NATO will enlarge together into East Central Europe and stop there. Barring rapid progress in Eurasia, an enlarged West likely will face a still-anarchical setting outside its new borders. Recognizing the dangers of this situation, this strategic end game endeavors to take whatever additional steps are possible to stabilize affairs in this outside region. It attempts this task by spinning a web of interlocked institutions over the east. Whereas the single-community and collective-security end games each rely on one powerful institution to accomplish their strategic missions, this end game relies on *several* institutions. It appraises each of these institutions as having a specialized role and, therefore, only limited powers, in the hope that, together, their combined effect will be powerful.

Affordability enters this strategic end game's calculus: The West may not be willing to pay high costs for efforts to stabilize the region outside its enlarged borders. Consequently, it endeavors to make something of the limited departures that will be possible and the modest resources that will be available, turning to institutional endeavors that create only limited commitments and will be inexpensive.

This end game would use its institutions to achieve several strategic purposes. The highest-priority goal is establishing constructive relations with Russia: convincing it to accept Western enlargement, encouraging its democratic reforms, drawing it closer to the West, and constraining it from destabilizing conduct. Its second priority is to help safeguard Ukraine's independence. Its third priority is to offer stabilizing benefits to other states that do not gain admission to NATO and the EU. This end game thus aims at ensnaring the biggest country—Russia—while catching Ukraine and many smaller countries in its web. By catching enough of them strongly enough, a positive outcome could be achieved.

This end game is pragmatic, realizing that institutions cannot produce miracles when countries are intent on opposing one another and the normal sources of stability are weak. Yet it emphasizes the integrative powers of institutions and the possibility of international cooperation and willingness of countries to enter arrangements that allow them to gain even if other nations also gain in equivalent ways. Moreover, it relies on institutions to help establish rules of conduct, encourage trust and collaboration, provide openness, and elevate negotiations over coercion as a prevailing norm. This end game proposes to take advantage of these features, and to expand upon the scope for cooperation as its institutions gain credibility. It aims to achieve whatever can be attained at limited cost. It offers no illusions of producing strategic utopia outside the West's enlarged borders, but it does offer hope of creating a sufficiently stable setting so that the dangers to the West are minimized.

Institutional Vehicles

This end game employs two types of institutions: security and economic. Security institutions would offer Russia close ties to NATO through such steps as a security treaty with it, the 16+1 format, regular attendance at NATO summit meetings and ministerial sessions, bilateral talks with NATO's leaders, the NACC, and collaboration in such crisis-management forums as the Balkan Contact Group. It also would use the Partnership for Peace to develop cooperative military relations with Russia in a variety of areas, including peacekeeping operations. Another institutional forum for reaching out to Russia is arms-control negotiations, including CFE, START, and related talks. Finally, this end game envisions a gradual if modest expansion of OSCE's functions so that Russia gains a measure of the stronger collective-security framework that it seeks.

In the economic realm, this end game proposes steady bilateral and multilateral ties aimed at helping Russia build market democracy, including continuing aid from the IMF and other international assistance bodies, and eventual membership for Russia in such key bodies as the G-7, the WTO, and any regional trade organizations that might be established in the coming years. This end game envisions a similar institutional mix for other countries, albeit treating them as less important and deserving of attention than Russia.

Feasibility

The strength of this end game lies in its affordability and feasibility. It provides a clear sense of its game plan and policy instruments to be employed. Many of its institutions already exist or can be readily created, and they appear to be able to perform their tasks and to work together. Their efforts are likely to produce beneficial results, provided the recipients are willing to take advantage of the limited ties the West offers them. This end game thus offers a favorable cost/benefit ratio, few risks of overentanglement, and the possibility of major returns if events go well.

Desirability

The big question about this end game is whether it passes the test of desirability. Will the benefits achieved be enough to satisfy the West's primary objectives? Or will the institutional web merely have a marginal effect on an otherwise turbulent situation? These questions are hard to answer because the institutional web suffers from a major flaw: It offers no well-elaborated theory of how and why it would promote a stable regional system. It says nothing about the underlying geopolitics of the region. *In essence, it offers a program in search of a strategic concept.*

Because this end game is not anchored in a strategic concept, the task of gauging the nature and combined effectiveness of its operations is rendered difficult. As acknowledged by its own rationale, the individual strands of the institutional web will have limited powers. NATO membership will give powerful defense commitments to the Visegrad Four. But although PFP will allow the West to develop cooperative military relationships with other countries, it will not render them secure. Nor will OSCE provide guaranteed security. Barring success by arms-control negotiations in fashioning major disarmament—an unlikely outcome—the problem of security anarchy and military imbalance will remain.

This end game's economic institutions may help promote market capitalism and restored prosperity, but the effects will be constrained by the limited resources made available by the West. Major success for this end game would ride on the hope that modest efforts in each domain will work together synergistically: that the whole will be greater than the sum of its parts. However, the causal mechanisms are unclear. If synergy is not achieved, the outcome could be marginal in each area. If so, the future will be shaped primarily by events occurring outside the institutional web, not within it.

The West and Russia

A major issue is the extent to which this end game will allow the West to achieve its objectives for Russia. This end game's theory, that establishing an institutionalized dialogue with Russia will help achieve better relations with that country and influence it to accept Western enlargement, is correct in that the act of giving Russia formal, high-level links to NATO and other Western institutions will help confirm its status as a European power and allow it to regularly express its views *as* Western decisions are being made, not afterwards.

Yet, the existence of permanent communications channels can count for little if the policy gaps are too wide to be bridged. A core issue affecting enlargement is that Russia is now contesting the transformation of Eastern Europe from a neutral zone into a region permanently bonded to the Western community. Russia's position is that this transformation violates its legitimate interests and would not benefit European security. Any change of heart will occur for substantive reasons—Russia's acceptance of the new geopolitical order—not because it is given the status of being allowed to voice its concerns about the transformation.

In the final analysis, the key is whether Russia emerges as a satisfied country. If it does not, the institutional web will matter little or will be broken down by destructive political forces.

The West and Other Countries

A different calculus applies to other countries remaining outside the Western community, but the implications for the institutional web are the same. Ukraine is an important example. Key is whether the institutional web provides Ukraine with the security assurances and economic support it needs to survive as an independent country, not one subservient to Russia. As matters now stand, the security assurances being offered Ukraine by PFP, other relationships with NATO, and OSCE membership do not seem strong. Although Ukraine has been given assurances that its borders are regarded as inviolate, none of the West's measures offers it formal collective-defense guarantees; it has no more than the right to diplomatic consultation with the West if it is menaced. Ukraine's economic relationship with the EU is growing only slowly under present policies. The overall outcome will be determined by whether the West establishes a strong strategic relationship with Ukraine, not by the institutional web existing today. In the years ahead, although this web may grow stronger, the West must have goals for Ukraine and be willing to forge the relationship needed to realize those goals. What applies to Ukraine also applies to the Baltic states and East European countries that remain outside the Western community.

The Other CIS Countries

As for the remainder of the CIS, the West's institutional web could be of minor importance because it does not provide a powerful framework for ordering Eurasia's strategic affairs. The future will be determined by whether the CIS countries survive and by the nature of their relations with Russia and with each other. If reintegration gathers momentum, at issue will be the nature of the new security and economic arrangements taking shape on CIS soil. The institutional web may allow the West to influence somewhat the goals, norms, and rules taking shape within the CIS. But absent Western involvement on behalf of a Eurasian structure that can be embraced by the CIS members, the web will not give the West great power to shape the outcome. It may influence how Russia conducts itself within the CIS, but it is unlikely to be a determining factor if Russia perceives powerful strategic incentives to behave in ways contrary to Western preferences.

Summary

In summary, the institutional web offers the West useful avenues to, procedures for, and ways of influencing strategic affairs outside its enlarged borders. But if it is given only modest resources, it will not provide the West with a highly powerful instrument for putting its own imprint on strategic affairs there. Its utility will depend not only on resources but also on the strategic goals being sought by the West, and by the vigor with which those goals are pursued.

A stand-alone end game requires a strategic theory to animate its activities. To the extent that the web is animated by a strategic theory capable of being realized and of maintaining stability in the aftermath, its contribution to managing the new geopolitics will be enhanced. To the extent that it is not, the web will be directionless, and it will have only a marginal effect because it lacks a strategic vision and the power to achieve a more stable and integrated outcome.

OPEN-DOOR ENLARGEMENT

Theory

In this end game, core strategic issues would be grappled with in a bold way. In a second-stage expansion, the West would enlarge farther than the Visegrad Four states, extending membership to several other countries, including the Baltic states and Ukraine. The rationale is that the Baltic states belong in the Western fold because they are European countries and that Ukraine should be admitted because its survival is a vital interest to the West. The Baltic states and Ukraine probably would join NATO and the EU a few years after the Visegrad Four join.

This end game would keep the door open to further enlargement, including the possibility that Russia could eventually join, but as a distant endeavor that at best will happen some years after stage 2. In the interim, it would aim for constructive relations with Russia and would support the spread of market democracy across Eurasia. However, it calls for Eurasia's interstate relations to remain geopolitically plural, asserting that the West's gradually expanding bodies—the EU and NATO—should be the vehicle for bringing integration to Eurasia—not the CIS.

This end game's theory of strategic stability reflects a distinct view of how to handle emerging geopolitical realities. The second-stage enlargement would benefit the countries involved as well as producing a larger zone of security and democracy around Eastern Europe than would come from admitting only the Visegrad Four. The underwriting of Ukraine's independence is especially critical to this goal, and to the larger purpose of producing a peaceful Europe. Keeping Eurasia pluralistic by discouraging CIS reintegration not only opens the region to a phased Western enlargement but also inhibits any organized bloc from emerging that might menace the enlarging West.

Whereas the first three end games endeavor to solve the Russia problem by giving Russia a substantial stake in the new strategic order for East Central Europe, this end game offers Russia a smaller immediate stake and partly proposes to solve the problem by rendering Russia less able to contest the new order. In this end game, Russia eventually would achieve market democracy and join the West; however, by drawing Ukraine into the West's orbit and keeping the CIS pluralistic, it takes out insurance against the risk that Russia may evolve differently.

The attraction of this end game is that enlargement is broader than the Visegrad Four. Its drawbacks are reflected in four key questions: Will the West be prepared to take the controversial steps of absorbing Ukraine and the Baltic states? Will relations with Russia remain stable if enlargement goes beyond the Visegrad Four? Is the idea of preserving a pluralist Eurasia for many years a contribution to stability? Is Eurasia's regional structure likely to produce a stable system? To the extent that the answers are different from those postulated by its theory, the consequences of this end game require careful appraisal.

Institutional Vehicles

Before this end game can be evaluated, we must elaborate on its theoretical components. The idea that enlargement should be limited to the Visegrad Four implies that NATO will be an exclusive club with somewhat larger, but still-closed, membership. This end game adopts a broader vision: that the doors should be open to *any* Continental nation that can demonstrate its democratic credentials and contribute to the common good, but that enlargement beyond the Visegrad Four nonetheless should be cautious and pragmatic.

Additional countries invited to join must fit into the West's scheme of strategic priorities, have stable relations with their neighbors, and meet many other political and economic criteria normally used as the basis for judging applications to the EU and NATO. Therefore, while it favors only the Baltic states and Ukraine, it might also admit Romania and Bulgaria, but without enthusiasm about their candidacy unless they fully adopt Western values.

This end game seeks strategic flexibility in dealing with Russia and the remainder of the CIS by either admitting them into the fold at a later stage or keeping them out while forestalling any threat to the West. It deems Russia an uncertain practitioner of market democracy for many years, and a questionable member of the EU and NATO in any event, for the following reasons: Russia's huge size and precarious economic condition make near-term membership in the EU improbable; Russia has no need of military protection from NATO and likely will not want to commit itself to defend NATO's members; and NATO will not be likely to be willing to extend collective-defense guarantees to Russia's borders—including its Siberian and Far Eastern borders.

Hence, in this end game, Russia will remain outside the Western club for many years, as will the other CIS countries, because the Caucasus and Central Asian states are too far removed from Europe geographically, strategically, and economically to be likely candidates for admission. This end game concedes that Belarus likely will draw close to Russia, but it endeavors to keep the Caucasus and Central Asia out of Russia's orbit. *A core goal is to prevent Russia from reacquiring the allies, resources, and territory that could allow it to conduct major opposition to Western enlargement.*

To a degree, then, this end game adopts a Janus-faced stance toward Russia and Eurasia. Its theory of how to produce a stable regional security system for stage 2 enlargement is based on a combination of a well-buffered Eastern Europe, a Ukraine that is secure because it is a member of the West, a Russia that is isolated and deprived of allies or subordinates, and a Eurasia that is composed of many states that are largely separate from each other. In theory, this regional system could change in stage 3 and beyond as more countries, including Russia, are brought into the Western fold. But if these countries fail to make the transition to market democracy and constructive relations with the West, the regional system presumably would retain its stage 2 character in perpetuity.

Preliminary Evaluation: Desirability and Feasibility

How can this end game be evaluated? The answer is that it defines enlargement in more-ambitious terms than are being considered in many quarters today, and it would call upon the West to invest considerably greater resources in the endeavor. Rather than admit four nations into NATO, it would admit up to eight or ten new countries in the coming years, and it would have the Western community enter into the CIS. It passes the tests of offering a clear portrayal of the geopolitical future, a coherent strategic theory, and a broad game plan for implementation. The larger issue is whether it is feasible and desirable. The proper judgment is that it meets both criteria— only if its underlying assumptions prove valid. We examine these assumptions next.

Assumption: Baltic States and Ukraine Want NATO Membership

One of this end game's key assumptions is that the Baltic states and Ukraine will want membership in NATO. At the moment, the Baltic states seem eager to join, and Ukraine, potentially so. But by joining, they will take on heavy responsibilities, and they may run the risk of engendering troubled relations with Russia. Will the Baltic states and Ukraine be willing to commit to defending all of NATO's other members and to accepting the impingements on their sovereignty that alliance membership will require? Will they judge the gains in additional security worth the costs if Russia is offended? If their relations with Russia lie in the gray area—neither warm nor cold— will they be willing to risk a worsening in order to gain NATO security assurances of defending them against this outcome? To the extent they feel nervous in addressing these questions, their enthusiasm for NATO may weaken.

An equally important question is whether NATO is willing to extend Article 5 guarantees of collective defense to them. If NATO is willing to extend its security perimeter this far, will it be physically able to carry out the necessary military commitments? Defending the

Visegrad Four is a viable proposition because of those states' proximity to Western Europe; protecting the Baltic states and Ukraine would be harder. The entrance of the Visegrad Four into NATO may reduce the difficulty of projecting power to the Baltic states and Ukraine, but NATO forces would be required to travel fully 1,000–1,500 kilometers from their bases in Western Europe in a crisis. The problem could be eased by basing NATO forces in these countries, but the budget cost would be high and the provocation to Russia could be considerable. Even with such basing, NATO forces would be required to accept demanding new security missions in the immediate shadow of Russian military power.

If the consequence is potential trouble with Russia, NATO might balk at the proposition; even the invitees might have second thoughts if their security can be preserved through less-demonstrative measures. If sour relations with Russia are a foregone conclusion, the Baltic states and Ukraine doubtless would be desperate for NATO membership, but this situation would sharply elevate the costs and difficulties facing the West. In a more tranquil setting, admission to the EU and a PFP-like association with NATO might be more appealing to the Baltic states and Ukraine. For the West, admission of the Baltic states to the EU but not to NATO might be acceptable; Ukraine's entrance to the EU but not to NATO may be a different matter, because the difficulty of backdoor commitments through the WEU could prove formidable. Ukraine's status as a member of the West thus is not easy to resolve.

Assumption: Russia Will Acquiesce to Baltic States and Ukraine Joining the West

The assumption that Russia will either acquiesce to the Baltic states and Ukraine joining the West or lack the power to contest it seems equally fragile. The Russian government has already made clear its opposition toward NATO enlargement into Poland if Russia is kept out of the alliance. It may ultimately acquiesce in this step, because throughout its history, Russia has tolerated the ebbs and flows of its fortunes west of the Bug River. Its stance toward the lands east of the Bug River has been far less flexible. It drove foreigners out of Ukraine in the 1600s and out of the Baltic states in the early 1700s. Since then, a cardinal principle of its strategic policy has been that both the

Baltic states and Ukraine should be in Russia's sphere of influence, if not under its outright control. If it does not foresee a stage 3 Western enlargement as benefiting itself, Russia might well react to stage 2 with deep alarm.

Russia's military doctrine makes clear its aversion to the presence of any hostile military coalition on its borders. Russia might interpret NATO and EU enlargement into the Baltic states and Ukraine as evidence of a hostile coalition being formed, or at least as a serious threat to its right to a zone of security around its borders. One of its geopolitical concerns could be a German-American axis with menacing designs. Another concern could be re-creation of the old Polish-Ukrainian axis of the sixteenth century, which threatened Russia's security: In Russia's eyes, a new Polish-Ukrainian axis could enjoy the backing of NATO military power and EU economic strength.

At a minimum, the combination of Western enlargement into the Baltic states and Ukraine, coupled with efforts to deny Russia control over the remainder of the CIS, could raise the prospect of Russia becoming isolated on the Eurasian landmass. If Russia's reaction is hostile, its capability to resist would depend on its strategic power. Perhaps it might lack the strength to mount a countervailing effort. But if Russia rejuvenates only partly in the coming years, the West could, at a minimum, find itself facing a stiff contest over control of lands that are far from its own power center and within easy reach of Russia's military forces.

If Western enlargement into the Baltic states and Ukraine were to occur in a hostile atmosphere, this step almost inevitably would trigger a strong Russian effort to reintegrate the remainder of the CIS and to create a military alliance. If it were to succeed, the West's goal of keeping Eurasia pluralist might go up in smoke. At a minimum, the region could be cast into a lengthy period of stressful interstate politics between Russia and the West that could have larger negative consequences. Indeed, if the West succeeded in keeping Eurasia pluralist, the question becomes, Would this outcome itself be stabilizing? A pluralist Eurasia might become a hotbed of local chaos that could bring about the strife, violence, and Russian interventionist activities that Western policy seeks to prevent.

Core Issues

The core issues are whether the West is prepared to admit the Baltic states and Ukraine, and whether stage 2 would be followed by a stage 3. To the extent that a stage 3 is not in the cards, this end game runs the risk of taking Russia's geopolitical interests and power too lightly. Enduring stability normally requires a balancing of interests based on a shared theory of legitimacy. The risk is that Russia may see this end game as tilting the geopolitical balance too far against it and as not being legitimate. A related concern is that, in its quest to keep Eurasia pluralist, this end game may try to squelch positive forms of reintegration that could prove healthy. If so, this end game leaves the CIS countries no viable alternative but to pursue integration on their own, under Russia's leadership.

Summary

In the final analysis, the concept of fashioning an interim regional order based on an ever-enlarging West, an isolated Russia, and a pluralist Eurasia seems plausible if Russia emerges as a democracy that places its strategic trust in the West, wants to join Western institutions, and is confident of its eventual admission into them. If Russia emerges as a country with paranoid reactions or even traditional geopolitical imperatives, this concept could fall apart, or at least place dangerous burdens on the West.

The consequence of enlargement beyond the Visegrad Four could be the opposite of what this end game seeks: not an acquiescent Russia and a pluralist Eurasia but a hostile Russia and a reintegrated Eurasia in the form of a new military bloc willing to engage the West in a struggle for control of Ukraine, and possibly the Baltic states as well. The key issue, therefore, is whether this end game's assumptions are vulnerable to being overthrown by real-world events.

THE TWO-COMMUNITY SOLUTION

The two-community solution grapples with core geopolitical issues, but quite differently than open-door enlargement. It would enlarge the EU and NATO only into Eastern Europe, offer membership to the Visegrad Four in the near term, and might eventually admit Romania and Bulgaria. It might bring the Baltic states into the EU, yet not into NATO. But it would deny any intent to enlarge into the CIS and Eurasia. It would seek close relations with Ukraine; however, it would not make this country a full-fledged member of either the EU or NATO. Nor would it make any pretense of eventually including Russia or other CIS countries in these two Western bodies. It would seek constructive relations with Russia and a stable Eurasian order through an entirely different mechanism from that pursued by open-ended enlargement. It would support the idea of a separate community of nations emerging on CIS soil. Thus, it would endorse—not oppose—certain forms of CIS reintegration: the kind that would make the CIS a genuine body of independent countries that work together democratically on behalf of the common good, and in ways that do not threaten the West.

Theory

Its theory of achieving a stable overall regional order is that an enlarged West and a properly reintegrated CIS would aspire to build normal neighborly relations in the manner of two separate but cooperative communities living side by side.

Similar to open-door enlargement, this end game offers a clear portrayal of the future regional system, a plausible theory of stability, and a game plan that can be implemented. If its policy is successfully pursued and the consequences are as advertised, the outcome could be a future in which a limited Western enlargement is carried out amid a stable regional security system and constructive relations with Russia. Yet it, too, is based on assumptions about how the future can be influenced. If these assumptions are flawed, the end game itself must be scrutinized carefully before it is adopted as policy.

Basic Assumptions

The two-community solution can be criticized for being less visionary than open-door enlargement about propagating Western values. Its distinguishing feature is its pragmatic acceptance of geopolitical realities. Its philosophical premises are fivefold:

- Owing to geostrategic priorities and resource constraints, the West is going to pursue enlargement only in limited ways.

- Irreversibly, two separate strategic clusters are going to evolve: an enlarged West that absorbs Eastern Europe, and a Eurasian cluster embracing different political and economic values from the West.

- Russia inevitably will emerge as the leader of this Eurasian cluster. If the West aspires to have stable relations with Russia, it must craft a policy that acknowledges this reality without issuing Russia a blank check to engage in illicit conduct.

- Some reintegration will take place in Eurasia. Only the nature of this reintegration is in question.

- The key to regional stability lies in ensuring that these separate strategic clusters achieve normal relations rather than sliding into rivalry with each other.

Priorities

The two-community solution's highest priority is to admit the Visegrad Four into the EU and NATO while avoiding high additional expenses for endeavors outside the new boundaries of both institutions. Yet its budgetary costs are uncertain. The key variable would be the West's willingness to support Eurasian integration with concrete resources. The cost could be greater than that of the institutional web, but probably would be less than that of open-door enlargement if primary financial responsibility is delegated to the CIS countries. The success of the endeavor nonetheless would depend partly on the level of Western resources committed (i.e., technical advice, assistance, and some financial support), but the outcome would be determined mostly by the CIS countries themselves.

Institutional Vehicles

This end game's approach to Eurasia calls for using Western Europe's gradualist experience in building community as a model for guiding reintegration of the CIS. Western Europe built slowly, from the ground up. In contemplating this model for Eurasia, the two-community solution opposes any imposition of a hierarchical federal model on the CIS, or even premature forms of confederation. What it would support is a gradual growth of the CIS's functional activities in areas that could help bring about stable government, economic recovery, and market democracy on CIS soil. It thus would allow for Russian leadership of the CIS, but only the kind of leadership that points toward creation of a truly democratic community, not a coercive power bloc led by Moscow and aimed at subordinating the identities of the CIS powers or contesting the West for geopolitical influence in East Central Europe.

This end game's model for achieving stable relations between Europe and Eurasia has several features. It would not aim to exclude Russia from Europe or to divest the Western community of responsibility for influencing Eurasian affairs. Under it, Russia and other CIS countries would continue to have membership in transcontinental institutions (e.g., OSCE) and would establish growing relations with NATO, the EU, and other Western bodies. The United States and Europe, in turn, would be granted the right to insist on proper codes of conduct and peaceful interstate relations within the Eurasian cluster.

In this end game, the appearance of divisive geopolitical lines would be avoided by having Poland, the Baltic states, Ukraine, Romania, and Bulgaria function as interlocking bridges between Europe and Eurasia. These seven countries would establish close ties with both communities and carry out normal diplomatic and commercial relations with them. Ukraine's status would be key, for although it might be regarded as a member of the Eurasian community in important ways, it would draw close to Europe in significant respects. Poland would do the same by conducting close relations with Ukraine, Belarus, and Russia. The borders between the two communities thus would be blurred, not distinct.

Economic Relations

Economic relations between the two communities would reflect present-day realities, coupled with a commitment to progress and cooperation in the future as the scope for collaboration gradually builds. For the near term, this end game assumes that Europe and

Eurasia will be operating on the basis of very different economic models. While Europe will be dominated by wealthy market economies, Eurasia will be dominated by less-wealthy countries undertaking the transition to market mechanisms. This situation will influence the extent to which common policies and full-scale commercial relations between them can be established. The long-term goal, however, would be to avoid the emergence of rival economic blocs and exclusionary zones. As a result, the Eurasian community would be allowed to enter the world economy as its market mechanisms and competitive capabilities develop. The EU would establish growing economic ties with Russia and its CIS neighbors. As the situation allows, open trade relationships between Europe and Eurasia would be established, and investments would flow back and forth. The guiding model would be to establish healthy economic relations between two different communities that are increasingly interdependent.

Political and Security Relations

Political and security relations would reflect the same model of normal neighborly relations. The two communities would work with each other, and with the United States and other world leaders, to carry out multilateral policies in such areas as peacekeeping, regional crisis management, and nonproliferation. They would endeavor to develop common diplomacy in key regions, including the Balkans, the Middle East/Persian Gulf, South Asia, and Asia. On the European continent, their security affairs would be coordinated to ensure that geopolitical rivalry does not emerge between them. The two communities would retain responsibility for their own security policies and defense strategies, but their actions would be guided by arms-control negotiations and stability-enhancing policies. The guiding concept thus would be two communities that provide for their common defense but do not menace each other. They would work together to ensure that the borders between them are peaceful and are not marked by large force deployments or other preparatory activities that could give rise to mutual suspicion and a competitive action-reaction cycle.

Desirability

If its vision can be created, this end game serves the West's core objectives at least minimally well. It allows for a vigorous enlargement into Eastern Europe. While its Eurasian policy is limited, its vision of a constructively integrated CIS led by Russia is more attractive than that of an anarchical region left vulnerable to chronic turmoil or a new Russian empire. An appraisal of this end game's desirability therefore hinges on the judgment of whether a better outcome in Eurasia can be achieved with a different approach. Could the West achieve something more satisfactory by embracing more-ambitious objectives? Would it be willing to pay the price of pursuing these objectives? If the West adopts the two-community solution, is it playing with fire by endorsing reintegration of any sort? Conversely, would a more intrusive Eurasian policy be likely to produce a better outcome, or would it squander resources and risk backfiring? The answers to these questions will affect how the two-community solution is judged in relation to the alternatives.

Feasibility

If the West adopts this end game, will the consequences be as advertised? The answer is that this end game's feasibility depends on the willingness of the major players—the West and Russia—to carry it out. For the West, the demands imposed by enlarging into Eastern Europe alone will be substantial. As a result, the West might lack the willpower and resources to carry out the Eurasian component of this end game.

One of this end game's critical features is its handling of Ukraine. Its concept is that Ukraine should not be a neutral state but, instead, a country that serves as the main bridge between the two communities. But will Ukraine evolve this way if the two-community solution is pursued? The West would run the risk that, by ruling out Ukrainian membership in the EU and NATO, it might push this country into Russia's camp. The risk would be all the greater if a Eurasian community takes shape that provides an acceptable home for Ukraine.

To avoid this outcome, the West likely would be compelled to pursue a vigorous outreach program to Ukraine in both economics and security affairs. De facto, Ukraine might gain the benefits of Western membership, even if it does not formally belong to the EU and NATO. Other, more comprehensive remedies to the Ukraine dilemma can also be contemplated. For example, Ukraine might establish a security relationship with the West and an economic relationship with the CIS, or vice versa. A more satisfactory model might be a Ukraine that enjoys strong associate membership status in both Western bodies and in the CIS—an arrangement that would give Ukraine an active voice in the West and in the CIS, and reassurances from both communities, without having its relationships with one become the cause of distancing from the other. In theory, this approach could work. The issue is whether the theory will be put into practice.

The feasibility of the two-community solution also depends on whether its model of a limited reintegration of Eurasia can work. Eurasia is not Europe. The major differences between the two define the barriers to grafting the European Community onto Eurasia in any literal sense. At a minimum, Eurasia would have to find its own way to build this reintegration model, and the outcome could be quite different from what has evolved in Europe.

The idea of pursuing this end game, however, is hardly beyond the pale. The Russian government lately is talking in these terms. While most other CIS countries shy away from all overarching concepts for the CIS, they have begun cooperating with Russia and their neighbors in specific functional areas. Their behavior suggests that if they come to endorse any end game, it likely will be this one—not something more ambitious.

For the West, the key issue is whether its own interests and the larger cause of a stable Continent are best served by an anarchical CIS region left to its own devices or by an approach that accepts reintegration as a probable dynamic and tries to channel it in healthy directions. The impending risk is that even a gradualist model of reintegration, once brought to life, could evolve into a Frankenstein's monster. Such an evolution could occur if Russia takes advantage of the opportunity to bypass the incrementalist approach in order to erect a hierarchy under its control. In the worst case, the outcome could be a new security bloc under Russian control, dedicated to menacing the West and contesting enlargement into Eastern Europe. Yet the dangers of this outcome already exist, and the risks may be greater in the current setting of anarchical instability than in a setting in which formal guidelines for reintegration have been established.

Summary

One of the best ways to ensure a cooperative Russia may be to embed it in a multilateral framework in which collaboration is the norm. This judgment lies at the basis of ideas to bring Russia into Western institutions. But if Russia is not to be allowed into the EU and NATO, a properly integrated CIS may be the best alternative. Indeed, it may be the *only* alternative, because an anarchical and unstable Eurasia is an open invitation to a unilateralist and coercive Russia. Moreover, if the West chooses to participate in a healthy form of CIS reintegration, it may have greater leverage for opposing unhealthy departures. Even so, this end game opens the door to a Russian-led reintegration without offering guarantees that events would unfold in the manner contemplated by it.

The bottom line is that the two-community solution is based on a set of assumptions that must be proven valid for this end game to make sense. Its chief attraction is its realism; its main liability is that Eurasian reintegration may take a wrong turn. It represents a less-inexpensive fallback position if more-ambitious end games are deemed too expensive, or too dangerous, or too unlikely to succeed.

POLICY IMPLICATIONS

Need to Plan Now

The central implication of this analysis is that the enlarging West has a broad spectrum of plausible end games for dealing with Russia, East Central Europe, and Eurasia. Which one it chooses will depend heavily on the West's priorities, resources, and judgments. The task of choosing is rendered complex because the West is uncertain about the future, the requirements being faced, and the consequences of its own actions. Typically, governments faced with uncertainty prefer to postpone decisions about final strategic plans. Often, they select policy actions that make sense for a variety of strategic theories, test the waters as they go, and wait until the future is better defined before making firm commitments.

This practice may be followed in the enlargement arena, but the West cannot delay indefinitely the task of sorting out its thinking on strategic end games. The Visegrad Four may well be joining NATO by the end of this decade, and they may join the EU a few years later. When they do, the West will acquire commitments to them and will be involved in their geopolitical setting. The West, therefore, is best advised to have a clear strategic end game by then that specifies how it plans to shape the surrounding regional security system.

End-Game Trade-Offs

Each of the end games surveyed here will require the West to set different objectives and to take different actions. Because of such differences and because its own resources are constrained, the West cannot hope to pursue all of these end games at once. The single-community solution implies that enlargement into Eastern Europe should be a small part of a much larger endeavor aimed at bonding Europe and Eurasia. If the West adopts this end game, it should focus its efforts on creating the comprehensive, transcontinental governing body needed to carry out this design. If the West embraces collective security, it should lower its horizons by focusing on regional security management, and it should focus on building a more powerful successor to the OSCE. If the West chooses the institutional web, it should plan on enlarging only into Eastern Europe; its efforts to fashion stability outside this zone should focus on several institutional endeavors, each with a limited charter. If the West chooses open-door enlargement, it should plan on enlarging further as its device to achieve regional stability. If it embraces the two-community solution, it should discount plans for additional enlargement and focus on measures to achieve a constructively reintegrated CIS and Eurasia.

If this analysis is correct, the single-community solution embraces an ideal outcome, but its total lack of feasibility disqualifies it as a serious strategic end game that would justify the efforts needed to bring it about or the sacrifices that would have to be made elsewhere. Collective security is realistic in its issues and goals, but it does not seem sufficiently comprehensive to qualify as a stand-alone end game. It will suffice only if the regional security system is already stability-prone, but not if there is potential for instability.

The institutional web is the end game most likely to be pursued. It is a viable, low-cost approach and is aimed at remedying a variety of problems that need addressing. Its drawback is that it may fail to address basic geopolitical issues brought about by enlargement and other dynamics. If so, the West may be put in the position of deciding between open-door enlargement and the two-community solution.

Open-door enlargement makes sense if the West is truly prepared to enlarge into Eurasia and if the effort seems likely to produce stable relations with Russia. The two-community solution is a viable alternative if the West either does not want to enlarge farther eastward or if enlarging farther eastward will produce unmanageable troubles with Russia.

If either open-door enlargement or the two-community solution is adopted, each can be combined with appropriate elements of the institutional web. For open-door enlargement, the institutional web can be used to establish relations with Russia and other CIS countries that do not gain admission in stage 2 of enlargement. For the two-community solution, the institutional web can be used to establish outreach programs aimed at encouraging constructive CIS reintegration and at creating friendly relations between Europe and Eurasia in reintegration's aftermath. In theory, the combination of the institutional web and one of these two end games could provide the West with a powerful strategic policy for coping with the geopolitical fundamentals ahead and for steering the regional security system toward stability. A key to the choice between these two end games—and to the success of both—will be Ukraine's status. Regardless of the end game selected, success can be achieved only if the West devotes effort to carrying out that end game. Much will depend upon the willpower, resources, and expertise of Western policy.

The Russia Factor

In the final analysis, the task of choosing a strategic end game will be heavily influenced by the approach adopted for how best to deal with Russia, its statist foreign policy, and its emerging disgruntlement with Western enlargement. The best way to placate Russia is not to enlarge at all. However, enlargement will occur to pursue Western interests, so Russia's stance will be shaped by basic geopolitical imperatives. Accordingly, if the West is to embrace open-door enlargement into Eurasia, it likely will need either to include Russia or to be prepared for enduring security troubles with Russia. If the two-community solution is adopted, the task of dealing with Russia will be eased, but the West will face the challenge of ensuring that reintegration does not lead to the wrong kind of reunited Eurasia. Nonetheless, Russia has a compelling interest in reaching a strategic outcome with the West, which provides reason for hope that a sensible strategic end game can be pursued and can provide a satisfactory role for Russia and a successful outcome. Enlargement thus can be embedded in a stable regional security system. The trick will be to fashion a proper strategic end game, then to implement it.

Chapter Eight

MILITARY END GAMES FOR ENLARGEMENT

The public attention that is now focused on the politics of Western enlargement will soon need to widen to include military affairs as well. Over the coming years, enlargement will interact with regional dynamics to produce a new military regime in East Central Europe. This new military regime will be more than a reflection of politics and diplomacy, however. It will become an independent variable likely to influence the emerging geopolitics of East Central Europe, including the manner in which NATO enlarges and relations form with Russia. How these military affairs evolve can either promote a satisfactory outcome or undermine it. The challenge facing the West will be to encourage the former and avoid the latter.

To meet this challenge, the central task facing the West is threefold:

- The West will need to craft the military aspects of enlargement so that security commitments to new NATO members can be carried out in a fashion that is affordable, promotes alliance cohesion, and brings about a well-conceived defense strategy.

- The West will need to act in a restrained manner and engage in strategic cooperation with Russia to ensure that offensive threats are not posed and that a competitive action-reaction cycle is avoided.

- The West will need to work with East Central Europe's numerous states—including those remaining outside NATO—to ensure that their military postures are adequately strong, but are defensive and contribute to regional stability.

Once again, the West will be pursuing multiple objectives that can pull policy in different directions, so the details will be crucial. Careful planning will be needed to ensure that these details are handled properly.

This situation mandates the forging of a military end game: a destination for emerging military affairs that is coordinated with the West's strategic end game. The act of designing a military end game will be carried out in three arenas:

- NATO's interaction with new members to shape common defense arrangements, including military strategy, forces, programmatic measures, and command structures

- Force modernization and weapon sales, which will involve not only countries joining NATO but other nations as well, including Russia

- Arms control, which will involve Western negotiations with Russia and other countries.

The complex task facing the West is to shape sensible policies in all three arenas that work together to bring about a well-conceived military end game.

The purpose of this chapter is to address the challenges and requirements confronting the West as it goes about trying to fashion a coherent military end game. To focus the analysis, this chapter assumes that NATO, not another institution, will be the West's primary vehicle for carrying out new security commitments. It further assumes that the Visegrad Four will join NATO within five years and that enlargement will not proceed further. If a different enlargement pattern emerges because fewer or more members join NATO, the details will change. But the underlying concepts are likely to remain constant. The analysis begins by discussing each of the three military policy arenas separately. At the conclusion, it views these arenas together: Coordinating their activities will be key if a sound overall military end game is to be fashioned.

SHAPING NATO'S NEW DEFENSE ARRANGEMENTS IN EAST CENTRAL EUROPE

Analysis can best begin by recognizing that the act of admitting new members to NATO is a truly strategic undertaking. Although the primary purpose of NATO enlargement into East Central Europe is not to erect a new military bloc, or to counterbalance a virulent threat, or to wage a new Cold War, NATO, nonetheless, remains a collective-defense alliance. Wherever NATO goes, a security agenda of some sort follows. Because East Central Europe has potential dangers, senior NATO military officials are likely to conclude that the worst outcome is a hollow military commitment: New members enter the alliance, but appropriate steps are not taken to fashion the military arrangements needed to meet their defense requirements. This is the starting point for putting NATO enlargement in proper military perspective.[1]

NATO will be seeking a confident sense of overall military security amid an unknowable future. Therefore, it will probably prefer to anchor defense planning not on specific threats but on future military capabilities and generic contingencies: classes of conflicts, from small to large, that could arise in different ways. Russia, because of its powerful military posture, will be one concern, but other concerns will matter as well, most of them embodying modest military requirements. Because most potential new members do not regard their own forces as adequate to the task, they will turn to NATO to provide military help. Owing to Article 5—the NATO Treaty's collective-defense clause—the alliance will be obligated to respond. Consequently, the forces of NATO and of new members will be drawing closer together to learn how to carry out new missions and combined military operations in Europe and elsewhere.[2]

---

[1]See Michael Dobbs, "Enthusiasm for Wider Alliance Is Marked by Contradictions," *Washington Post*, July 7, 1995.

[2]For a conceptual framework, see Ronald D. Asmus, Richard L. Kugler, and F. Stephen Larrabee, "NATO Expansion: The Next Steps," *Survival*, Spring 1995.

A Range of Missions Performed Together

In scope and the degree to which security operations are involved, the missions ahead will cover the gamut. At the low end will be peacekeeping and peacemaking, as well as specialized missions: border patrol, immigration control, disaster relief, hostage rescue, and counterterrorism. Combined military capabilities also will be required for local emergencies and management of various crises. NATO also will need to be prepared for minor and major regional conflicts, not only in the Visegrad Four but in other regions outside Europe to which NATO forces might be sent (e.g., the Persian Gulf). A final requirement will be the defense of new-member borders in situations where national forces are not up to the task. Unlike during the Cold War, the Article 5 commitment to border defense likely will be seen as an insurance policy against the unexpected rather than the centerpiece of NATO defense policy. Nonetheless, it will remain the ultimate *raison d'être* of alliance coalition planning and will play a role in determining defense activities by all countries. The implication of these diverse missions is that the forces of NATO and new members will need to learn how to perform many types of military operations *together*. Noncombat operations will be part of the task, but these forces also will be learning how to wage war by fighting alongside each other.

The coming military agenda likely will not necessitate any earth-shaking upheaval in NATO's defense plans. For the most part, the required forces already exist; the task is to prepare them for the new era. NATO therefore can approach this agenda knowing that its resources will not be overwhelmed and that the required measures need not pose a threat to Russia or any other country. Nonetheless, this agenda is not trivial. The forces of NATO and East Central Europe have Cold War heritages and, prior to PFP, have never worked together. Important changes will be required so that coalition operations can be conducted with adequate strength and effectiveness. As a result, a comprehensive defense program must be fashioned and will be *evolutionary:* carried out over a period of a decade or more. But it will embody a wide range of activities, and it will alter the military terrain in East Central Europe.

To carry out an adequate defense program, a large number of nations will have to participate, work together, and share the burdens fairly. As discussed below, the budgetary cost will be a variable that depends on the measures adopted. Provided that prudent goals are set, the effort should be affordable. NATO's nations in Central Europe are spending $110 billion annually on defense. Even if the U.S. defense budget is discounted, NATO will be spending about $1.5 trillion over the coming decade. A program of enlargement measures could be funded with only a modest diversion of these resources, but it could necessitate some scalebacks in lower-priority programs. NATO has pursued 10-year programs before: AD-70 (Alliance Defense for the 1970s), the Long-Term Defense Plan (LTDP), and the Conventional Defense Initiative (CDI), for example. This background provides confidence that enlargement's defense affairs can be handled if the alliance sets its mind to the task.[3]

Changes Required of New Members

What changes will be required of NATO's new members? Until only a few years ago, these countries were members of the Warsaw Pact and their defense ministries operated under Soviet control. Today, defense planning in each country is supervised by civilians and performed by democratic means (i.e., parliamentary scrutiny). Membership in NATO will introduce a further transformation. While retaining its national character, defense planning by new members will take place within the framework of NATO's established multilateral mechanisms. New members will be compelled to adopt the political and managerial model practiced by Western democratic states that work together within a large, well-oiled alliance. Because this model is so vastly different from that of the Warsaw Pact and current practices (as described in Chapter Five), it alone will bring about great changes in the ways that these countries go about their defense business.

The changes ahead in the defense strategies and forces of these states will also be profound. Throughout the Cold War, their forces were designed to support a Soviet-crafted strategy that aimed at posing a *blitzkrieg*-style offensive threat to Western Europe. The Visegrad Four provided about one-third of the 90 divisions and 4,000

---

[3]For supporting analysis, see Jeffrey Simon, ed., *NATO Enlargement: Opinions and Options*, Washington, D.C.: National Defense University, Ft. McNair, 1995.

combat aircraft arrayed against NATO in Central Europe. These forces played a specialized, but important, role in Warsaw Pact strategy and were designed accordingly. This historical legacy is important because the old Soviet/Warsaw Pact military model is so vastly different from the NATO model in many respects.

The most obvious difference lies in basic military strategy. Whereas Warsaw Pact strategy was offensive, NATO strategy was defensive throughout the Cold War, and remains so. Underlying this difference are major dissimilarities in the very fundamentals of military philosophy—differences that reflect not only the distinction between totalitarian and democratic values but also dissimilar geostrategic situations, economic systems, military theories, and historical experiences at waging war. These dissimilarities penetrated to the depths of the force postures on both sides. They resulted in very different combat forces, logistics systems, command structures, weapons, doctrines, training, and operating procedures. Taking everything into account, it is hard to imagine two military alliances so radically different in their approaches to coalitions and warfare.

To operate with NATO forces, the assets of new members must undergo many changes to achieve technical compatibility. For both combat aircraft and ground weapons, technical compatibility will need to be fashioned through multiple measures: common fuels, munitions, nozzles, radio frequencies, etc. New mobilization systems will need to be fashioned. The readiness of several air and ground units may need to be enhanced. NATO safety standards and routinized procedures will have to be adopted. An intensified exercise program with NATO may be needed at all levels. East Central Europe (ECE) military personnel will need to attend NATO schools in large numbers. These changes, however, are only the tip of the iceberg: To produce combat and support formations that can carry out NATO military doctrine, the force structures of new members will need to change.

Development of a Western air traffic control system already is under way, but this effort likely will require expansion to include a new air defense system with different command structures, radars and communications nets, and ground-based missiles. Beyond this, new members may be required to reconfigure their army divisions by reducing artillery and tanks, increasing infantry, and adding more rear-area logistics support units. Their old emphasis on divisions and regiments likely will give way to NATO-style emphasis on brigades and battalions. They likely will need to place less reliance on massed barrages in exchange for greater reliance on precision strikes directed by sophisticated C3I capabilities, and to change their logistics system of unit replacement in favor of NATO's individual replacement system. Their air forces might be obligated to place more emphasis on ground attack missions rather than on air defense, and to acquire better support assets to generate higher sortie rates. They also will need to learn how to use smart munitions—including real-time targeting, onboard computers, lasers, and infrared sensors—for ground-attack operations. These changes point to emergence of East European force postures that are very different from today's.

Also required will be alterations in the military infrastructures of the Visegrad Four. During the Cold War, these countries developed large infrastructures, but their assets were tailored to support the Warsaw Pact and its westward-oriented offensive strategy. Their new infrastructures will need to focus on territorial defense in different directions and on the absorption of reinforcing NATO combat and support assets. In some places, upgrades will be needed because the existing structure is eroded, or poorly configured, or inadequate for new requirements.

For example, the Visegrad Four likely will need to develop new petroleum, oil, and lubricants (POL) distribution systems so that NATO fuels can be available on short notice. They may be required to upgrade their roads, rails, ports, and air bases to meet NATO standards and requirements, to erect new command posts, and to install new telecommunications systems. They may need to procure quantities of ammunition, spare parts, and end-items; to build new reception facilities; to clear new assembly areas; to create new training grounds and firing ranges; and to construct new aircraft shelters and ammunition-storage sheds. Activities in these areas often escape public notice, but they are the heart-and-soul of defense preparedness and coalition membership. The required changes will take place only gradually, but as they occur along the Western model, they will stamp NATO's presence on Eastern Europe, even if U.S. and West European forces are not deployed there.

Changes in NATO's Defense Posture

How will NATO's defense posture need to change? NATO will have little difficulty providing C3I and logistics support to new members, but if it must back up its treaty commitments with combat forces, it will have a constraining legacy of its own to overcome. The United States has long planned for expeditionary missions, but the West European countries still have military postures designed mostly for defense of old Cold War borders. Despite recent downsizing, they maintain large forces. In Central Europe alone, the West Europeans have 27 mobilizable divisions, 1,800 combat aircraft, and 195 major naval ships. Yet only a small portion of these forces are prepared to deploy outside their territory and engage in significant combat operations.

NATO's primary capability is its Rapid Reaction Force (RRF). Logistics constraints limit any single deployment to 4 divisions and 300 aircraft. These forces, moreover, are intended for a wide spectrum of missions and are commonly associated with operations in NATO's southern region. NATO's AFCENT (Allied Forces, Central) command, which might carry out new commitments to the east, has 4 multinational corps under its control, but none is designed for projection missions. NATO's air forces can be prepared for eastern missions with only modest changes, but greater improvements will be required by the ground forces. Most West European divisions can operate away from their homeland, but they will need better mobile logistics assets at the corps and echelons above corps. Also important, a reception infrastructure for NATO forces—bases, assembly areas, and storage depots—will need to be developed on the territory of new members.

The willingness of NATO's members to undertake the necessary measures will depend on political decisions in alliance capitals. The task of carrying out new security commitments in East Central Europe is only one of several strategic missions requiring innovations in NATO's traditional ways of doing business. The alliance faces the challenge of broadening its planning beyond defense of old Cold War borders in several regions, not just Eastern Europe. In addition, NATO faces the task of crafting updated plans for each region and of allocating roles and missions among its members so that critical tasks are performed.

The manner in which East Central Europe is handled will be influenced by this overall allocation. In the past, NATO's strategic missions for different regions have been allocated on the basis of national interests, specialization based on comparative advantage, and a division of labor. If this practice is followed again, the primary responsibility for East Central Europe will be given to Germany, the United States, and Britain—perhaps aided by France and the Low Countries. The pattern of strategic cooperation likely to emerge thus will be composed of this subcoalition working with the new members, both individually and collectively.

That the ECE states might remain outside the integrated command—as is France—appeals to some for political reasons: It might be seen as a reassuring signal to Russia while minimizing disruption to NATO's current structure. However, powerful military incentives may arise for new members to join, not only to gain the benefits of NATO membership but to help empower the alliance to carry out its commitments to them. The real issue may not be whether they join the integrated command, but how new command relationships should be fostered.

A variety of models are available. NATO might elect to use a CJTF to handle ECE defense affairs, but task forces normally do not conduct long-range planning. Alternatively, NATO might create a new command (e.g., an AFEAST), but doing so would complicate a NATO command structure already in need of streamlining. A logical choice would be to rely on AFCENT by extending its zone eastward, which would allow for close coordination between new members and old. If so, a key issue will be whether multinational formations are fashioned in East Central Europe—an approach that would carry forth the current AFCENT practice but that might not be embraced by the Visegrad Four. Such an approach could, unfortunately, signal to the Visegrad Four that a military bloc has been created. The alternative would be to separate ECE forces from each other, thus replicating the AFSOUTH (Allied Forces, South [Europe]) pattern, in which defense planning is conducted largely on a nation-by-nation basis.

Three Different Military Strategies

While command relationships will be part of the military end game, the more important issue is the character of the defense posture to be created. The alternative end games at NATO's disposal can be gauged by analyzing three different military strategies that might be followed: new-member self-defense, power projection, and forward presence.

Under the first strategy, "new-member self-defense," the Visegrad Four would become largely responsible for protecting themselves; NATO would provide C3I and logistics support, but a minimum number of combat forces. Under the second strategy, "power projection," new members would still provide most of the required combat forces, but NATO would be responsible for having powerful combat forces available for prompt deployment in an emergency. The key feature of this strategy is that forces assigned by current NATO members would remain at their present bases in Western Europe. Apart from small-scale deployments to send a reassuring signal and to conduct normal peacetime training, they would not be permanently stationed in East Central Europe in peacetime. Under the third strategy, "forward presence," NATO would again accept major combat missions in East Central Europe. The key difference is that large U.S. and West European forces would be stationed there in peacetime, and they would be able to conduct operational-level (i.e., sizable) combat missions on short notice.

Each of these strategies responds to a unique theory of requirements and reflects a specific set of trade-offs. New-member self-defense provides the least amount of overall military capability, but at the lowest budget cost: Using standard planning tools that take into account acquisition and operations, we estimate that it would take an alliance-wide, 10-year cost of about $15–$20 billion to make ECE forces compatible with NATO forces, to upgrade their infrastructure, and to enable NATO to provide C3I and logistics support. Power projection would provide a medium level of capability through NATO reinforcement. Illustratively, it would cost about $35–$50 billion for improvements to ECE and NATO forces, including the capacity to project NATO forces eastward in a crisis. Forward presence provides the greatest capability, because it stations NATO forces on ECE soil, where they would be available on short notice. Because the costs of permanent stationing are quite high, its expense could rise to $70–$100 billion, depending on the number of forces deployed.

Evaluation of Three Strategies

How can these options be evaluated? The answer will be determined by how NATO decides to balance multiple objectives, including achieving credible Article 5 commitments at affordable cost, a responsive military posture, fair burden-sharing, a coherent theory of roles and missions, a cohesive alliance, and minimal provocation of Russia.

New-member self-defense makes sense if the Visegrad Four are deemed capable of defense, with NATO providing only C3I and logistics support. It thus is geared to local contingencies at the low end of the spectrum, not to larger regional conflicts including invasion by an overpowering external threat. This strategy has four attractions: It is inexpensive; it makes new members responsible for themselves; it imposes no new burdens on NATO; and, of the three strategies, it would be the least provocative of Russia or other countries. It also has four drawbacks: It might signal a weak NATO commitment to new members; it could provide insufficient capabilities for dealing with unexpected, but demanding, contingencies; it does not create a clear path to ECE military integration in NATO; and it provides little scope for NATO and ECE combat forces to work together so that they can conduct combined missions outside Eastern Europe.

Power projection makes sense if the goal is to develop a combined capability for a broader set of contingencies, including simultaneous conflicts that could threaten to overpower the forces of the ECE states. More expensive than new-member self-defense, it has attractions beyond that of amassing additional military power: It formally commits the United States and Western Europe to serious combat missions in East Central Europe; it sends a reassuring signal to new members; and it provides a basis for achieving a high degree of collaboration and cross-training among NATO and new-member forces, thus enhancing NATO's military integration and multilateral character. It might be more provocative to Russia than the self-defense strategy, but it avoids the inflammatory step of basing large NATO combat forces eastward in peacetime. Its viability, however, depends on NATO's willingness to develop adequate power-projection and reinforcement capabilities. Because it would require alterations in NATO's distribution of roles, missions, and burden-sharing policies, it could impose more internal stress on NATO than would the self-defense strategy.

Forward presence is quite expensive and far more provocative than the other two strategies. By requiring large peacetime stationing in East Central Europe, it doubtless would strain NATO's internal cohesion and cause political tensions in the host countries. Its main military attraction is that it provides forces that can readily undertake major combat missions on short notice. This strategy would be required only if NATO's new members face the threat of a major surprise attack. It becomes a viable choice if a Cold Peace or Cold War with Russia erupts. Even then, large forward stationing of NATO combat forces would be required only if major adversary forces are based close to the borders of new members and can attack before NATO reinforcements arrive on the scene. It thus is a strategy for an extreme situation.

Provided no sharp political downturn occurs, NATO's strategy likely will come down to a choice between self-defense and power projection. The deciding points will be the size and character of NATO forces to be affiliated with security missions in Eastern Europe. Even the self-defense strategy requires the commitment of NATO C3I and logistics assets—assets that could require some NATO combat forces to help protect them and ensure that they operate effectively. The power-projection strategy requires larger NATO combat forces, but their number is variable. For example, the strategy could be carried out with a small posture of only a few fighter wings or with a ground corps with 3 divisions and 3 wings. A larger option is a posture similar to the U.S. "building block": 5 divisions and 10 wings. A still-larger posture might be similar to the U.S. force deployed to the Persian Gulf: 10 divisions and 10 wings. Which alternative is selected would hinge on the missions to be performed, the contingencies to be guarded against, assumptions about simultaneity, and the military requirements growing out of these calculations.

Although contingencies at the low end of the spectrum (e.g., peacekeeping) will dominate NATO's defense planning as new members join, capacity for border defense against major threats will remain a key indicator of the alliance's ability to carry out Article 5 commitments. Poland and Hungary likely will be the two Visegrad countries most affected by this requirement. Because any future threats will themselves be of moderate size, NATO and its new members can aspire to deter and defend against them in realistic and affordable ways. Over several years, an adequate combined military posture can be built that provides the necessary assurances to the new members. Western military doctrine—with its focus on nonlinear concepts, joint operations, and sophisticated technology—provides the basis for protecting new members in the flexible-but-responsive manner required. NATO's current strategic concept makes clear that nuclear weapons will remain an option for situations in which they are needed. The combined forces of NATO and new members need not be outgunned in the years ahead, as they were during the Cold War. As a result, conventional defense—based on the capacity to assemble sufficient forces in the weeks required—can be the centerpiece of NATO's strategy.

NATO's multiple objectives likely point to an evolving power-projection strategy, with the ultimate defense capability to be decided on as the future unfolds. But if power projection is the strategy of choice, it will beget a particular kind of military end game. New members of NATO will be primarily responsible for their own self-defense, but they will work within the integrated command and they will receive assurances of NATO military support in a crisis. Small NATO forces, logistics sites, and command staffs might be based on the soil of new members, but they will be for political bonding and military training, not for immediate warfighting. Sizable NATO forces will be available to reinforce in a crisis, but they will be stationed in Western Europe, not to the east. In today's political climate, this strategy and posture would establish a zone of defensive security in East Central Europe while not suggesting hostile intent or posing an offensive military threat to Russia and other countries. It thus would square with a Western political strategy aimed at promoting regional stability through viable Article 5 commitments supplemented by military restraint.

GUIDING FORCE MODERNIZATION AND WEAPON SALES IN EAST CENTRAL EUROPE

The future arms market in East Central Europe will play a major role in determining how countries modernize their military forces. It therefore promises to be a second arena that will shape this region's future military structure. Today, ECE countries are too poor and beset with internal troubles to buy new weapons in any magnitude, but in the decade ahead they will be placing sizable orders to replace aging models and thereby modernize. The United States, various West European manufacturers, and Russia will be the primary sellers.

If left alone, the process of weapon sales and modernization could produce not only profits but an unhealthy outcome (i.e., distribution of sales) that erodes the West's interests and regional stability. It will also affect the manner in which NATO enlargement unfolds and the military postures that take shape in the aftermath (i.e., distribution of new weapons after they are bought). Consequently, weapon sales, too, will need to be guided by sound policy with a sensible end game.

Principal Buyers

The principal buyers will be the Visegrad Four, plus Ukraine, Romania, and Bulgaria. Together, their military postures add up to thousands of tanks, artillery pieces, aircraft, and other systems. Most of these weapons were procured during the Cold War and reflect technology of the 1970s or earlier. In the coming years, many will reach the end of their life cycles and will have to be replaced.

Poland is a good example of a country whose force is facing obsolescence. Its current tank inventory includes 1,000 T-55s—1950s technology that is obsolescent on the modern battlefield—and 700 T-72s from the 1980s. Poland's air force is dominated by 200 MiG-21s from the 1960s; its only current-era models are 12 MiG-29s. At least one-half of Poland's overall inventory will need replacing if only to avoid constant breakdowns, soaring maintenance costs, and poor safety.

The combined inventories of Hungary, the Czech Republic, and Slovakia are about equal to Poland's posture, and their weapons are older than Poland's. Romania's force posture is the oldest in the region, and Bulgaria's posture is similar to Poland's. Only Ukraine's posture is fairly modern, owing to an up-to-date stockpile when the Soviet Union unraveled. Even so, at least one-quarter of its weapons will need replacement, thus making it one of the region's biggest buyers.

If old weapons are well-maintained, they can be usable against similarly equipped armies, but not against enemies armed with new-generation weapons—one reason why these countries fear Russia: Not only does Russia have larger forces and uncertain political intentions, but its forces are more modern. Unmodernized East European forces also will be hard-pressed to work with NATO's forces, which are more modern even than Russia's. Their ability to participate in PFP and NATO after admission will depend on their access to the modern military technology needed to implement NATO's doctrine and procedures.

Several countries have modest defense industries that can meet some of their acquisition requirements. For example, Slovakia manufactures tanks and other army equipment, as does Poland. Ukraine has the industry to make major parts for several different systems; however, because it was integrated into the old Soviet military-industrial complex, it builds few entirely finished weapon systems. Other countries manufacture small arms, ammunition, logistics-support vehicles, and various types of spare parts. These efforts aside, the seven countries do not produce major weapon systems in the large quantities that may be needed. In particular, they do not make modern combat aircraft, which will be the most expensive items procured, and will have to buy from manufacturers outside their national boundaries and the region itself.

The exact number of weapons facing compulsory retirement is uncertain, but if 40 percent of the inventories become obsolete, the following will require replacement by the year 2005: 3,500 tanks, 3,500 infantry fighting vehicles, 3,000 artillery tubes, 800 combat aircraft, 1,500 SAM launchers, 180 helicopters, 70 air transports, 10 major naval combatants, and 30 patrol craft. Along with these major weapons will come a need for missiles, electronic gear, C3I systems, ammunition stocks, maintenance equipment, and spare parts.

If all the expensive Western equipment is bought, the total bill could be roughly $70 billion: $16 billion for ground weapons, $28 billion for aircraft, $15 billion for SAM systems, and $13 billion for new ships. The cost could be driven down by several factors:

- Some countries likely will seek less-expensive systems.

- Some countries also may turn to procuring used but refurbished models that, while not offering a full life cycle, will cost less.

- Some countries may seek to lease major weapons—e.g., Tornado aircraft from Germany.

- Others may resort to the practice of buying new components that can be fitted onto old models, although modernizing this way is not cost-free and merely postpones for a few years the need to buy new frames.

These factors taken into account, this study's estimate is that the coming weapons market will total about $40–$50 billion of international procurement in the coming decade.

Can the East European states afford purchases of this magnitude? At present, these seven countries are spending about $11 billion annually for defense.[4] Assuming a modest recovery, their combined spending could rise to about $15 billion annually over a decade, even if no capitalist boom takes place. During the coming decade, these countries thus may be spending about $130 billion total. If normal spending patterns are followed, roughly $30–$40 billion may be available for purchase of foreign equipment items.

If funds are lacking, the difference can be bridged by loans and grants provided by friendly governments. NATO governments may need to provide security assistance to the Visegrad Four as they join the alliance, and they may face incentives to give financial aid to Romania, Bulgaria, and Ukraine as well. If these East Central European states receive about $1–$2 billion annually in loans and grants, they may be able to combine this aid with their own revenues to fund most of their high-priority requirements. Many countries likely will seek co-production agreements that can help them develop stronger defense industries of their own. If such agreements are forthcoming, their incentive to engage in the necessary belt-tightening to permit robust foreign procurement policies will increase.

---

[4]Estimate based on official exchange rates. Using purchasing-power parity as the basis, defense expenditures rise to $25–$34 billion.

Potential Sellers

What sellers likely will enter this market will depend on strategic motives and economics. Developments likely will be influenced by trends in the global sales market, which in recent years has shrunk from its Cold War high of $65 billion annually to only $20 billion annually. This market is projected to grow to only $30 billion annually a decade from now. Moreover, domestic procurement has dropped off in most countries to a level about one-half that of the 1980s. Force reductions are under way almost everywhere. To save money, many countries are taking advantage of current sophisticated technologies to postpone new major procurements until the next decade, when new generations of weapons become available. The net result is that the East Central European market could expand to become 20 percent of the international sales market and even 10 percent of total sales volume (includes domestic sales and foreign sales), taking into account home-grown procurement. Thus, it may be big enough to attract many sellers.[5]

U.S. manufacturers will face obvious incentives to corner a satisfying share of this market. In early 1995, the U.S. government announced its willingness to begin selling weapons to ten East European countries (Ukraine was not included).[6] This decision reflected an effort to help support PFP and NATO enlargement, but its effect has been to open the region to U.S. defense industries.

At the moment, the United States is the world's largest exporter of weapons, with a volume of $11 billion annually, and its weapons are widely regarded for their outstanding quality and suitability to modern doctrine, owing partly to the recent Persian Gulf War. U.S. weapons can be relied upon to undergo qualitative improvements, because the Pentagon continues to research, develop, and modernize them. U.S. weapons also bring highly valued links to the U.S. economy, defense industry, and military services. Also important, U.S. manufacturers have developed good reputations for providing high-quality technical services, maintenance, training, and product

---

[5]U.S. Department of Defense, *World-Wide Conventional Arms Trade: A Forecast and Analysis*, Washington, D.C.: U.S. GPO, December 1994.

[6]Dana Priest and Daniel Williams, "U.S. Allows Arms Sales to 10 in Ex-East Bloc," *Washington Post*, February 20, 1995.

improvements over a weapon's lifetime. The chief disadvantage of U.S. weapons is that they are costly: often marginally more expensive than West European models, and significantly more expensive than less-sophisticated Russian models. Even so, U.S. manufacturers will enjoy a competitive position with the East Central European countries wanting close ties to the United States and possessing the money to pay for excellent military hardware.

A key determinant may be whether the U.S. government is willing to provide security-assistance loans to the East European states. At the moment, Congress has put a tight lid on security assistance and regulates the countries that receive this aid. The FY95 budget for grants and aid was only $4 billion, of which over $3 billion went to Egypt and Israel. Turkey and Greece claimed most of the rest. Unless this ceiling is lifted or the distribution of assistance is changed, little security assistance will be available to the ECE states, including those that will be joining NATO. Lack of security assistance will either inhibit these countries from modernizing their postures or, more likely, will force them to go to other suppliers willing to offer attractive financial-assistance packages.

West European suppliers particularly may perceive the strategic reasons and market incentives to offer this aid, because East Central Europe is in their own backyard. The West Europeans play a smaller role in the global market than does the United States, but that role is far from trivial: Britain, Germany, and France together have annual sales of $6 billion. Several West European countries have banded together to form consortia for producing such major weapons as the new European fighter, air transports, helicopters, and tanks. As the EU pursues a common defense identity, its reliance on multinational consortia will grow.

Owing to its proximity to and its growing economic involvements in Eastern Europe, Germany is well-situated to gain a large share of the weapons market. It produces most of the weapons wanted by the ECE states: combat aircraft, tanks, infantry fighting vehicles, frigates, and coastal patrol vessels. With annual sales of $4 billion, Britain is best known for its warships, but it also produces the low-cost Hawk aircraft, as well as tanks, infantry fighting vehicles, artillery pieces, missiles, electronic equipment, and other gear. The French defense industry produces weapons across virtually the entire spectrum. Its

Exocet anti-ship missile is a rival to the U.S. Harpoon, and its fighter aircraft are quite good. Italy sells transport aircraft and small naval vessels. Spain does the same. Sweden sells combat aircraft, submarines, and small naval craft.

Russia is a wild card. When the Cold War ended, it lost what had been a flourishing East European sales market worth about $4 billion annually. This loss was part of a larger global catastrophe for Russia. In the 1980s, the Soviet Union annually delivered about $26 billion in weapons abroad. Roughly $9 billion took the form of grant aid (i.e., gifts) to impoverished allies. Even so, the Soviet Union earned $15 billion in hard currency each year: a major plus for its struggling economy. As of 1993, Russia was exporting only $2.6 billion annually. Together with the rapid downsizing of its own military establishment, this loss created further troubles for its bloated defense industry. In an effort to recover lost ground, Russia in 1993 announced a policy of seeking new markets. Selling weapons to the seven ECE countries would be an ideal way not only to gain profits and bolster its flagging defense industry, but also to reclaim a measure of political influence through military ties.

The main selling point for Russia's weapons is that they are well-suited to *current* East European force structures and doctrine. As those countries move to the Western model, the attractiveness of Russian weapons will decline. Even so, they are relatively inexpensive, durable, and effective for most missions. Russia will be least likely to make headway in the Visegrad Four states, which will be trying to draw close to NATO. It may be better able to sell weapons to Romania and Bulgaria—countries that will be outside the NATO fold. Russia may stand its best chance with Ukraine, which, owing to its large defense establishment and need for some modernization, may compose 15–25 percent of the ECE market. In an ideal world, Ukraine might want to buy Western weapons. However, because it depends on Russia for energy and other economic goods and because Russia will be Ukraine's biggest export market, Ukraine may face incentives to buy weapons from Russia to maintain a trade balance and a favorable political climate. If the West proves unwilling to sell weapons to Ukraine, Ukraine will have nowhere else to turn.

Competition

This portrayal of buyers and sellers adds up to a large arms bazaar in future years. East Central European countries will be seeking to purchase sizable quantities of new weapons, and, with the global market tepid elsewhere, manufacturers from the United States, Western Europe, and Russia will be striving to corner this market. Consequently, they may fall into competition with each other. The immediate stakes will be sales and profits, but this competition will also have larger implications.

The countries that capture the largest shares of the market will acquire political influence in key capitals and defense establishments. Also important, weapons sales will significantly shape the military arrangements in East Central Europe over the coming decade. They will determine the types of capabilities bought by all seven countries, and they will affect the coalition relationships that develop. They will influence how NATO enlargement plays out in political and military terms, and they will play a major role in determining whether Russia regains influence in the region's security affairs.

International trade theory argues for an end game determined by market dynamics. But in this sensitive arena, the potential exists for a negative strategic outcome. One risk is that the Western nations might become so engrossed in winning market share that they develop serious political rivalries with each other, thereby weakening their capacity to cooperate in shaping a coherent PFP and NATO enlargement. A second risk is that Russia might gain a market share that is either too large—leaving it unduly influential in some countries—or too small—leaving it as an angry outcast feeling that its legitimate economic and strategic interests have been shunned. A third risk is that of an unhealthy military outcome in East Central Europe. NATO's new members might fail to procure the weapons needed to smooth their transition into alliance military membership. Some countries could buy weapons in unbalanced ways and wind up with force postures that are gleaming in a few areas but that lack overall readiness and joint capability. Other countries might gain access to too many offensive weapons, thereby destabilizing the region because they pose threats to their neighbors. These market-driven dangers are real enough to call for political control of the weapon-sales process so that sensible strategic and military outcomes are attained.

Leadership-Dominated End Game: Political Control of Weapon Sales

From the West's standpoint, a sound end game likely would call for sales to be dominated by countries willing to assume leadership as NATO enlarges eastward. This approach would call for the sale of weapons by countries whose military forces will be performing most of the work in developing close ties with new NATO members—most likely, the United States and Germany. This does not rule out sales by Britain, France, and others. It merely means that the countries accepting the strategic burdens are entitled to fair-market shares and to assurances that new members will be using weapons familiar to these leaders. Regardless of which countries do the selling, a key outcome likely to affect NATO planning is that new members would acquire weapons that will facilitate their ability to become integrated into NATO's military mechanisms.

A risk is that market-driven dynamics could result in political polarization of the region between the West and Russia: for example, if the Visegrad Four buy exclusively from NATO countries but Ukraine, Romania, and Bulgaria buy exclusively from Russia. The unintended outcome could be the drawing of de facto geopolitical lines. The need to reduce this risk argues for a Western effort to make NATO weapons available to Romania and Bulgaria and, above all, to Ukraine.

If Ukraine buys weapons only from Russia, its military forces will be drawn into Russia's orbit, irrespective of the policies of its civilian leadership. If Ukraine is given access to NATO technology and military support, it will be more likely to develop close political ties to the West, even if it does not gain formal membership into NATO and the EU. Selling weapons to Ukraine is only one part of a larger military equation for dealing with this country. The situation requires a robust PFP aimed at building a Ukrainian defense posture capable of defending its borders and working informally with NATO military establishments in a variety of missions.

The West has an interest in ensuring that Russia is not frozen out of the market. One reason is that some Russian weapons can make cost-effective contributions to regional defense and stability. For example, the Russian SA-10 surface-to-air missile may be an adequate substitute for the U.S. Patriot system at about one-half the cost. Russian combat aircraft can be rewired to meet NATO standards at an incremental cost of about 5 percent above fly-away purchase price. As well, allowing Russia access to this market will enable it to gain economic profits from the strategic changes taking place there and will give it an incentive to work cooperatively with the West, confident that it will enjoy a measure of political influence as a result.

What the situation requires is a heterogeneous pattern of weapon sales, whereby the West dominates the Visegrad Four market but Russia maintains a significant position, and purchases by Ukraine reflect a mixture of Western and Russian sales according to Ukraine's preferences. What applies to Ukraine also applies to Romania and Bulgaria. Such an outcome could blur sharp political distinctions, encourage multilateral cooperation, and dilute any propensity to polarization.

Finally, political control of the weapon-sales process argues for an effort aimed at producing East Central European defense establishments that themselves are contributors to regional stability. One important goal will be to ensure that the ECE states do not spend so much on weapon procurement that they unbalance their overall defense planning and damage their prospects for economic recovery. This goal can be advanced by Western assistance policies, but it can also be promoted by acquiring weapons at the less-expensive, lower end of the technology scale. For example, F-16 and Tornado fighters can meet legitimate defense needs at far less cost than the F-22 or the European fighter. The application of this standard to procurement of aircraft and SAM systems seems especially important, because these systems are expensive and will dominate procurement budgets everywhere. Along with this emphasis on inexpensive technology can come efforts to ensure that, insofar as possible, *defensive* weapons are bought—not systems that greatly enhance offensive military capabilities. Moreover, steps can be taken to ensure that the sales process works to ensure that the East European countries remain as close to military balance with each other as is feasible. The guiding concept can be better-armed countries that can defend themselves, draw closer to the West, not provoke Russia, and minimize military threats to each other.

Summary

In summary, a sensible military end game for this arena could produce an outcome very different from what might evolve if market dynamics go unchecked and an uncontrolled armaments bazaar emerges. This end game calls for proactive Western management of the weapon-sales process and political-military goals that go beyond profit maximization. It envisions appropriate Western security-assistance policies for needy nations in East Central Europe. It begins with Western policies aimed at managing tensions within NATO and at enhancing NATO's ability to exert effective leadership and integrative objectives across the region. It includes collaboration with Russia's legitimate interests and is focused on promoting multilateral political cooperation, not polarization. It reaches beyond the Visegrad Four to include Ukraine, as well as Romania and Bulgaria. It culminates with the shaping of East Central European defense establishments that are affordable and integrated with PFP and NATO, and that enhance self-defense without posing offensive threats to neighbors. This outcome could be difficult to achieve, but it offers the prospect of using the weapon-sales process as an instrument to help promote regional stability, not undermine it.

IMPROVING THE CFE ARMS-CONTROL REGIME

An assessment of the third arena begins by recognizing that the Conventional Forces in Europe (CFE) Treaty regime will need to be strengthened if arms control is to make a satisfactory contribution to military stability in East Central Europe and nearby regions. The treaty greatly reduced conventional armaments in Europe: No sensible theory of future stability would scrap it. The problem is that the treaty is founded on the old bipolar order and does not address key new-era geopolitical and military issues, because it neither achieves a balance in the new multipolar setting nor precludes offensive military strategies and aggression. This problem is likely to worsen as the military dynamics of the new era unfold. The solution likely does not lie in pursuing an end game of further deep cuts, but in orchestrating practical changes that respond to legitimate security requirements while reducing the incentives to confrontation and instability.[7]

The CFE Treaty

The CFE Treaty of 1990 was designed to stabilize the Cold War confrontation between NATO and the Warsaw Pact. Its intent was to strip away the Warsaw Pact's large offensive potential and to leave a defensive strategy in its place. Because NATO's smaller forces were deemed closer to a defensive strategy, the CFE Treaty imposed only marginal reductions on them. As a result, the treaty required the Warsaw Pact bloc to reduce by about 50 percent and the NATO bloc, by about 10 percent, thereby achieving equal force levels on both sides. Its jurisdiction stretching from the Atlantic to the Urals, the treaty imposed restrictions on manpower and five types of weaponry: tanks, armored fighting vehicles, artillery, attack helicopters, and combat aircraft. At its heart was the provision for each side to have a treaty-limited entitlement (TLE) of about 70,000 major ground weapons and 6,700 combat aircraft.

In addition, the treaty established four subzones within the overall Atlantic-to-Urals zone, the sublimits of each providing for numerical balance between NATO and the Warsaw Pact. See Table 8.1. The three central zones are concentric; inner zones are contained in the outer zones. In today's world, the smallest—subzone 4—regulates force levels in inner Central Europe (Germany and the Low Countries, plus today's Visegrad Four). Subzone 3 reaches out to include larger parts of Western and Eastern Europe, including Belarus and northern Ukraine. Subzone 2 includes western Russia. Finally, the CFE Treaty establishes a special flank zone governing force limits in the northern and southern regions, including the Caucasus.

The CFE Treaty paved the way to a wholesale destruction of Warsaw Pact weapons, a sense of emerging bloc-to-bloc equality as the Cold War ended, greater military transparency across all of Europe, and strict limits on how forces could be shifted among the various subregions. In these ways, it contributed to stability. But it did not call

---

[7]For analysis, see Richard A. Falkenrath, "The CFE Flank Dispute: Waiting in the Wings," *International Security*, Spring 1995.

Table 8.1

CFE Subzones

Subzone	Western Countries	Eastern Countries
Subzone 4	Germany, Belgium, Netherlands, Luxembourg	Visegrad Four
Subzone 3	Subzone 4 plus Denmark, France, United Kingdom, Italy	Subzone 4 plus Belarus, Northern Ukraine, Kaliningrad
Subzone 2	Subzone 3 plus Spain, Portugal	Subzone 3 plus western Russia and Kazakhstan
Flank Zone	Greece, Iceland, Norway, Turkey	Romania, Bulgaria, southern Ukraine, Moldova, Russia (St. Petersburg and North Caucasus), the three Caucasian states

for numerical equality among Europe's countries: Indeed, it allowed for big asymmetries. The treaty's principal effect thus was to ratify the post–Cold War distribution of military power that has evolved in unbalanced ways because of multiple different national defense policies.

Owing to the disappearance of the old bipolar structure, many problems are beginning to emerge with the CFE Treaty. Some problems reflect specific difficulties being encountered by several countries in honoring the treaty's restrictions while attending to their new security requirements. A more fundamental problem is that, because so many military imbalances have emerged since the treaty's signing, many countries are left still-fearful for their security. Their response is to turn toward unilateral measures or collective-defense guarantees.

The bottom line is that, notwithstanding its huge contributions, the CFE Treaty does not provide a comprehensive, enduring, new-era theory of military stability for East Central Europe and the surrounding regions. The looming risk is that the efforts of many nations to progress to a safer future will interact in ways that cause the entire treaty to come unraveled.

One of the biggest problems will be Russia's stance. Russia is becoming skeptical that CFE still serves its interests. Russia's immediate objection has been that CFE constraints on forces in its North Caucasus region are equivalent to only 1–2 divisions. The Russian Ministry of Defense has been seeking authorization for roughly four times this many. As of late 1995, an accord seemingly has been fashioned to allow Russia greater flexibility in interpreting its flank entitlements.

A larger problem for Russia may derive from its need to handle security requirements in Europe and Asia with a defense posture only one-fourth the size of the Soviet Union's Cold War posture. This development leaves Russia having to shift forces back and forth between Europe and Asia to meet unanticipated upsurges in requirements. CFE leaves Russia free to move forces toward Siberia and the Far East, but it constrains Russia's capacity to move additional forces into the country's western areas, as well as into the northern St. Petersburg region and the Caucasus region.[8]

Beyond this, Russia may be developing reservations about how it perceives the new European military balance being fostered by CFE and recent geopolitical changes. The old bipolar equality no longer has strategic meaning. As Table 8.2 shows, changing geopolitical dynamics are altering how the new military balance is likely to be perceived in Moscow. The main development is that the TLEs and forces of the Visegrad Four likely will be joining NATO, thereby increasing the total military power in the Western camp. Whereas Russia formerly could count the entire Warsaw Pact on its side of the ledger, now it is reduced to the CIS. To the extent that CIS countries are not deemed reliable allies, Russia is left with its own posture for gaining a sense of comfort that its security is intact and that a regionwide military balance is being maintained.

The new geopolitical reality is that, although Russia will overpower its immediate neighbors, its forces alone will fall well short of

---

[8]Douglas Clarke, "The Russian Military and the CFE Treaty," *RFE/RL*, October 23, 1993.

Table 8.2

CFE Ground Entitlements[a, b]
(thousands)

NATO Total	NATO/ Central Europe	ECE/ Visegrad Four	Ukraine/ Belarus	Russia/ CIS	Russia Alone
67	45	13	19	46	24

[a]Includes total numbers of tanks, armored fighting vehicles, and artillery.
[b]Romania and Bulgaria, not shown here, are allocated 10,000 weapons.

providing a numerical counterweight to NATO forces. Because NATO is a defensive alliance, this situation imparts no strategic threat to Russia in military terms. But in Russia's eyes, it may affect political perceptions across the region, and it may leave some Russians nervous about their country's strategic standing.

NATO might also acquire problems with CFE restrictions on its own flexibility. When the Visegrad Four join NATO, their national force postures will be large enough to use their TLEs. At issue is whether NATO will be allowed room to deploy sufficient West European and U.S. assets onto Visegrad Four soil to carry out the military dimensions of enlargement. Small peacetime deployments can be accommodated, but NATO will want the freedom to deploy sizable forces in a crisis. Whether a problem will exist depends on the interpretation given to the CFE Treaty.

In theory, the treaty allows for flexible movement of forces within subzone 4, which could permit large NATO deployments eastward without violating treaty provisions. Yet the treaty's spirit reflected the assumption of two opposing blocs and of Eastern Europe's remaining apart from the West. If the treaty is interpreted as allowing for only one-half of subzone 4's TLE on Visegrad Four soil, it could become a barrier to any large-scale NATO troop movements eastward. Beyond this, what will happen if the Baltic states, Ukraine, Romania, and Bulgaria all join NATO? Would CFE allow NATO to reinforce them in a crisis? If overly stiff restrictions prevail, CFE could become a problem not only for Russia but for NATO as well.

Other countries could find themselves hampered. For example, CFE subzones 2 and 3 divide Ukraine into two parts. As a result, Ukraine is not free to move its forces within its own national boundaries. What will happen if basing imperatives, or demography, or a crisis leads to a need for troop distributions that violate CFE limits? The larger issue is whether, in the more multipolar setting of tomorrow, the many small and medium-sized countries of the region are content to live within CFE's limits. To the extent they worry about their security, some may develop preferences for larger forces, or differently configured forces, which are not permitted by CFE.

If the goal is to retain the CFE Treaty's best features, revisions to its specific provisions seem inevitable. Otherwise, several countries could be led to withdraw from the treaty entirely. Russia likely will seek changes beyond its Caucasus demarche, NATO may want alterations of its own, and other countries may feel likewise for their own reasons. The risk is that the CFE Treaty may gradually be twisted out of recognition, although some of the changes may be desirable or at least not greatly damaging.

The proper stance for the West appears to be open-minded flexibility, coupled with firmness on the CFE Treaty's enduring principles. If all participants react this way, the future likely can be marked by a process of negotiations and adjustments that preserve the still-valid core of CFE.

New-Era End Game: Deep Cuts

Yet the West's arms-control strategy should be marked by something more visionary than damage-limiting tactics. What can be done by way of fashioning fresh arms-control concepts aimed at remedying the negative military features of the new era? An end game with surface appeal is to pursue further deep cuts that render all countries able to defend their borders but unable to attack their neighbors.[9] The outcome presumably would be a stable region, because no nation would fear for the future or be able to wage offensive warfare.

---

[9]For an in-depth analysis and advocacy of this idea, see Janne E. Nolan, ed., *Global Engagement: Cooperation and Security in the 21st Century,* Washington, D.C.: The Brookings Institution, 1994.

Although this concept sounds attractive in principle, it suffers from drawbacks in practice.

One of the key problems is Russia, which is more than a European state. A huge country spanning two continents, it perceives a need for a large army not only to maintain internal control but also to defend against threats from Asia and South Central Asia. As a result, it likely will be unenthused about reductions well below the already-scaled-back posture now being designed. A large Russian army is a worry to nearby European countries and will lead them to want large forces of their own. Beyond this, general uncertainty about the future may influence many countries to want as many forces as can be afforded. In today's climate, most countries seem willing to spend about 3–5 percent of GDP on defense. Since this spending will normally permit full use of CFE entitlements, many states may feel little urgency for further drawdowns. If the common consensus favors the status quo, deep cuts will not gain the political support needed to make it a viable arms-control strategy.

In addition, the idea of deep cuts suffers from a logical flaw in its theory. It assumes that major reductions to levels below CFE will strip countries of offensive potential and thereby bring about regional stability. The flaw is that the relationship between military strategy and force levels is more complex than this simple formulation. Even if most states favor regional stability, not all will want to part entirely with offensive power—especially countries with vital interests located outside their borders. If a consensus does emerge in favor of border defense as the sole determiner of military strategy, two troublesome questions arise: How are the requirements of a purely defensive strategy to be measured so that the target for reductions can be determined? How can analysis determine when a country has enough military power to defend itself but not enough to attack its neighbors?

The answers uproot the premise that force postures can readily be designed that are configured for defense but not offense, because *strategy* and *capability* are not the same thing. A defensive strategy normally will give rise to a force posture that may be large and, almost irrespective of its size, can be used to carry out offensive operations in some form. The consequence is that defensive strategies and commensurate forces do not necessarily yield stability. If military stability is to be achieved, the act of reducing the size of Europe's military arsenals another step or two will not achieve this goal in some comprehensive way.

Normally, defensive requirements are measured by two standards: the size of a country's borders and the ability to field a force posture that cannot easily be overwhelmed without the attacker suffering heavy losses in the process. For small states, these standards typically give rise to a perceived requirement for fully 3–5 divisions and 3–5 fighter wings: a fairly large force capable of serious fighting. For bigger states, the requirements typically are higher, because there is either more territory to be defended or a desire for greater margins of insurance. This is the reason medium-sized countries such as Germany, France, Poland, and Ukraine typically choose to deploy 8–12 divisions and 400–600 combat aircraft—a great deal of military power. These large force levels reflect what is typically deemed necessary for nations intent on protecting themselves, not on threatening their neighbors.

What the idea of deep cuts fails to recognize is that the current CFE regime was inspired by the goal of creating defensive strategies. For the most part, the force postures of today reflect this goal. The problem is that they can perform a broader range of military missions than just border defense. To be sure, there are differences between forces designed for offense and those designed for defense; e.g., an offensive force has more tanks, fighter-bombers, mobile logistics units, bridge-crossing equipment, and other assets for power projection. But the difference is a matter of *degree*, not type. A defense-tailored force is still well-armed, and typically it has a significant number of weapons and capabilities that can be employed for offensive purposes. On the modern battlefield, moreover, defensive strategies require joint operations, firepower, maneuver, and local counterattacks. As a result, the distinction between defensive and offensive capabilities is blurred at the tactical level. Virtually all modern armies can go on the offensive.

This military reality has a key implication for analyzing how force size affects military options. Doubtless, bigger forces have greater offensive power than smaller forces. But the lethality of modern weapons means that smaller forces are not necessarily punchless. A single fighter wing armed with modern munitions can inflict major damage on neighbors as far away as 500 kilometers. A single division can enter a neighbor's territory, occupy a zone 50 kilometers wide and 100 kilometers deep, and inflict great damage in this zone. An indicator of the potential to carry out offensives and inflict damage is Bosnia, where most of the killing has been done by fairly small but persistently active infantry forces. Consequently, even Europe's small powers will possess considerable military strength that can be used for limited but potent offensive purposes. Europe's medium powers will be better-equipped for this purpose. Its major powers, coalition blocs, and alliances will be even better-equipped.

Not Distribution of Arms but Distribution of Power

The proper conclusion is that further arms reductions perhaps can help promote stability if they are attainable, but they should not be viewed as a potential cure-all if wholesale disarmament is not in the cards. Once modern forces have been created, the capacity for offensive strategies is quite hard, if not impossible, to eliminate. In theory, a defense-only region can be created, but this step would require far deeper cuts than anything imaginable for a continent in which an all-encompassing political community is still a dream.

A counterproposal to deep cuts holds that the best route to stability lies in increasing military power everywhere so that no state can be defeated easily—not in decreasing power in ways that yield many weak states vulnerable to predators. Perhaps this proposal makes a bad idea sound good, but it does illuminate a basic point: All countries will need enough forces to defend themselves by making aggression against them a difficult proposition. These requirements are not small. If they are not met, the burden on NATO to make up the deficiency will be all the greater. Perhaps further arms-control cuts make sense, but not necessarily if the consequence is to threaten minimum military sufficiency.

Summary

In the final analysis, the best guarantee of stability is not the absolute level of military power held by single nations but the relative distribution of power among the nations making up the region. Stability will result if individual countries and coalitions have no disproportionate power advantages over their neighbors that could create temptations for aggression. The problem today is not merely that East Central Europe houses still-large military inventories but that it is afflicted with multiple military imbalances. The region's structural characteristics make achieving the goal of across-the-board numerical balance unrealistic. As a result, arms-control strategy needs to focus on how to deal with existing realities and emerging dynamics so that the situation does not worsen and so that pragmatic steps are taken to foster improvements.

If deep cuts are not forthcoming, control of military modernization across East Central Europe ranks as a potentially important contributor to stability. Modernization is typically not a subject of conventional arms control, but because technology is a key determinant of combat power, it likely will be a major variable in determining whether stability is preserved. Modernization policies motivated by defensive concepts and self-restraint can help ensure that no country gains qualitative supremacy over its neighbors. Agreement on common readiness levels can have similar effects, as can accords on training practices, doctrines, exercises, logistics systems, and stationing policies. Stability-enhancing practices in all these areas can help buffer the destabilizing effect of large forces and multiple imbalances across the region.

Properly conceived force commitments by NATO can also have a similar stabilizing effect by reassuring the vulnerable and by warning would-be predators. As these NATO commitments are made, however, an important task will be to help head off the risk of a military rivalry between NATO and Russia in East Central Europe. Political factors will be the most important determinant of their relationship, but the military interaction between them will be influential as well. The danger is that, if this interaction is not guided by arms-control concepts, it could acquire an unhealthy dynamic of its own, and thereby poison the political atmosphere.

A new bipolar confrontation could emerge if Russia were to decide to pose an offensive military threat to NATO and the EU as they enlarge eastward. A more insidious and likely danger is that of a confrontation arising even with both sides pursuing defensive military strategies. Confrontation could gradually take shape if the two sides are suspicious of each other's intentions, are uncertain of their own footing, and decide to err heavily on the side of cautionary prepared-ness in their defense planning. Enlargement by NATO could degen-erate into a process of building a forward-presence strategy that deploys large West European and U.S. forces and of molding new-member forces into a tightly integrated multinational force posture. To the east, Russian actions and reactions could result in CIS military reintegration and the deployment of sizable forces near NATO's bor-ders. The resulting action-reaction cycle could give rise to a new geopolitical dividing line, growing rivalry, and increasingly powerful postures on both sides, poised to fight each other.

Arms-control efforts can focus on regulating the military details of how NATO enlarges and how Russia responds. The dominant theme can be to gain consensus from both sides on the need to keep mili-tary preparations moderate and transparently defensive. If this goal is to be achieved, NATO will need to design its military preparations with Russia's sensitivities in mind. Russia will need to reciprocate by not stationing large forces in Belarus and by not building an offense-oriented military infrastructure there. Provided both sides behave prudently, the risks of an action-reaction cycle can be avoided. This agenda is very different from CFE's today, but it may be arms control's most important challenge for the future.

TOWARD A COMPREHENSIVE MILITARY END GAME

This chapter has argued that NATO needs a sensible military end game if it is to enlarge successfully, because emerging military affairs will have a major impact on how the future takes shape in East Central Europe. The worst nightmare is a militarily hollow NATO en-largement that results in weak Article 5 commitments, a bipolar con-frontation with Russia, an uncontrolled arms bazaar that intensifies already-existing military imbalances among key nations, and the collapse of conventional-arms control.

This or any other nightmarish outcome is far from inevitable. Indeed, this region's emerging military affairs can be brought under control and steered to a stable conclusion that advances the West's interests. Doing so, however, will require skillful defense manage-ment. A well-conceived military end game will need to be fashioned and then carried out by paying close attention to the details.

Assuming that enlargement incorporates the Visegrad Four, the West's overall military goals are as follows: credible but affordable Article 5 commitments to these new members, a noncompetitive military relationship with Russia, and a stable regional balance of power that leaves neighboring countries able to defend themselves while not threatening each other. Achieving all these goals will not be easy, because they can pull Western policy in different directions. To pursue all these goals at once, the West will require sensible policies in the three arenas discussed here: NATO's defense arrangements with new members, the weapon-acquisition and force-modernization process, and conventional-arms control. Equally important, Western policies in all three arenas will have to be coordinated so that their effects can be mutually reinforcing.

Of the decisions facing the West, perhaps the most important will be NATO's military strategy for carrying out enlargement, which will play a major role in shaping NATO's military arrangements with new members and will help define the policy agenda for ECE modernization and arms control. Will NATO choose self-defense, or power projection, or forward presence? If the choice is self-defense, NATO may lessen the burdens on itself and face few troubles with Russia; however, it may fashion a weak Article 5 commitment, and it likely will confront intensified pressures to open the gates of arms sales and modernization so that new alliance members and PFP participants can defend themselves virtually alone. If the choice is forward presence, the problems will be the reverse: NATO's Article 5 commitment will be strong and pressures for ECE modernization will lessen, but the burdens on NATO will be large, the risk of confrontation with Russia will mount, and prospects for continuing arms control will be damaged. The attraction of power projection is that it will allow the West to pursue all of its objectives without risking grave damage to any of them.

If NATO is propelled toward a power-projection strategy, a coherent military end game can be fashioned by determining the logical policy implications in each arena. NATO defense arrangements will need to be designed so that new members can carry out most missions affecting their security, with NATO reinforcements available to help meet unfulfilled requirements. Modernization in East Central Europe can proceed on the assumption that because NATO will be available to help new members and PFP countries, the weapon-acquisition process can be guided by the defensive strategies and moderate goals that are consistent with regional stability. Because NATO can affordably meet its Article 5 commitments while refraining from military steps that might provoke strong Russian counteractions, arms-control strategy can be refashioned to focus the practical goals discussed earlier while preserving the CFE framework.

The ultimate destination would be an enlarged NATO backed by collective-defense guarantees and adequate military forces dividing labor between new members and old. This militarily prepared NATO would pose no offensive threat to Russia and the CIS, and the stage would be set for the two sides to cooperate in showing military restraint so that a competitive action-reaction cycle does not ensue. The countries of East Central Europe would gain sufficient access to new military hardware to ensure that their legitimate defensive needs are met, but their modernization efforts would unfold at a measured pace, and care would be taken to ensure that modern technology is distributed symmetrically. Arms control might aim for further reductions if a consensus exists on this goal, but its main objective would be to regulate readiness, doctrine, and modernization so that a stable balance of power is preserved or so that at least the present imbalances do not worsen. As a result, new military arrangements would take shape in East Central Europe, but the risk of a slide into intensified competitiveness and multipolar rivalry would be dampened. Beyond this, regional military affairs could evolve in a way that supports the West's strategic goal of fashioning an enlarged EU and NATO that fits into a stable regional security framework.

Chapter Nine

CONCLUSIONS

This book has put forth the thesis that the United States needs to think deeply and plan wisely in handling the emerging geopolitics of East Central Europe. The United States and its allies will be moving east, but they cannot afford to view enlargement in isolation. The challenge facing them will be to fashion a larger Western community within the framework of a stable security system for the entire region. This outcome is feasible, but it will not be accomplished easily, given the many trends that are not propelling events in favorable directions.

Enlargement offers the opportunity to admit new European democracies into the Western community, but it also entails demanding challenges because it will draw the West into a turbulent region and closer to Russia's borders. Moreover, the act of enlargement will set in motion waves of changes that extend beyond the countries joining the West. These changes will need to be guided toward a favorable outcome. Consequently, an era of hard strategic labor lies ahead.

A stable relationship with Russia must be part of the solution. However, relations with this country threaten to be part of the problem. Russia's new statist foreign policy calls for CIS reintegration and opposes NATO enlargement. The West will need to deal with the possibility that statism may endure and that Russia may acquire greater strength for carrying it out. Yet it also will need to view Russia as one important part of a larger enterprise. The risk of mollifying Russia by not enlarging is that East Central Europe may slide into instability as a result of the geopolitical dynamics affecting the region. The risk of enlarging in a way that alienates Russia is that a new bipolar confrontation may result—most likely, a Cold Peace. The task ahead is to craft an enlargement and an overall regional design that steer clear of both risks.

To achieve a favorable outcome, the West will need to develop a strategic end game: a destination coupled with a plan for getting there. In this book, we have identified five strategic end games that might be considered. Each would pull Western policy in different directions, and the choice among them is not obvious, because each offers its own strengths, weaknesses, and trade-offs.

The West most likely will pursue the institutional web for the near term. But it will ultimately face the task of adding to the institutional web by choosing between open-door enlargement and the two-community solution. How it decides to handle Ukraine will play a major role in its decision: Will the West's goals and the larger cause of regional stability best be served by a Ukraine that belongs to the EU and NATO, or by a Ukraine that remains outside? If Ukraine remains outside, how can its security and economic affairs be designed so that it maintains its independence and enjoys stable relations with both the West and Russia?

The West also will need to fashion a military end game. Because the current regional setting creates an imbalance of power and insecurity for almost all countries, military affairs promise to play an influential role in determining whether a stable political outcome is attained. NATO will need to forge sensible defense arrangements with new members that carry out Article 5 commitments while not posing an offensive threat to Russia or other countries remaining outside the alliance. The West also will need to assert control over the weapon-sales process and modernization so that political polarization is avoided and military stability is encouraged. Further, it will need to forge a new conventional-arms-control strategy so that the CFE framework is preserved and new problems are addressed.

NATO may pursue a power-projection strategy for guiding defense arrangements with new members. If so, this strategy offers the promise of attaining the West's core objectives. It also will permit appropriate approaches toward modernization and arms control to be crafted, but only if concrete agendas are fashioned for handling the challenges posed by both.

As the West goes about the task of enlarging, managing East Central Europe's geopolitics, and dealing with Russia, strategic thinking will be required. Although policy can succeed only if it is implemented effectively, implementation can take place only in a setting in which goals, premises, and postulates are spelled out. The West cannot afford to deal with the challenges ahead by muddling through. It needs to think clearly about its objectives and to fashion policies for attaining them—and a positive outcome.

BIBLIOGRAPHY

Alexeyev, Alexander, "Security from the Atlantic to the Urals and Beyond," *International Affairs*, February 1993.

Allison, Graham, and Robert Blackwill, "The Grand Bargain: The West and the Future of the Soviet Union," in Graham Allison and Gregory F. Treverton, eds., *Rethinking America's Security: Beyond Cold War to New World Order*, New York: W. W. Norton and Company, 1992.

Arbatov, Alexei, "Arbatov Urges Civilian Control over Armed Forces," *Nezavisimaya Gazeta*, March 18, 1995.

——, "An Empire or a Great Power?" *Novoye Vremya*, December 1992.

——, "Russia's Foreign Policy Alternatives," *International Security*, Vol. 18, No. 2, 1993, pp. 5–44.

Aron, Leon, and Kenneth M. Jensen, *The Emergence of Russian Foreign Policy*, Washington, D.C.: U.S. Institute of Peace, 1994.

Aslund, Anders, "Eurasia Letter: Ukraine's Turnabout," *Foreign Policy*, Fall 1995.

——, "Russia's Success Story," *Foreign Affairs*, Vol. 73, No. 5, September/October 1994.

Asmus, Ronald D., Richard L. Kugler, and F. Stephen Larrabee, "NATO Expansion: The Next Steps," *Survival*, Spring 1995.

Atkinson, Rick, "Germans Invest in East Europe, but Curb Image of Empire," *Washington Post*, April 17, 1994.

——, "Russia Warns NATO on Expansion," *Washington Post*, March 20, 1995.

Atkinson, Rick, and John Pomfret, "East Looks to NATO to Forge Links to West," *Washington Post*, July 7, 1995.

Barynkin, Victor, Col. Gen., "Military Infrastructure of the State," *Krasnaya Zvezda*, April 11, 1995.

Belyayev, D., "Statistics on Deepening Crisis in Defense Industry," *Rossiyskiye Vesti*, June 1, 1994.

"The Black Sea Fleet: Documents and Comments," *UCIPR Survey*, Kiev, Ukraine, June 1995.

Blackwill, Robert D., and Sergei Karaganov, *Damage Limitation or Crisis? Russia and the Outside World*, Washington, D.C.: Brassey's Inc., 1994.

Boyd, Charles G., "Making Peace with the Guilty," *Foreign Affairs*, September/October 1995.

Bozmolov, Oleg, "Russia and Eastern Europe," *International Affairs*, August 1994.

Braithwaite, Rodric, Robert D. Blackwill, and Akihiko Tanaka, *Engaging Russia: A Report to the Trilateral Commission*, New York: Trilateral Commission, June 1995.

Brzezinski, Zbigniew, *The Grand Failure: The Birth and Death of Communism in the Twentieth Century*, New York: Collier, 1990.

——, *Out of Control: Global Turmoil on the Eve of the 21st Century*, New York: Scribner's, 1993.

——, "A Plan for Europe," *Foreign Affairs*, Vol. 74, No. 2, January/February 1995.

——, "The Premature Partnership," *Foreign Affairs*, March/April 1994.

Bush, Keith, "Aspects of Military Conversion in Russia," *RFE/RL*, April 8, 1994.

Checkely, Jeff, "Russian Foreign Policy: Back to the Future," *RFE/RL Research Report*, October 16, 1992.

Clarke, Douglas, "The Russian Military and the CFE Treaty," *RFE/RL*, October 23, 1993.

Cohen, Saul B., *Geography and Politics in a Divided World*, London: Methuen, 1964.

Crow, Suzanne, "Russia Debates Its National Interests," *RFE/RL Research Report*, July 10, 1992.

————, "Russia Plans to Take a Hard Line on Near Abroad," *RFE/RL Research Report*, Vol. 1, No. 32, August 14, 1992.

————, "Russia Seeks Leadership in Regional Peacekeeping," *RFE/RL Research Report*, April 9, 1993.

d'Encausse, Helen, *The End of the Soviet Empire*, New York: BasicBooks, 1993.

Davenport, Brian A., "Civil-Military Relations in the Post-Soviet State: Loose Coupling, Uncoupled?" *Armed Forces and Society*, Winter 1995.

Devroy, Ann, "President to Urge Yeltsin to Press Reform Agenda," *Washington Post*, January 6, 1994.

————, "U.S., Russia Sign Variety of Pacts," *Washington Post*, September 28, 1994.

Devroy, Ann, and Fred Hiatt, "U.S., Russia Cite Discord at Summit," *Washington Post*, May 10, 1995.

Devroy, Ann, and Margaret Shapiro, "Yeltsin Says Reforms to Continue," *Washington Post*, January 11, 1994.

Dobbs, Michael, "Christopher Predicts Progress on NATO Expansion Issues at Russian Summit," *Washington Post*, April 27, 1995.

————, "Enthusiasm for Wider Alliance Is Marked by Contradictions," *Washington Post*, July 7, 1995.

————, "NATO Has Initial Talks with Russia," *Washington Post*, May 31, 1995.

————, "Summit Negotiators Agree on Security Issues, but Hill GOP Opposes Deal," *Washington Post*, May 4, 1995.

————, "Wider Alliance Would Increase U.S. Commitments," *Washington Post*, July 6, 1995.

————, "Yeltsin Survives Impeachment Vote," *Washington Post*, March 29, 1993.

"Document Presents Theses of Council," *Nezavisimaya Gazeta*, August 19, 1992.

Dokuchayev, Anatoliy, "The Russian Army: Footnote to Assets and Conclusions," *Krasnaya Zvezda*, May 6, 1994.

Drozdiak, William, "Russia, European Union Sign Historic Pact," *Washington Post*, June 25, 1994.

————, "Yeltsin Warns NATO in Expansion," *Washington Post*, December 9, 1994.

Drozdiak, William, and John F. Harris, "Russia Asks Fuller Ties with NATO," *Washington Post*, May 25, 1994.

"The Economy of Ukraine in January Through September 1994," *Uryadovyy Kuryer*, Kiev, October 27, 1994.

Ellison, Herbert J., *History of Russia*, New York: Holt, Rinehart and Winston, 1964.

Falichev, Oleg, "Building Up the Armed Forces to the Proper Strength Is Our Common Cause," *Krasnaya Zvezda*, March 23, 1995.

Falkenrath, Richard A., "The CFE Flank Dispute: Waiting in the Wings," *International Security*, Spring 1995.

Federal Ministry of Defense, *White Paper, 1994*, Bonn, Germany, 1994.

Felgengauer, Pavel, "Call-Up: No Professional Army Yet in Sight in Russia," *Current Digest of Post-Soviet Press*, May 31, 1995.

————, "Expert Appraisal: The Russian Army Employs New Tactics," *Current Digest of the Post-Soviet Press*, February 8, 1995.

————, "Year of Military Reform," *Current Digest of the Post-Soviet Press*, March 22, 1995.

Foreign and Defense Policy Council, "Document Presents Theses of Council," *Nezavisimaya Gazeta*, August 19, 1992.

"Foreign, Defense Policy Council Revises Strategy for Russia," *Nezavisimaya Gazeta*, May 27, 1994.

Foye, Stephen, *CIS Joint Command Scuttled: Russian Defense Organs Shuffled*, Washington, D.C.: RFE/RL Research Institute, June 1993.

————, "Latest Figures on Contract-Military Service," *RFE/RL*, April 5, 1994.

————, "On Budget, Baltic Fleet and Kaliningrad," *RFE/RL*, March 24, 1994.

————, "Plans for Mobile Force Outlined," *RFE/RL*, March 3, 1993.

————, "Russian Security Council Discusses Border Regions," *RFE/RL*, July 14, 1994.

————, *The Soviet Legacy*, Washington, D.C.: RFE/RL Research Report, June 1993.

Furtado, Charles F., "Nationalism and Foreign Policy in Ukraine," *Political Science Quarterly*, Spring 1994.

Gareyev, Mahmut, "Russia's Priority Interests," *International Affairs*, June 1993.

————, "Some Problems of the Russian Military Doctrine," *International Affairs*, August 1993.

Gareyev, Thomas W., "Russia's Priority Interests," *International Affairs*, Moscow, June 1993.

Garnett, Sherman, "The Integrationist Temptation," *The Washington Quarterly*, Winter 1995.

———, "Russian Power in the New Eurasia," *Carnegie Endowment for International Peace*, Washington, D.C., Fall 1994.

Goble, Paul, "Russia and Its Neighbors," *Foreign Policy*, Spring 1993.

Gompert, David, "How to Defeat Serbia," *Foreign Affairs*, July/August 1994.

Gorski, Valeri, and Yelena Chebotareya, "Maastricht and Russia," *International Affairs*, March 1993.

Goshko, John, "Yeltsin Claims Russian Sphere of Influence," *Washington Post*, September 26, 1994.

Grachev, Pavel, "Defense Minister Says Army of 2 Million Needed," *ITAR-TASS*, February 4, 1994.

"Grachev: Strapped Army at Minimum Level," *Trud*, Moscow, June 7, 1994.

Gray, Colin S., *The Geopolitics of Superpower*, Lexington, Ky.: University of Kentucky Press, 1988.

"Great Russia Revives," *The Economist*, September 18–24, 1993.

Haneider, Wolfram F., *Germany, America, Europe: Forty Years of German Foreign Policy*, New Haven, Conn.: Yale University Press, 1989.

Hiatt, Fred, "IMF Flunks Russia's 1995 Budget," *Washington Post*, December 6, 1994.

———, "Pitch for Pragmatic Partnership," *Washington Post*, March 19, 1994.

———, "Russia's Army: A Crumbling Giant," *Washington Post*, October 21, 1993.

———, "Russia May Now Delay Joint NATO Program," *Washington Post*, March 31, 1994.

———, "Russia Speeds Plan for Link to NATO," *Washington Post*, March 17, 1994.

———, "Russia's Military Machine Bares Rust," *Washington Post*, January 17, 1995.

———, "Yeltsin Names Cabinet of Reformers," *Washington Post*, January 16, 1994.

———, "Yeltsin's New Cabinet: Reformers' In-Out, Out-In Ideology Unclear," *Washington Post*, November 21, 1994.

———, "Yeltsin Promises Assertive Russia," *Washington Post*, February 24, 1994.

———, "Yeltsin Promises to Hold Course Despite Election," *Washington Post*, December 22, 1993.

Hiatt, Fred, and Margaret Shapiro, "Move on Chechnya Shifts Political Alignments in Moscow," *Washington Post*, December 15, 1994.

———, "Yeltsin Assumes Special Rule over Russia," *Washington Post*, March 21, 1993.

Hockstader, Lee, "Moscow Ties Return to Mount Georgia," *Washington Post*, October 24, 1993.

———, "Rebels Overrun Georgia City," *Washington Post*, September 26, 1993.

———, "Russia Absorbs High Price of Victory," *Washington Post*, July 9, 1995.

———, "Russia Pours Troops into Breakaway Region," *Washington Post*, December 11, 1994.

———, "Russia Troops to Guard Georgia Rail Line," *Washington Post*, October 21, 1993.

———, "Will Yeltsin Try to Save Russia or Himself?" *Washington Post*, January 3, 1994.

———, "Yeltsin Backs Stringent Budget and Predicts Economic Turnaround in 1995," *Washington Post*, November 26, 1994.

———, "Yeltsin Vents Anger at NATO," *Washington Post*, April 12, 1994.

Hrushevsky, Michael, *A History of Ukraine*, Kiev: Ukrainian National Association/Archon Books, 1970.

Huntington, Samuel, "The Clash of Civilizations," *Foreign Affairs*, Summer 1993.

Ianin, Sergei, "Factors of Tension in the Army Environment," *Russian Social Science Review*, January 1995.

International Institute for Strategic Studies (IISS), "Fissile-Material Protection: A New Challenge," *Strategic Survey*, 1989–1990.

———, *The Military Balance*, London: Brassey's Inc., annual editions, 1989–1995.

———, "Security Concerns in Central Europe," *Strategic Survey*, London: Brassey's Inc., 1993–1994.

———, *Strategic Survey*, London: Brassey's Inc., 1992–1994.

———, "Transcaucasus: Hell Is Other People," *Strategic Survey*, 1993–1994.

———, "Ukraine: Rising from the Ashes," *Strategic Survey*, 1994–1995.

Itskhoki, Alexander, "National Interests and National Dignity," *International Affairs*, July 1994.

Kaplan, Robert D., *Balkan Ghosts: A Journey Through History*, New York: Vintage, 1993.

Karaganov, Sergei, "After the USSR: Search for a Strategy," *Krasnaya Zvezda*, February 19, 1993.

———, "Expanding NATO Means the Isolation of Russia," *Moskovskiye Novosti*, September 19, 1993.

———, "Post Economic Boom, Balanced Conservative Image," *Segodnya*, January 4, 1994.

Karatnycky, Adrian, "The Ukrainian Factor," *Foreign Affairs*, Vol. 71, No. 3, Summer 1992.

Kasatkin, Anatoly, "Will the Middle East Become a Russian Priority," *International Affairs*, July 1994.

Kegley, Charles W., and Gregory Raymond, *A Multipolar Peace: Great Power Politics in the Twentieth Century*, New York: St. Martin's Press, 1994.

Kennedy, Paul, *Preparing for the Twenty-First Century*, New York: Random House, 1993.

Keohave, Robert O., and Lisal Martin, "The Promise of Institutionalist Theory," *International Security*, Summer 1995.

Kholodov, Dmitriy, "Admiral Chernovin's Submarines?" *Moskovskiye Komsomoletsi*, March 26, 1994.

Khristolyerbova, Irina, "Hearings: Chief of the General Staff Considers Professional Army an Unaffordable Luxury," *Current Digest of Post-Soviet Press*, May 10, 1995.

Kincade, William, and Natalie Melsiyczak, "Unneighborly Neighbors," *Foreign Policy*, Spring 1994.

King, Charles, "Moldova with a Russian Face," *Foreign Policy*, No. 97, Winter 1994–1995.

Kipp, Jacob W., "The Zhirinovsky Threat," *Foreign Affairs*, Vol. 73, No. 3, May/June 1994.

Kissinger, Henry A., *Diplomacy*, New York: Simon and Schuster, 1994.

Kolesnikov, Mikhail, Col. Gen., "Army: Problems, Solutions," *Armeyskiy Sbornik*, January 1995.

Koropeckyj, I. S., *The Ukrainian Economy: Achievements, Problems, and Challenges*, Cambridge, Mass.: Harvard University Press, 1992.

Kozantsev, Boris, "First Steps Toward Russia's Partnership with NATO," *International Affairs*, December 1994.

Kozin, Vladimir, "New Dimensions of NATO," *International Affairs*, March 1993.

Kozyrev, Andrei, "And Now: Partnership with Russia's Democrats," *Washington Post*, October 13, 1993.

————, "The Lagging Partnership," *Foreign Affairs*, May/June 1994.

————, "A New Russian Foreign Policy for a New Era," Russian Federation Permanent Mission to the United Nations, Press Release No. 41, September 24, 1992.

————, "Partnership or Cold Peace?" *Foreign Policy*, Summer 1995.

————, "Russia: A Chance for Survival," *Foreign Affairs*, Spring 1992.

————, "Russia's Interests: Country's Military Doctrine and International Security," *Krasnaya Zvezda*, June 14, 1994.

————, "What Is to Be Done with NATO?" *Moscow News*, No. 39, September 24, 1993.

Krauthammer, Charles, "The Romance with Russia Is Over," *Washington Post*, December 16, 1994.

Kugler, Richard L., "The Defense Program Question: The Military Dimensions of NATO Enlargement," *National Defense University*, May 1995.

————, *Toward a Dangerous World: U.S. National Security Strategy for the Coming Turbulence*, Santa Monica, Calif.: RAND, MR-485-JS, 1995.

Kupchan, Charles A., and Clifford A. Kupchan, "The Promise of Collective Security," *International Security*, Summer 1995.

Larrabee, F. Stephen, *East European Security After the Cold War*, Santa Monica, Calif.: RAND, MR-254-USDP, 1993.

Lebed, Alexander, General, "Senior Officer on Army's Problems," *Komsomal Saya Pravda*, February 3, 1994.

Lederer, Ivo J., ed., *Russian Foreign Policy: Essays in Historical Perspective*, New Haven, Conn.: Yale University Press, 1962.

Leshkov, Sergey, "Defense Industry's Future," *Izvestiya*, December 30, 1995.

Lipisky, Andrei, "The Community of Central Asia," *International Affairs*, October 1993.

"Lopatin Analyzes History, Results of Military Reductions," *Novaya Vezhednevnaya*, Moscow, May 26, 1994.

Lukacs, John, *The End of the Twentieth Century and the End of the Modern Age*, New York: Ticknor and Fields, New York, 1993.

Lukin, Vladimir, "Our Security Predicament," *Foreign Policy*, Fall 1992.

———, "No More Delusions: Reform in Russia Will Never Fit American Ideals," *Washington Post*, August 1, 1994.

Lynch, Allen, "After Empire: Russia and Its Western Neighbors," *RFE/RL Research Report*, March 1994.

Mackinder, Sir Halford, *Democratic Ideals and Reality*, New York: Norton, 1962.

Mahan, Alfred T., *The Influence of Seapower upon the French Revolution and Empire, 1793–1812*, Boston: Little, Brown, 1898.

Makarevskiy, Vadim, General, "Military Reform Is Proceeding," *Obshchaya Gazeta*, April 1994.

Maley, Mikhail, "Future Role of Defense Industry in Economy," *Delovoy Mir*, April 11, 1994.

Marcus, Ruth, and John F. Harris, "Behind U.S. Policy Shift on Bosnia: Strains in NATO," *Washington Post*, December 5, 1994.

McFaul, Michael, "Why Russia's Politics Matter," *Foreign Affairs*, January/February 1995.

McMichael, Scott, "Russia's New Military Doctrine," *Military Affairs*, October 1992.

Mearsheimer, John J., "The Case for a Ukrainian Nuclear Deterrent," *Foreign Affairs*, Vol. 72, No. 3, September 1993.

———, "The False Promise of International Institutions," *International Security*, Winter 1994/95.

————, "A Realist Reply," *International Security,* Summer 1995.

Migranyan, Andranik, "Chechnya as Turning Point for Russian State," *Nezavisimaya Gazeta,* January 17, 1995.

————, "Presidential Council Member Migranyan Assesses Policy Toward FSU," *Nezavisimaya Gazeta,* January 12, 1994.

Miller, Steven E., "The Case Against a Ukrainian Nuclear Deterrent," *Foreign Affairs,* Vol. 72, No. 3, September 1993.

Mizir, Viktor, and Sergei Oznobishchev, "Security After the Cold War," *International Affairs,* August 1993.

Motyl, Alexander J., *Dilemmas of Independence: Ukraine After Totalitarianism,* New York: Council of Foreign Relations Press, 1993.

Moynihan, Daniel Patrick, *Pandaemonium: Ethnicity in International Politics,* New York: Oxford University Press, 1993.

"Narodnoe Khoziaistvo SSSR za 70 let: Yubileiny statistichesky yezhegodnik," *Finansy I Statistika,* Moscow, 1987, pp. 219–263.

NATO, *Study on NATO Enlargement,* Brussels, Belgium: NATO Headquarters, September 1995.

Nolan, Janne E., ed., *Global Engagement: Cooperation and Security in the 21st Century,* Washington, D.C.: The Brookings Institution, 1994.

Oberdorfer, Dan, and Ann Devroy, "Clinton Said to Have Ordered Bolder Ideas on Russian Aid," *Washington Post,* April 2, 1993.

Olcott, Martha Brill, "Central Asian Independence," *Foreign Affairs,* Vol. 71, No. 3, 1992.

Ottaway, David, "Russia Pledges to Back Ruble on World Currency Markets," *Washington Post,* July 5, 1995.

Pfaff, William, *The Wrath of Nations: Civilization and the Furies of Nationalism,* New York: Simon and Schuster, 1993.

Pichnigiv, Boris, "The EC and Russia in the All-Europe Context," *International Affairs,* March 1994.

Pleshakov, Konstantin, "Russia's Mission: The Third Epoch," *International Affairs,* January 1993.

Pozdnyakov, Elgiz, "Contemporary Geopolitical Challenges and Their Influence on Security and Stability in the World," *Voyennaya Mysl'*, No. 1, January 1993.

———, "Russia Is a Great Power," *International Affairs,* January 1993.

———, "Russia Today and Tomorrow," *International Affairs*, February 1993.

Priest, Dana, and Daniel Williams, "U.S. Allows Arms Sales to 10 in Ex-East Bloc," *Washington Post,* February 20, 1995.

Pushkov, Alexei, "Building a New NATO at Russia's Expense," *Moscow News,* No. 39, September 24, 1993.

———, "Russia and America: The Honeymoon's Over," *Foreign Policy,* Winter 1993/94.

Ragsdale, Hugh, ed., *Imperial Russian Foreign Policy,* New York: Woodrow Wilson Center Press, 1993.

Rahr, Alexander, "Atlanticists vs. Eurasianists in Russian Foreign Policy," *RFE/RL Research Report,* Vol. 1, No. 22, May 29, 1992.

"Results of Winter Training Period," *Krasnaya Zvezda,* Moscow, June 2, 1994.

RFE/RL Daily Digest, 1992–1994.

Rissanovsky, Nicholas V., *A History of Russia,* London: Oxford University Press, 1984.

Robinson, Thomas W., "National Interests," in James N. Rosenau, *International Politics and Foreign Policy: A Reader in Research and Theory,* New York: Free Press, 1969, pp. 173–190.

Rumer, Eugene, "Will Ukraine Return to Russia?" *Foreign Policy,* Fall 1994.

Rupert, James, "Between Russia and Ukraine's Key Region in Crimea Is Focus of Diplomacy," *Washington Post,* March 30, 1995.

————, "Striking at Separatists, Ukraine Abolishes Crimea's Charter, Presidency," *Washington Post*, March 18, 1995.

————, "Ukraine Votes Austerity Spending Bill," *Washington Post*, April 6, 1995.

————, "Yeltsin Criticizes Ukraine's Crimea Policy," *Washington Post*, April 15, 1995.

"Russia, Belarus Scrap Border Checkpoints; Ex-Soviet States Reach Partial Accords on Rights, Debt," *Los Angeles Times*, May 27, 1995.

Russian Government, *Main Provisions of the Military Doctrine of the Russian Federation*, Moscow, 1993.

"Russian Interests in the CIS," Conference Report, *International Affairs*, November 1994.

Sakwa, Richard, *Russian Politics and Society*, London and New York: Routledge, 1993.

Saunders, David, *The Ukrainian Impact on Russian Culture 1750–1850*, Edmonton: Canadian Institute of Ukrainian Studies, University of Alberta, 1985.

Semenov, Vladimir, Col. Gen., "We Will Not Permit a Decreased Level of Combat Readiness," *Armeyskiy Sbornik*, January 1995.

Sestanovich, Stephen, "Russia Turns the Corner," *Foreign Affairs*, January/February 1994.

Shafiqul, Islam, "Rough Road to Capitalism," *Foreign Affairs*, Vol. 72, No. 2, Spring 1993.

Shapiro, Margaret, "Belarus Voters Support Renewed Ties to Russia," *Washington Post*, May 15, 1995.

————, "Russia Congress Moves to Reduce Yeltsin's Power," *Washington Post*, March 11, 1993.

————, "Russia's Parliament Passes Tough Budget," *Washington Post*, June 24, 1995.

————, "Yeltsin Appeals for Truce on Powers," *Washington Post*, February 13, 1993.

——, "Yeltsin Sets Constitutional Talks in June," *Washington Post*, May 12, 1993.

——, "Yeltsin Vows to Protect Reforms," *Washington Post*, May 6, 1993.

Shaposhnikov, Yevgeny, "A Security Concept for Russia," *International Affairs*, October 1993.

"Shirshov: R55 Trillion Is Subsistence Minimum for Defense Budget," *Krasnaya Zvezda*, Moscow, June 4, 1994.

Sidorova, Galina, "Kozyrev's Policy Adviser Responds to Migranyan on FSU Policy," *Nezavisimaya Gazeta*, January 19, 1994.

Simes, Dimitri, "America and the Post-Soviet Republics," *Foreign Affairs*, Vol. 71, No. 3, 1992.

——, "The Return of Russian History," *Foreign Affairs*, January/February 1994.

Simon, Jeffrey, ed., *NATO Enlargement: Opinions and Options*, Washington, D.C.: National Defense University, Ft. McNair, 1995.

Solodobvnik, Sergei, "The Community of Central Asia," *International Affairs*, October 1993.

Soroka, Mikhail, Gen., "Air Force Commander: No New Combat Aircraft Expected," FBIS-translated text, April 1, 1995.

Southerland, David, "Azerbaijan Picks Exxon Over Iran for Oil Deal," *Washington Post*, April 11, 1995.

Spyckman, Nicholas J., *The Geography of the Peace*, New York: Harcourt Brace, 1944.

Stankevich, Sergei, "A Sphere of Russia's Vital Interests," *International Affairs*, March 1994.

"START II Impact on Strategic Forces Viewed," *Segodny*, Moscow, June 1, 1994.

"State Counsellor Views Foreign Policy Goals," *Nezavisimaya Gazeta*, March 28, 1992.

Subtelny, Orest, *Ukraine: A History*, Toronto: University of Toronto Press, 1988.

"Summing Up the Results of the Past Year and Looking to Next Year," *Mocskoy Sbornik*, Moscow, December 28, 1993.

Thomson, David, *Europe Since Napoleon*, New York: Alfred A. Knopf, 1964.

Tsygichko, Vitaliy, "What Kind of Army Do We Need? The Political Context of Russian Military Doctrine," *Nezavisimaya Gazeta*, April 13, 1994.

Ukraine and Ukrainians: A Reference Outline, Ukrainian National Association, February 1993, p. 5.

Ulam, Adam B., *Expansion and Coexistence: The History of Soviet Foreign Policy, 1917–1967*, New York: Praeger, 1968.

Ullman, Richard H., *Securing Europe*, Princeton, N.J.: Princeton University Press, 1991.

U.S. Department of Defense, *World-Wide Conventional Arms Trade: A Forecast and Analysis*, Washington, D.C.: U.S. Government Printing Office, December 1994.

Velychenko, Stephen, *Shaping Identity in Eastern Europe and Russia: Soviet-Russian and Polish Accounts of Ukrainian History, 1914–1991*, New York: St. Martin's Press, 1993.

Vernolin, Vladimir, "Army Needs Worthy Budget," *Krasnaya Zvezda*, Moscow, June 9, 1994.

Vogel, Steve, "U.S. Proposes NATO Partnership for Former Warsaw Pact Nations," *Washington Post*, October 20, 1993.

Volkov, Lev, Lt. Gen., "STARTII and the Topol Mobile Intercontinental Missiles," *Segodnya*, June 1, 1994.

Williams, Daniel, "Bosnia: Europe's Lesson or Problem?" *Washington Post*, December 7, 1994.

———, "Russia Joins NATO Plan," *Washington Post*, June 22, 1994.

————, "Russia Minister Balks at NATO's Expansion Plans," December 1, 1994.

————, "Russia Vows Bosnia Peace Role, Sidesteps U.S. Military Force Proposal," *Washington Post*, May 6, 1993.

————, "Yeltsin, Clinton Clash Over NATO's Role," *Washington Post*, December 5, 1994.

Williams, Daniel, and Lee Hockstader, "NATO Seeks to Reassure East as Russia Warns Against Expansion," *Washington Post*, January 6, 1994.

Wolfe, Thomas, *Soviet Military Power and Europe, 1945–1970*, Baltimore, Md.: The Johns Hopkins University Press, 1970.

Wolfers, Arnold, "The Pole of Power and the Pole of Indifference," in James N. Rosenau, ed., *International Politics and Foreign Policy: A Reader in Research and Theory*, New York: Free Press, 1969.

Wolfowitz, Paul D., "Clinton's First Year," *Foreign Affairs*; January/February 1994.

Yermolin, Vladimir, "Army Needs Worthy Budget," *Krasnaya Zvezda*, June 6, 1994.

Zagorsky, Andrei, "The Commonwealth: One Year On," *International Affairs*, February 1993.

————, "Russia and Europe," *International Affairs*, January 1993.

————, "Tilting from the CSCE to NATO?" *International Affairs*, March 1994.

Zelikow, Philip, "Beyond Boris Yeltsin," *Foreign Affairs*, January/February 1994.

Zimmermann, Warren, "Origins of Catastrophe," *Foreign Affairs*, March/April 1995.